FUEL

F

E

blue
rider
press

 SPECIAL DELUXE

ALSO BY NEIL YOUNG

Waging Heavy Peace

BLUE RIDER PRESS
A MEMBER OF PENGUIN GROUP (USA)
NEW YORK

SPECIAL DELUXE

Neil Young

Illustrated by the Author

blue
rider
press

Published by the Penguin Group
Penguin Group (USA) LLC
375 Hudson Street
New York, New York 10014

USA · Canada · UK · Ireland · Australia
New Zealand · India · South Africa · China

penguin.com
A Penguin Random House Company

Library of Congress Cataloging-in-Publication Data

Young, Neil, 1945–
Special deluxe / Neil Young.
p.   cm.
ISBN 978-0-399-17208-3
1. Young, Neil, 1945–   2. Rock musicians—Canada—Biography.   I. Title.
ML420.Y75A3   2014   2014026830
782.42166092—dc23
[B]

Printed in the United States of America
1   3   5   7   9   10   8   6   4   2

BOOK DESIGN BY CLAIRE NAYLON VACCARO
ENDPAPER PHOTOGRAPHY BY ADAM VOLLICK

Penguin is committed to publishing works of quality and integrity.
In that spirit, we are proud to offer this book to our readers; however,
the story, the experiences, and the words are the author's own.

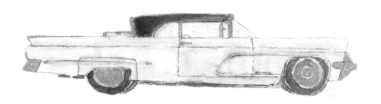

Dedicated to Bruce Falls,
a true electric transportation
pioneer, and to L. A. Johnson,
"Long May You Run"

1959 Lincoln Continental "Lincvolt"

1957 Eldorado Biarritz Convertible "Aunt Bee"

THIS IS A STORY about the proud highway of second thoughts. Because I have already written a book about my life, some events will be familiar to those who have read that book. In this book, I am looking at my relationship with cars over many years.

Originally, my idea for this book was Cars and Dogs. That seemed like a nice enough idea for my second book, basically an outgrowth of the first one. I reasoned that I have had a love affair with cars my whole life, so that would be a really good thing for me to share in this second effort. I also have had some really great dogs, and I thought that both cars and dogs would be perfect vehicles to tell some more stories.

Drawing on my pedigree as the son of a great Canadian writer, Scott Young, and my family history of author friends, I could surely pull something together that would be of interest to somebody and potentially keep me busy for a while, which I really would appreciate. It was my original hope that I could write an interesting book and continue the fun I had with my first one. The only problem I had was the feeling that the book was going to get serious and obsessive about some of the things that I really care about. That had been something I had to face with my first book. In writing about cars I would have to come clean about a lot of my feelings concerning fossil fuels, global warming, and American politics that might end up driving away readers. Unlike the cars themselves, a fun and innocent topic, the subject of politics and legislation might change the book significantly from the way it started, making it not that much fun for some people to read. I had my fair share of doubt.

To complicate things further, upon closer inspection and a great deal of soul-searching over a period of more than one hour, I realized late one night that I was perhaps the worst master of a dog that the world has ever seen. I have done almost everything wrong that one can do with a dog, and that would surely be a royal turnoff for any dog lover reading my new book if I called it *Cars and Dogs*. With that in mind, I changed the title to *Cars I Have Known* just to make sure that I did not attract any dog lovers who might really hate the book and me after the first few dogs. That said, I hope I have made the right decision in still including my dogs, and indeed some other dogs. I am trying to underplay their presence in the story by not mentioning them officially, yet including them whenever it seems appropriate.

 SPECIAL DELUXE

1948 Monarch Business Coupe

Skippy was a Labrador mix. We had Skippy when I was a young boy, about four or five, I reckon. He was basically a yellow Lab, with some sort of other dog thrown in for seasoning and personality, as well as endurance, I am sure. I say that because my dad used to take Skippy for runs on the weekends or any other time it seemed right. The dog runs were a wonderful family experience. It was about 1950, gasoline cost twenty-seven cents a gallon, and we had a 1948 Monarch business coupe with a huge trunk. Skippy would jump right in the trunk happily, as far as I can remember, his tail wagging and ready to go, because he knew we were going for a run in the country. After my dad closed the trunk door with Skippy safely inside, we would all jump in the car.

Omemee, our little town with a population of 750, was on Highway 7 between Lindsay and Peterborough, in the province of Ontario in the vast country of Canada, and the open and wild countryside was only about three miles away. We would ride out there together, past the dump, along the swamp, and across the low bridge—which enabled the water to slowly run under it, joining one part of the swamp, or "bog" as it was called locally, to the other part. On one side was a large expanse of water with stumps sticking out of it where trees once stood, before the mill and dam were built, forever changing the natural flow of the river. On the other side was the marsh, which was mostly cattails and swamp grass.

At the far end of the bog, at the dam, farmers would bring in their crops to the mill to have them ground by the grinding wheel, which was turned by water running under the mill, hitting a big paddle wheel. Where the water entered the mill from the bog, it swirled and kind of boiled and was really deep. That's where the fish were living. Once, while my mom and dad were visiting friends who lived near the mill for dinner, instead of sitting around bored while they talked and drank, I went down to the mill at sunset and caught some frogs, put them on my line, and nabbed three or four really big bass, which I proudly brought back to the party.

Back in the car, though, when we got across the low bridge, it was obvious that we were on a road that was built on an old abandoned railroad line. It was straight, narrow, and all overgrown with trees. The surface was smooth for miles. We would cruise along on our old gravel road through a beautiful leafy tunnel of multicolors, the sun streaming down through them. When Daddy stopped the car I would get out with him while he opened the trunk and let Skippy out, then we would get back in the car and away we would go, with Skippy running behind. After a few miles we would reach the Hog's Back, a road that took off into the hills. Cedar-rail fences anchored every fifty feet or so with rock piles ran along on both sides of the Hog's Back, a more primitive and much rougher road. It went up and down hills, had big rocks on it, and had grass growing right out of the middle of it. We had to go real slow. Often

Skippy would see a groundhog and take off after it, howling and barking. Daddy would stop and let him chase the groundhog for a while until Skippy eventually came back to the Monarch with his tongue hanging out, covered with burrs and all manner of sticky things.

Skippy never caught a groundhog to my knowledge, although he had a great time trying, then we would slowly crawl along the Hog's Back in the Monarch until we got to a little pond in a farmer's field where Skippy would drink and drink. Then Daddy would open the huge trunk door and Skippy would happily jump inside and curl up on the blanket Mommy had put there for him. We would make our way home and open the trunk, finding Skippy curled up on the rug, but instantly ready to jump out and go in the house, happily wagging his tail.

A Monarch is actually a Canadian-made Mercury, the same as the American one but with a different name. Ours was kind of light in color and was called a businessman's coupe, so named I think because it had that huge trunk for putting products in to make an instant sale. This was really a workingman's car. No frills. I seem to remember ours had a small backseat, although some of them didn't. It was simple and comfortable with cloth upholstery. My earliest recollection of the 1948 Monarch was at a place called Jackson's Point, where we lived on the lake for a while before the family moved to Omemee. I vividly recall it in our driveway in Omemee, but it was soon replaced with a four-door sedan.

1951 Monarch Sedan

It was a stormy and rainy night on Labor Day weekend and the traffic was intense. We were on a family car ride to the Toronto Hospital for Sick Children. I had contracted polio and our house had quarantine signs on it, warning people to stay away. We drove to Toronto in our new four-door sedan, a black 1951 Monarch that looked a lot bigger than the old one. On long trips I usually slept on the floor, listening to the wheels turn and feeling the little bumps on the highway, but that night I was feeling stiff in my back, wondering why my mother was crying so much, and why we were driving in the middle of the night. We eventually arrived at a very big, drab-colored, and imposing building: the Toronto Sick Children's Hospital.

I was treated for polio there, starting with a lumbar puncture, which was scary and intimidating, not to mention painful. It was performed with a large needle that looked surprisingly like a fishing lure, with colored, featherlike things on the end and the big needle protruding. As I write this, I am amazed that my memory of this needle is so vivid. How could it look like that? Was it a dream?

Then Mommy and Daddy had to go home, and I was in bed in the hospital for a long time until they returned, and I finally shuffled across a small room with a shiny linoleum-tile floor, from my dad to my mom, to prove that I could walk. I was very happy to get back into the Monarch and go home. I rolled down the window and played airplane with my hand as I smelled the Ontario countryside. By sticking my hand out the window and tilting it up or down, I could "fly" my arm like an airplane wing.

Once at home again, I moved pretty slowly for a while and couldn't keep up with the other kids around town, but I was getting better, and in the fall of 1951, as soon as I was well enough, I began grade one at Omemee Public School. Miss Lamb was my teacher. She used to pick me up off the floor by my chin to get my undivided attention when I misbehaved.

The school was a three-story brick building and I remember King George's picture hanging above the blackboard. We sang "God Save the King" every morning. Still recovering from the polio, I couldn't run very well when playing with the other kids at recess, although I had no problem getting into trouble with my pal Henry Mason by making faces and weird sounds to disrupt the class. Henry and I were always cutting it up. Ultimately, we both were hanging by our chins at the hand of Miss Lamb.

That was the year I started driving, probably late 1951. There was an old Model A or Model T Ford parked on the road near school and when we walked home for lunch every day we would pass it. It was black and boxy, unlike any of the newer cars, and we were curious about it. Perhaps *I* was most curious. One day I got in it and turned the key. The car started to move! I was driving! It was my first drive. As long as I held the key on, the car would move! The owner came out and busted me right there. He told me he was going to tell my mom and dad. I was scared as hell. I walked and walked, terrified to go home for lunch. I missed lunch and went back to school, which got my mom and dad upset. I got in big trouble and confessed to my driving episode myself, without the man who owned the car ever having to tell them anything.

The seasons came and went with great regularity and the snows in Omemee were always big and deep. The pure white snow was bright in the sun, almost blinding. When spring arrived, the trees exploded in green and flowers popped out of everyone's gardens, planted in front of and around their houses. Summer came right on time with the tourists from the States and the countless wonderful afternoons at the swimming hole on the Pigeon River under the big cement highway bridge. Then fall would sweep in on schedule, changing the colors of the maple trees to red, brown, and gold, all along our Highway 7, right through the heart of town.

With the changing seasons, I could feel something in my bones, an occasional chill and tremor through my body. My soul felt it. I think it was life itself as I grew. Those multicolored leaves soon became brittle and started to fall, dying on the ground. They then were gathered with rakes into piles and burned by the roadside, filling our little town with the sweet smoke of burning leaves, marking the end of another season. Year in and year out, right on time, that was how I grew up, and I was happy with the changes as they paraded through our little town of 750 souls.

After Christmas 1951, my parents decided to take the family to New Smyrna Beach in Florida. On that first trip down to Florida, I slept on the floor in the back of the Monarch, with the sound of the wheels on the road putting me in dreamland. My brother, Bob, would sit on the seat. The back windows opened and that was really cool. I played airplane. I spent hours doing that on our long trips south every winter, as the journey became an annual tradition for our family. We would pack up and go to New Smyrna Beach right after Christmas, and Daddy would write there in our little cottage on the beach. I loved those family trips. We were all together and really happy.

Stopping at motels for the night, my mom would put hot towels on my eyes because I had sties, sort of little infections like boils on my eyelids that really hurt. I don't know why Bob and I both got those. Maybe it was the chocolate bars and candy we ate on the trips. Anyway, we were back in the car in the morning and away we would go!

When we got to Georgia we would always see the signs reading LAST CHANCE FOR PECANS! Those signs would go on for miles and miles. We always knew we were getting closer to Florida when we saw them. Once in Florida, we would travel on A1A, the route that ran from beach town to beach town. We were never in a hurry and it was the time of our lives. Gas was around twenty-seven cents a gallon. Our family's Monarch would shed about 1,296 pounds of CO_2 into the atmosphere every time we made that great trip to Florida, and on the way back we would do it again.

Our little rented cottage in New Smyrna Beach on Atlantic Avenue was right on the sand dunes and we had a path through the sand directly to the ocean. We stayed in the same cottage every year. Skippy went to Florida, too, and we would run with him on the beach. Cars could drive on the beach, so we could run Skippy right there! It was so fantastic doing that. Dog lovers: In case you are wondering, Skippy did not ride in the trunk on those long trips to Florida. He rode with Bob and I in the back.

Of course, we had to go to school, and there was one named Faulkner Street School that both Bob and I went to. We started after Christmas holidays and left after Easter holidays, returning up north to finish the year at Omemee Public School. Growing up, I went to a lot of schools—twelve before I dropped out—but it never dawned on me that I was different from most kids in that respect.

While we were in New Smyrna Beach, every Thursday we would pile in the Monarch and go to Buck's Barn and the drive-in. Buck's Barn was a Quonset hut with wood chips and peanut shells on the floor and a lot of picnic benches with checkerboard tablecloths all set up inside. They served fried chicken and French fries. We had that every week! Families and kids were everywhere. After dinner we would get in the Monarch and go to the drive-in theater to watch a new movie. Car speakers hung on posts at every parking spot. Daddy would set up the speaker in the window of the car and turn it up for the cartoons, which started just as it was getting dark. We were there with hundreds of other cars and it is one of the best memories of my life. Our family was together and all was perfect in the world.

Another thing we did very often was go out for dinner at a special place that had a buffet. I remember standing in line there one night, looking at some incredibly red apples. The apples were right in the center of everything and they were huge and bright shiny red, very appetizing. I reached in as far as I could and got one of 'em and put it on my plate. When we got back to the table everybody was laughing at me! They were totally cracking up that I had taken an apple from the big display. It was made of wax. I had to give it back.

Monday night was bingo night at our house. People from the neighborhood would come, and my mom would serve some good food. The grown-ups drank beer and got real loud, having a good time. One night, I had just learned the alphabet and went down from my bedroom and recited it for the first time in front of everybody. At the end, everyone cheered for me. What a great feeling! I really liked that approval. Pretty soon Easter came along with the big Easter egg hunt, then when we returned from Florida in the Monarch, it was the last time, probably early 1953. We didn't stay very long in Omemee.

1954 Monarch Lucerne

For reasons unknown to me at the time, having to do with my parents' marital problems, we left Omemee, where we had lived for years, and moved to Winnipeg, back where my mommy and daddy had come from originally. At that time, gas prices had risen to about twenty-nine cents per gallon. On the trip out there to Winnipeg, we put around 1,382 pounds of CO_2 into the atmosphere with the Monarch, but we weren't alone. In 1954, 58 million other registered motor vehicles drove a total of 557 billion miles.

When we arrived in Winnipeg, Mom and Dad were trying to get their marriage back together again. We lived on a little street called Hillcrest Avenue, at number 145, marking the first time I can remember having a street number on our house. I went to Nordale School there for the last couple of months of grade three, the new kid. I was always the new kid. I was used to that. I didn't mind.

There was a store on the corner near our house where I saw a little sailboat in the window. I would go down and look at it every day. It reminded me of the freedom I felt while playing on the river or the lake back in Ontario. It grew on me until I knew I had to have it. In an early sign of the obsessions I would have later in life, I dreamt about it every night. When Christmas came, I didn't get the sailboat, but I did get a Werlich bicycle from my grandpa Bill Ragland! It came in a big cardboard box and Daddy put it together with a screwdriver and some pliers, then I went out for my first ride. It was cold outside and the lawns still had some snow on them but the sidewalks and streets were bare. Soon, after riding on the street and falling a few times, I got the hang of it. With the wind flying through my hair, I was free! I cruised around the neighborhood, learning all the streets. I rode to school! I rode home. I rode everywhere I could. I really loved moving through the world with my hair blowing in the wind.

Every Thursday night there was a square dance at the community center, and I, at eight or nine years old, would go down there and try to do it. I was a fish out of water, not knowing any people and more importantly not knowing how to "do-si-do with the old left hand" as some guy called out instructions over a squeaky speaker while records were playing, but I did see some girls there and that was interesting. Fascinating, actually. Sometimes, when I got to dance with them, it was a thrill. I was really nervous and self-conscious, but I was having a good time. By the beginning of spring I was starting to know kids, making friends, and getting into the groove.

We used to ride to many places, my new friends and I. It seems we all got our bikes at the same time, and the freedom was infectious. There was a river, the Assiniboine, that flowed through town, and a natural trail (no cement or pavement) followed the banks going up and down through the trees and little canyons. It was called the Monkey Trail.

Created by the First Nations peoples centuries before when *they* first settled in Winnipeg, the trail was just like a roller coaster and we used to ride out there with lunch bags packed by our moms, eat lunch, ride some more, and then ride home. That would take a full day, and I remember getting home a few times after the streetlights came on and getting a real earful from my dad and mom. Of course, we could not call and check in from a pay phone, because that would not have been a good use of a dime. I probably did not have a dime anyway.

Pulling wagonloads of things around with my bike brought a new dimension to my bicycle riding experience. One day, I was out riding along pulling my wagon, and it hit a rock or something and I went flying! I landed on my head and was knocked out on the curb. I remember waking up on the road with some people I didn't know looking down at me. I had a concussion, and it took a while to come back to my senses. The front wheel of my bike was all bent. It sure was a hell of a year there in Winnipeg, and it came to an end as suddenly as it started. We moved back to Ontario.

Back in Toronto, my dad had gotten a job working for the *Globe and Mail*, writing a daily human interest column on the front page of the second section that was maybe a little like this book. We got a new car, a 1954 Monarch Lucerne, a metallic-silver four-door sedan, and if it wasn't brand-new, it was only a year old. The most fascinating aspect of this car is that, later on, absolutely no one re-membered it except for me, and I remembered it very vividly. My brother, Bob, who has helped me remember a lot of things for this book, was pretty sure we never had the car. Perhaps I just imagined it. Perhaps not! It was real to me, and when I recently found a pic-ture of it from my childhood that proved it existed, I was ecstatic. I had almost been ready to admit that it was just a figment of my imagination until I found this little photo.

1957 Mercury Turnpike Cruiser

Because of my upbringing in rural Canada, where the houses we lived in were in rural areas and were not numbered, it meant something special to me when we began living in houses with numbers on them; it meant I was in the big city. When we settled in Toronto, it was on another city street of houses with numbers called Rose Park Drive. I was in grade four and was going to Whitney Public School.

That year, we took a big family trip to New York City. It was my first time going there, and when we got on the New Jersey Turnpike, I saw the new 1955 Pontiacs with the two bars of chrome on their hoods. New cars always showed up first in the States, and for me it was exciting just to see them. I was always looking for the latest models and could name them all. In New York City, we went up to the top of the Empire State Building and I stood on my toes to see down over the ledge. There I was, with my chin on the cement, peering over the edge, down to the street below, where tiny yellow taxicabs jockeyed for position on ribbons of asphalt. It was almost a quarter mile down to the street from the top of the building. New York City was the biggest place I had ever seen in my life.

Back in Toronto, I got to know some kids, and as a way to meet more, I started a club that was called the St. Lawrence Committee. I had a bunch of cards and we all wrote the name "St. Lawrence Committee" and our own names on them. I got those cards from my dad's study, where he wrote his daily column. These white, heavy-stock cards were three inches by four inches with blue lines on them, and they were very official looking. We were an exclusive club, and I was the president. When we would meet at recess, it felt good to belong to something.

Near the school was a store called Dot's, where the kids all went to buy licorice candy and hang out. There was usually a car parked there that I particularly remember. It had big fins on it and a lot of chrome. I think it was a DeSoto Firedome or a Dodge Adventurer or something like that. Advertisements on TV called it the "Forward Look." I was very impressed with that car and went back every day to see it. I would get some candy at Dot's for a few cents and look at the car, imagining myself driving it and being so cool. It had a lot of push buttons and that was the new thing. Push buttons even changed gears, and I was quite impressed. I could not imagine how pushing a button could change a gear. The car was like a rocket ship. I was already obsessed with cars. The designs were fascinating to me. The power was interesting, but it was the styling that really caught my eye.

During my life, I have collected many cars and have had lots of experiences with every one of them. They were a major part of my life. I did not collect perfect cars, expensive cars, or exotic cars. No; I collected cars for their uniqueness, with little concern for their condition. Because of that, most of my cars were dirt cheap. The great majority of my proud collection was clunkers. I just loved the way they looked and got a lot of joy from just observing them from every angle, as I considered their histories and the possible places they had traveled. They talked to me. And I talked to them.

I want to tell you two little car stories. My memory doesn't always make sense, so I am not sure of the locations and times. Because new cars were always introduced late in the year preceding the year of the car, it must have been late 1956 at the earliest, since these stories are about cars from 1957. I remember this happening near Rose Park Drive in the area near the Whitney school, but I was not there in 1956. I was living somewhere else. So here is the first of my two stories, lost in time.

Walking home from school one day I took a different way and went down a new street with big maple trees and impressive brick houses, each one with a long driveway. I saw a car parked in front of one of the big houses. It was a convertible with really sharp fins and beautiful curves. I had never seen one like that before, and I walked over to view it right up close and read the writing on it to see what it was. It was an Eldorado. I was very impressed, having never seen one. I knew that it was one of the best Cadillacs ever made. Upon close inspection I could read the word Biarritz *written in a stylish script in gold metal applied to the front fender. This was a car I had only heard of and had never seen! The epitome of Cadillac quality! I was knocked out with the beauty of the sculpted body, chrome, and glass, the lush leather seats with chrome medallions in the backrests, and the overall presence of this magnificent car. I looked at the license plate. "Michigan." Of course it had to be an American who actually owned one of these. I vowed that someday I would be down in the States, living the life I dreamt of, heard about, and read about. That was where all the cool music came from, all the great cars. How did those people do that? I wanted to know.*

And now I want to tell you the second story, lost in time as well.

I was at a friend's house, playing with his Lionel trains down in his basement. He had started building a really big layout down there, with his dad working on it with him. It had a plywood foundation with a lot of hills, bridges, and curves. It was under construction and going to be really amazing. I don't remember ever seeing it finished, but it left a mark on me. I can still see it clearly in my mind. I hope he and his dad finished that layout. As I was walking along on my way home from playing trains there, I noticed a stylish new car parked on the street. Walking up to it I saw that the electric rear window went up and down by pushing a button inside. I was very impressed with that feature, having never seen, or even imagined, anything like it. Also, there were little chrome ornaments on each fender with lights in them. This car was unreal. Looking at it further, I discovered it was a 1957 Mercury, a Canadian car with Ontario plates. I read the words Turnpike Cruiser *on the side. I had never seen so many new and different features on any car. A spare tire, cloaked in shiny chrome, was located on the extended back bumper that hung way out over the back. It was huge. My mind was blown. It made an indelible impression on me that I can still feel. Why? It is part of me. New designs I have never seen before seem to stay with me forever.*

While I was living on Rose Park Drive, I put my own design energy into making a submarine out of two-by-fours and nails. Near our house there was a park called Moore Park with a wading pool in the center of it. Even when it was filled with water it was not deep enough for swimming. That is where I tested my submarine. I designed the submarine based on aerodynamic principles I had learned with my airplane hand sticking out the side of Daddy's car. Using a wooden two-by-four as the main body, I cut a downward-sloping, wedge-shaped front end onto it with a handsaw. The sub was about sixteen inches long. Pulling the submarine along on a string connected to the front end caused it to submerge and travel underwater. For stabilization I added a conning tower made of another two-by-four cut into a different pointed vertical shape, and cutting through the water, it straightened out the slight wobble I had noticed. My wooden submarine would pop up to the surface whenever I stopped pulling it forward. It had to be moving to stay submerged. I drove big nails into it to represent guns, and it looked increasingly formidable. In fact, it was so formidable that it was banned from the pool by the authorities. They viewed it as a dangerous weapon.

The Wing brothers, a couple of Chinese boys I kind of knew from school, lived across from Moore Park and had a band. That year, in 1955, I went to Mayfair, a yearly event that was held every spring in Rosedale Park, which was a lot bigger than Moore Park, and watched the Wing brothers play on a little stage. I watched the whole thing go down, thinking it was really cool. People clapped after the band played, and the guys were very happy. That was something special to me. I saw they were doing what they liked and that other people were clapping for them.

At Mayfair, after watching the Wing brothers and their band, I won a very ornate and colorful leather collar with marbles and studs on it by throwing tennis balls at a rubber rabbit. I decided to give it to the girl I particularly liked, Mary Ellen Blanche. I felt more than a little nervous, walking up to her house to ring the doorbell and give her the gift. She was very pretty with blondish-reddish hair and a light complexion, a lot like my wife Pegi looks now, come to think of it. Her mother came to the door, and when I asked if Mary Ellen was home, she said no, so I had to leave the gift with her. Years later I was told that maybe she might not have thought that a dog collar was a good gift. I still had a lot to learn about boys and girls, to say the very least. It's the thought that counts, though.

It was around this time that I saw my mom and dad have a big fight, and Mommy was screaming at Daddy and he hit her. I don't know what they were fighting about and I guess I wasn't supposed to be there. Later Daddy said that my mother was hysterical and that's why he had hit her. Up to that point I had only heard the word *hysterical* associated with laughter. I really didn't like what I had seen, and I spent a lot of time during the following days in the basement with my little secondhand Lionel steam engine. Down there below the house on the cement floor, where I was in my own world with my electric train, the furnace, and the musty-smelling water pipes. I forgot about everything else.

It was a little damp in the basement, and sometimes I got a shock when I touched certain things. Bare feet did not work. One hanging lightbulb illuminated my little train set. I would sit on the floor and experiment with the transformer, holding the train and watching the wheels spinning and throwing sparks. That was the beginning of my long relationship with electricity.

1956 Volkswagen

In the summer of 1955, when I was nine years old, our family moved again; close to Pickering, Ontario, about thirty miles from Toronto, and into a new clapboard bungalow my mom and dad had purchased on Brock Road. My dad later wrote that this move was to be a new start for my family, referring to the problems that had been brewing in our house back in Toronto. My mom single-handedly painted the entire outside of the house a beautiful white. She painted everything inside the house as well. She really loved the place, and planted some trees in the front field that eventually became a lawn that Bob and I mowed with a gasoline-powered mower. My mother poured her love into that house, making it look great and doing everything she could to make it feel like a good home. I realize now, she was trying everything she could to make our little family work.

Once we settled in, I entered grade five at Brock Road Public School, a one-hundred-year-old stone schoolhouse with two classrooms—grades one through four in one room and five through eight in the other.

Some cars were known as "bombs" back then, when they were customized and "souped-up." There was a guy who had a cool bomb on Brock Road in 1955. He used to stop at Middleton's confectionery store across from our old stone schoolhouse and buy cigarettes, which he would roll up in his T-shirt sleeve, like the movie star James Dean. His bomb had blue lights under it and it made a low rumbling sound. He always left it running, and when he got in it to pull out onto the road, he crowded up by the steering wheel with his elbow out the window so you could see the cigarette pack rolled up on his sleeve. His posture was very different from a normal driver like Daddy.

At Middleton's confectionery store, bubble gum cards were big, with Elvis having his own line of cards. I remember this guy and his car well because I would go in to buy a five-cent pack of gum and cards and he was in there a lot. He and guys like him were known as "hard rocks" or just "rocks." His hair was greased back and came down on his forehead a little, and it came together in the back with a DA (duck's ass) or ducktail. His bomb was so cool. It had no door handles. I wondered how he got in and out and locked it and everything without any door handles. I would watch him outside Middleton's and still couldn't figure it out. It was a 1950 Monarch, maybe a 1949, because it was a little different from my dad's 1951. As he drove away looking so cool, his two exhausts made that low rumble, unless he was in a hurry and stepped on it, then it got really loud like a machine gun. Daddy's old Monarch did not do that at all. The rock's bomb really had a lot of attitude.

We had a gang of boys, maybe four or five of us, who walked home from school together every day. The gang did not include my two best friends, Chuck Bent and Reggie Taylor. Chuck lived up a side road behind the school, right near an old railroad bridge, in a big house full of kids, and Reggie lived the opposite way from me on Brock Road, about a mile past the school. The gang of boys walking in the direction of my house must have looked like a scene from *Huck Finn* or *Tom Sawyer*, scrubby-looking youngsters, ready to go fishing or investigating. A gang unified by scruffy hair and curious faces, always intent on some goal.

Walking along the road the same way from school every day, we were pretty predictable. There was a guy who lived in a house on our road, and he started waving to us from his front steps as we walked by. After passing him a few times, we waved back. One day, he asked us to come in. Curious as ever, we accepted and went inside the house. He sat us down in his living room in a big circle like we were at a meeting and told us he was going to teach us something he called "whacking off." He unzipped his pants and pulled out his pecker. Then he began. He encouraged us all to do the same thing. So we did. We never got the results he did. He said you had to use your imagination, or something to that effect.

The whole thing took a bit too long and I couldn't wait to get the hell out of there. We all agreed he was weird and we never went back, at least I know I didn't. I never told my mom and dad about it, either, and we made a pact that it would just be our own little secret. Every day when we walked by after that, we just kept going straight ahead and walked on, never looking over at that house again.

While we were living on Brock Road, we got a brand-new record player. It was a Seabreeze, and I think it was my mom who got it. It had a rectangular shape with a lid that opened on the top and three control knobs on the outside. There was a cloth on the front that had some shiny metallic threads in it and a speaker behind it. The finish was a blond wood, and I remember how excited my mother became because she had found a cabinet that matched it perfectly, a wonderful place to store all of her old records by Lena Horne and Satchmo. She loved those records. She arranged all the furniture so the record player was the center of attention.

My own 78 rpm record collection began there at Brock Road and consisted of Jerry Lee Lewis, Larry Williams, Little Richard, Elvis, and a few others. Rock and roll was just in its infancy when I played those records in the house alone, pretending *I* was singing those songs while I stood in front of a mirror, the Seabreeze blasting at full volume. I sang the songs right along with the singer and played my own imaginary guitar, making all my Elvis moves and soaking up the wild applause I was hearing in my head. I imagined I was winning some talent contest. I only did that when no one else was around; those moments alone in the house when Mom and Dad had gone out and Bob was at a high school dance or something. That Seabreeze had a magical transporting sound, and I would look forward to being left all alone in the house with my dreams.

Well, come along my baby, whole lotta shakin' goin' on.
Yeah, come along my baby, we really got the bull by the horns.
We ain't fakin'.
Whole lotta shakin' goin' on.

—Jerry Lee Lewis, "Whole Lotta Shakin' Going On"

We were all very happy to be out of the city, with a lot of land behind our house like we used to have in Omemee, but Daddy had a job working at Orenda Engines near Toronto. He had to drive to work every day and was gone a lot. Orenda made the engine for a famous Canadian plane of the time, the Avro Arrow, a delta-winged interceptor aircraft that was touted to be superior to its American counterpart, the F-35. Daddy was a public relations assistant to the vice president, or something like that. That is the only time I can remember him doing something other than writing for a living and I imagine it was not that great for him. I guess sometimes his stories just didn't sell.

Daddy sold his 1954 Monarch and got a 1956 Volkswagen shortly after we moved out to Pickering. It was fun to ride with him in it because it was small and we were close together. My mom had to have something to drive since my dad was gone so much in the city. For the first time, we were a two-car family! The little Volkswagen parked in our gravel driveway with my mother's 1950 Ford coupe.

One birthday, I guess it was my eleventh, I got a plastic Arthur Godfrey ukulele. It had a picture of Arthur Godfrey right on it, with some musical notes. With its nylon strings to tune to the little whistle that came with it and an instruction booklet full of chords, I was ready to go. One day, getting nowhere, I was trying to play it in the backyard when Daddy came out and said something about showing me some old songs. I was dumbfounded when he started to play and sing "Bury Me out on the Prairie." I had never heard him sing or play and didn't even know he knew how to play. I knew Uncle Bob played uke and piano and sang; we had all sat around listening to him and my girl cousins, but not Daddy, and there he was, singing and playing great. He looked so different; so light and happy. I will never forget it. I learned a few chords from him and started to learn to play myself. That was my beginning in music, that and the Seabreeze. I never saw my dad play again, though. I don't know why. There was some reason I didn't understand.

In 1956, Daddy got simultaneous jobs with the *Globe and Mail* newspaper and also on TV! That was very exciting. He was hosting *Hockey Night in Canada*'s intermission program, *The Hot Stove League*, every Saturday night. Those two jobs returned him to the kind of work he loved, writing and sports. Of course, for our family that meant another move. It also meant more money than we had ever had before.

1956 Monarch Richelieu

When we moved back to Toronto, our new house was at 49 Old Orchard Grove in North York. I checked into school at John Wanless Public School, a beautiful old brick-and-cement four-story building between Fairlawn and Brookdale Avenues, with a huge playground surrounded by a fence. I finished the last few weeks of grade seven there and then went for a full year, completing grade eight. I was then ready for high school at Lawrence Park Collegiate. Probably all that early moving around is why I am so happy traveling now. A lot of the kids I knew in school were reluctant to move. I always liked to go to new places, so that didn't scare me at all.

During this time, my dad did something quite unusual and different. He purchased a very cool and deluxe car, a 1956 Monarch two-door hardtop convertible. It was an attractive and sporty design with no post between the windows, so when they were down there was an openness. I was an avid follower of all the car designs, fascinated by every new twist and turn. When my father purchased this car it was the first time we had ever had a car that was more than just a standard sedan or coupe. This really got my attention. Perhaps he was rewarding himself for all of the success he was enjoying. It was a very big and stylish car, a statement, new in every way! I was thinking to myself, *Wow! Daddy has a cool car. This is really something.*

Life in the city rolled on. I had only a few friends at my new school. I never really had a lot of close friends anywhere we lived, though, usually just one or two. One I met was Brian (Bunny) Stuart, who lived one block over from Old Orchard Grove. He was into sports and I was into music and cars, but somehow we related really well and he became my best friend there at old John Wanless Public School. We spent a lot of time together, and I got to know his family well and spent many hours at his house. His brother had a 1958 Chevrolet Biscayne. I knew that the Impala was the nicest Chevrolet model that year, but that Biscayne of his brother's was really sharp. Every time I visited Bunny's house, I checked it out thoroughly when it was parked in the driveway, imagining the differences between it and the Impala. The Impala had a very sexy treatment over the rear window and more taillights than the Biscayne.

I missed my dad. He was in and out of our house and was writing in an apartment in the city a lot. I would always look for the big Monarch in the driveway when I came back from school in the afternoon, but it wasn't there much.

At noon hour, I would regularly stop by another friend's house where I could listen to some records. I don't remember his name, but music was always playing at his house and I really liked that. Every afternoon after school we would gather there to watch *American Bandstand* on TV. I couldn't wait to get to that part of the day!

Dick Clark gave us the music news as Conway Twitty and Johnny Burnette served up hits along with Roy Orbison, the Everly Brothers, Jack Scott, the Kalin Twins, Marty Robbins, and several others. Music was taking up most of my spare time as my interests were all starting to revolve around it.

> *Once you told me long ago,*
> *To the prom with me you'd go.*
> *Now you've changed your mind it seems.*
> *Someone else will have my dreams.*
>
> —MARTY ROBBINS, "A WHITE SPORT COAT
> (AND A PINK CARNATION)"

That fall, I started grade nine at Lawrence Park Collegiate. During this time there was a group called the Sultans that played at some of our local dances, and I would go to watch them every week with my friend Comrie Smith. Comrie was a schoolmate one year ahead of me who had dreams of a life in music, dreams like mine. We were the best of friends and used to buy records at a local store, Robinson's Radio and Appliances, on Yonge Street, located conveniently between our houses, about three blocks from mine and two blocks from his. When we started jamming in his attic with my uke and his guitar and bongos, it was the beginning of me playing music with others.

About Christmastime, Comrie failed math and was put back into my class for that subject. We walked to school together a lot after that, becoming good friends, listening to a little transistor radio and talking about music, music, music. We built a solid friendship, and he was one of my two best friends during that time of dreams and big plans of a life in music.

Every day on our walk to school, at some point we would leave Yonge Street and pass through residential streets, crisscrossing our way toward Lawrence Park Collegiate and listening to Gene Vincent or Bo Diddley on the transistor as loud as it could go. Sometimes we would try to play these songs at home on our instruments. We were pretty primitive. I don't think we even knew how to find those chords yet, but we were exploring.

> *Well, she's the gal in the red blue jeans*
> *She's the queen of all the teens*
> *She's the one that I know*
> *She's the one that loves me so.*
>
> —Gene Vincent, "Be-Bop-A-Lula"

Comrie had a car called Priscilla. She was an old Plymouth, a fun old car. He and his girlfriend, Lynda, a really happy, friendly, and pretty girl, used to spend a lot of time with me. Often the three of us would get in Priscilla and go for a ride to a nearby park overlooking Yonge Street, the main drag, where we would hang out and talk about music and life. Just sitting there on a bench or on the grass, talking together, looking through the trees at the cars going down the hill into Don Valley, dreaming about music and bands; we became three good friends. I always thought Comrie and Lynda would be together forever.

> *Well, pretty soon I met a friend,*
> *He played guitar.*
> *We used to sit*
> *On the steps at school*
> *And dream of being stars.*

We started a band,
We played all night.

—"Don't Be Denied"

Comrie and I dreamed about how someday we would make it in music. I don't remember any specific plans, but we were big dreamers. Every time there was a dance with a live band, we would go and watch them play. Church dances were popular and we would travel around Toronto, following the bands. The Sultans were one of our favorites, but we would go anywhere we could to see any band. Sometimes we went to areas where the dances were a little dangerous, with gangs fighting and older kids around, drinking. We stayed away from that, but still we always went to see the bands. Sometimes we were too young to get in and had to listen from outside. Occasionally, we could watch through a window in the side of the building, standing on something to get enough elevation to see. Each time we would take note of the equipment, the outfits they wore, the singers, the guitar players, drummers, and organists, anything to do with the music being made. We knew who was hot and why, and we had our own favorites.

On weekend afternoons, a lot of the kids I knew would go to the Glendale Theater on Avenue Road and Brookdale Avenue. It was just a couple of blocks from John Wanless school. We would go to the matinees. I loved horror movies and sci-fi and I would watch the westerns, too. We would go there and have popcorn and meet girls. Every weekend it was the greatest fun. Saturday morning at the end of my paper route, I would see the marquee and know what movies I would see at the double feature later in the day.

I can still smell the popcorn and see the girls. That's where we would all hang out. One weekend I saw *The Blob* in living color.

The advertising said, "See the Blob in living color." It didn't say that everything else in the movie was in black and white. I saw *Invaders from Mars*, *The Day the Earth Stood Still*, *The Crimson Pirate*, *Dracula*, *Frankenstein*, *Bride of Frankenstein*, *The Hound of the Baskervilles*, *Jack the Ripper*, and *The Adventures of Robin Hood*, just to name a few, and every week there was a serial as well as the double feature. It would have a fifteen-minute episode continuing on from the prior week. The hours there at the Glendale went by so fast. It usually started around noon or so. Week in and week out, I was in a groove, having the time of my life.

Late 1950s Triumph TR3

Near the beginning of my first year at Lawrence Park Collegiate, my dad picked me up at school and took me for a weekend trip to a sportswriters' golf tournament. When he showed up, I was surprised to see him riding in a sharp little yellow Triumph TR3 convertible. He had borrowed it for the trip because it was a fun car. We traveled along for some time in the little sports car; completely different from the many cars we had ridden in together. Somewhere on the trip he told me that, someday, if the family was not together, it did not mean he didn't love me. Then we went on with the rest of the weekend trip, arrived at the golf course, and played in the tournament, hanging out with NHL hockey players and sportswriters who were Daddy's friends. The next day he dropped me off near school and went back to his studio apartment to finish some stories he was working on. I don't remember him ever coming back to our house or ever seeing the TR3 again.

A couple of weeks later I came home from school and Mommy was crying and crying. Daddy had left a letter that said he was leaving and would not be back. Bob, Mommy, and I were all in the living room. Then it dawned on me what Daddy had been telling me in the TR3, and I blurted out, "I knew it. I knew it!" Crying loudly, I ran upstairs to my room and closed the door. Mommy came up and said, "You knew what?" Then I told her about the trip and what Daddy had said to me about not always being together. My mother was really beside herself, with tears running down her face, and I just held on to her.

A few days later, I came home from school and found Mommy in the driveway in front of the garage. She had her record collection out, a big pile of 78s from a couple of boxes. At first, it looked like she was organizing something. But Mommy was crying now, taking out each 78, looking at it, and breaking it on the cement driveway. That was one of the saddest things I have ever seen. I try to block it out of my mind. Just a late afternoon, sun getting ready to set, and there is this picture of her crying and breaking each record, making a little comment with each one.

We used to listen to Lena Horne and a lot of other old popular records that Mommy would put on the Seabreeze record player, which she always set up in our living rooms, wherever we were living. Lena Horne's *Stormy Weather* was one of her favorites. That Seabreeze was a big part of our family. Music is full with memories of love and happiness from the times of our lives. Songs are like little time capsules that take us back to those good times. That is part of music's magic. The other side of this is the music that brings back sadness, waking it up inside of you with just a few familiar strains of a song.

After a few quiet days, we started getting back to a routine, and things around the house got a little looser than they had ever been. About that time, Mommy decided she did not mind it if we called her Rassy, which was her nickname and what everyone else called her. She became very supportive of the musical dreams my friends and I were having. From that point on, she was behind everything we wanted to do and gave us a lot of freedom.

I was allowed to buy some cool clothes that I had seen down at Halpern's Men's Store on Yonge Street. One was a shirt that had a shiny front on it that looked like something a rock and roll singer would wear. A few blocks away was Robinson's Radio and Appliances, where Comrie and I were allowed to listen to records in the bargain bin, but not the Top 30. A nice lady there really treated us well. I got "Only the Lonely" by Roy Orbison there and that was my first 45 rpm record, all the others I had were 78s. I think "Only the Lonely" was the first time I put the plastic adapter in a 45 rpm record and switched the turntable speed to 45 rpm, but it may have been "Book of Love" by the Monotones, back while we were still at Brock Road.

There goes my baby
There goes my heart
They're gone forever
So far apart.

But only the lonely
Know why
I cry.

—ROY ORBISON,
"ONLY THE LONELY"

That Christmas, Rassy got me a banjo uke that I had seen at the music store. It had quite a folk sound. I would listen to a Kingston Trio LP my brother Bob had bought, and try to play along. There was a song called "They Call the Wind Maria" that I almost learned. It had a lot of minor chords and I liked the sound of them. That may have even been my first introduction to the minor keys I love so much and have used throughout my life.

> *Before I knew Maria's name*
> *And heard her wail and whinin',*
> *I had a girl and she had me*
> *And the sun was always shinin'.*
>
> *But then one day I left my gal,*
> *I left her far behind me.*
> *And now I'm lost, so gol darn lost*
> *Not even God can find me.*
>
> —Kingston Trio, "They Call
> the Wind Maria"

When I finished the ninth grade at Lawrence Park Collegiate, Rassy had just purchased a small English car. It was a four-door Ensign, light blue, made by Standard Motors. Rassy asked me if I would like to move to Winnipeg and make a new start. She painted a bright picture of her growing up there, the things she did, the people she knew, all the good times she had, and I decided it would be fine to move there.

Bob elected to stay in Toronto when he heard about the planned move. He had friends there and did not want to leave and start again. I was used to moving, but this was the first time I had moved away from half of the family, and it felt different. I was fourteen. So that was it for our family living together in one house.

Rassy and I packed up the Ensign, loaded a moving van, and began the long drive to Winnipeg. She elected to take a route across the northern United States because the roads were better down there. When we got below Manitoba, which is in the center of Canada, we headed north across the border back up into Canada and to Winnipeg. Gas cost us about 31 cents per gallon, and Rassy's Ensign got a little more than 23 mpg, so during that trip to Winnipeg we put 1,139 pounds of CO_2 in the atmosphere with that little car without our noticing. All the way there, she talked about the fun we would have, telling me how supportive and friendly the people in Winnipeg were. I think her time there was the best part of her life. When we stopped at motels, she would let me smoke a few of her cigarettes, Black Cat Plains, with no filter, which was very kind of her. Eventually we arrived in Winnipeg and set up house in an apartment in the suburb of Fort Rouge, on Corydon Avenue, kind of a main street.

The Gray Apartments, 250 Hugo Street, apartment number 5, greeted us. Our apartment was in the basement and my bedroom was right on the corner of Corydon Avenue and Hugo Street. My window, at the top of the wall near the ceiling, looked out on the feet of people standing on the sidewalk at the bus stop, waiting for a bus. Traffic was fairly heavy. The buses came and went, shaking the room just a little, but they were electric trolley buses. I noticed that these buses were fast and quiet, not like the noisy and dirty buses I had seen growing up in Toronto. There was no exhaust or fuel smell, just electricity from the two wires that ran above the street. I had never seen buses like that before.

Our building was not far from the Dorchester Apartments, an old apartment building where Grandpa and Grandma lived on Dorchester Avenue, and we would visit them about once a week for a while after we arrived. Rassy's parents were old and the place was very quiet. We would sit and drink tea, and Mom would talk with them and smoke cigarettes while I fidgeted. Something about that place made me feel a bit nervous or sad or something. I didn't know what it was. I wanted fresh air.

At our apartment, the Ensign was parked in a lane behind the building, and it was a five- or six-block walk to school. I attended the Earl Grey School, taking grade nine for the second time. I had failed to pass it at Lawrence Park.

MY FIRST BIT of good luck in Winnipeg was in somehow landing the best paper route in the world. The route consisted of approximately one hundred customers, who were mostly in apartment buildings, and was only a couple of blocks long. The winter came right on time, and I could still feel that thing in my soul, that growing feeling that was still with me like an invisible, chilly coat I wore beneath my skin and that showed up on its own occasionally. Since the temperature was often way below zero, my paper route was a huge bonus in wintertime. While other paperboys were trudging through the snow in below-freezing temperatures, I was delivering papers in heated buildings.

The route was a great source of income for me, and I was able to buy things. First off, I bought a Harmony Sovereign guitar with a DeArmond pickup added to it. This gave me a foothold as a guitar player, and I practiced night and day. I did not need an amp because the Harmony had F-holes and could be played acoustically at home.

I had gotten into the habit of writing little signs and posting them on my bedroom walls. Most of them said WHO CARES? These messages were a great cause of concern for Rassy. She was upset by my posted wall messages. I had to keep writing them, though, and now I see them as an early indication of my need to write and express myself. I played my Harmony Sovereign guitar all the time and I began writing in that room, playing little songs I had made up.

The Seabreeze was set up in our living room, which faced out onto the Hugo Street sidewalk. Through the living room window, a regular parade of footwear could be seen traversing the sidewalk outside. I listened to LPs by the Ventures and the Shadows with a sprinkling of 45s by the Fireballs, Johnny and the Hurricanes, Bill Black's Combo, the Viscounts, the Mar-Keys, and a great instrumental track called "Hide Away" by Freddie King.

Cruising up and down the streets and finding the best ways to get to school and back, I got to know the new neighborhood. As soon as school started, I met a few guys who liked music, and actually got a band going called the Jades, my first band. Right around New Year's, we played the Earl Grey Community Club. That was the only engagement the Jades ever had, but it was a start, and that's all we needed. The group was made up of myself on rhythm guitar, and schoolmates Jim Atkin on bongos, congas, and vibes; David Gregg on bongos; and John Daniel on lead guitar. He had a real good Gibson Les Paul Standard. John was the real musician. I had one instrumental song called "Wendy's Walk" that I played lead on. That may have been my first actual composition. On all the others, John played lead and I played rhythm. John had an amp, so I plugged into it as well. John was an accomplished guitar player who taught me a lot in the beginning at get-togethers we used to have in his house on Corydon, a couple of blocks from our apartment. His dad had a business there called Dot Transfer. Signs were all over the outside of John's house reading DIAL DOT AND DOT DASHES. Those were my musical beginnings in Winnipeg.

There was a guy at school named Koobie. His full name was Ken

Koblun and he was about six-five. He was the tallest kid in our school and we quickly found out that we had a lot in common. Ken was a foster child who had become adopted and was now part of the Clayton family. I was from a broken home, and divorce was a rarity, even somewhat of a stigma at that time, so we had something in common there, but music was our real bond.

Richard Clayton, Ken's brother, was English. All of the Claytons were in touch with England and had the latest music and news from there. The Shadows were hot. They were an instrumental group that backed heartthrob singer Cliff Richard, who was incredibly popular in England. The Shadows released a lot of instrumental records, which were quite great, and we aspired to be as good as them. We read about the Shadows in *Melody Maker* and *New Musical Express*, two English music papers with the latest skinny on groups in England and around the world.

Ken and I loved the Shadows, and the best band in Winnipeg, Allan and the Silvertones, had a guitar player who played all of the Shadows' songs. He played them great! His name was Randy Bachman. He had an echo sound on his guitar that he got from a tape recorder that was just like the one the Shadows' lead guitarist, Hank B. Marvin, had.

We all need heroes to get started. Hank and Randy were mine. They used an Echoplex tape delay, and I started to as well, and still use mine today. The combination of using tape repeat while a Bigsby vibrato tailpiece bends the pitch of a note and adds a ton of depth. Because there is a delay, the delayed note is always a different pitch from the original note as you use the Bigsby, bending the pitch, widening the sound by creating two close pitches, varying from each other, manually, at your fingertip. One sound chases another, always a little behind, and the pitches are slightly different. Of course, back then all I had was my Harmony Sovereign with one pickup and it had no Bigsby, so I couldn't actually play that sound. I had no echo. I just *knew* how to play it. Randy had a Gretsch guitar with two pickups and a Bigsby. I thought Randy's was the greatest guitar sound in the world. All I wanted was to have a shot at being that cool, and playing that sound.

In the North End of Winnipeg on Main Street there was an area that had a lot of pawnshops. It was the seedy part of town and there were always a lot of drunken Indians walking around, homeless. It never really dawned on me why that was. I just viewed it as a reality of life at the time. I didn't think about them being here first, or how Winnipeg, where the Red River and the Assiniboine River came together, used to be one of the largest Native centers, a hub of their civilization. The artifacts that have been found at the river fork indicate that tribes from as far south as Arizona were trading goods there with the Canadian tribes long before the white man came. The river fork was a traditional meeting place where the Native peoples from North America came together regularly every year to trade. Now we don't call them Indians anymore. We refer to them as First Nations people, which I like better because it is true.

I would visit those pawnshops often, looking at guitars and amps, trying to find something I liked. I would look at the Kay and Supro electric guitars in the window. National guitars were there, too. Lots of guitars from Japan or other Asian countries would be on display, some with many pickups and features like tremolo arms. They were flashy-looking and caught my eye. I was listening to Jimmy Reed, the blues player, a lot then, and he played a Kay guitar on his album cover.

You don't know me, baby,
Like I know myself.
I couldn't live if you should give
Your love to someone else.
Better get some insurance on me, baby,
Take out some insurance on me, baby.
'Cause if you ever, ever say good-bye,
I'm gonna haul right off and die.

—JIMMY REED, "TAKE OUT SOME INSURANCE"

Silvertone guitars were sold at Sears, and Jimmy played one of those, too, in a picture I had seen on one of his album covers. I would leave those album covers on display, standing up on top of the Seabreeze, so I could look at the pictures. Jimmy's guitars were all inexpensive ones compared to the Gibsons and Fenders from the USA. Those Gibsons and Fenders always caught my attention. I dreamed of owning one.

Around Christmastime, Ken got a guitar from his dad. This was very good, and I talked to Ken about our band needing a bass. He decided to trade the guitar and get a bass. With the help of Jimmy Kale from the Silvertones, Ken got a Danelectro bass from Cam's Hardware in the area of Winnipeg known as St. Vital, near where Jimmy lived. Hardware and appliance stores were places you could order amps and electric guitars back in those days.

Once Ken and I had good instruments, we started playing with more people in little bands at school. We had a band, the Stardusters, and played a little at the community clubs and churches near our school. After Christmas, I did a couple of shows with a band called the Esquires, but I was not good enough. The Esquires were ahead of me. I was struggling to play the chords and remember the fingerings for their songs. I guess I wasn't thinking so much about the beat. That's not too good for a rhythm guitarist. It didn't last. They dropped me. Those were some of my first performances.

Linda Fowler was a girl in the neighborhood. She did not go to our school and I never found out what school she went to. She was always dressed up. She was a pretty girl, very reserved, and usually wore all black—black dresses, jet-black hair—and red lipstick, all perfect. Her house welcomed us and it seemed that anything musical was welcomed there. Linda was fascinating and mysterious, nothing like other girls I knew at the time. She was more like a beat poet or something, very bohemian. Linda played piano and she really played it beautifully. Jim Atkin introduced her to me and we played with Linda under the names the Classics and the Stardusters. We had a vocalist, John Copsey, and Jim Atkin on vibes and bongos and congas. Ken was on bass. We had no drummer. We practiced and tried to get some engagements but couldn't get any, so we just kept on practicing, working at arrangements, trying things. With no style of our own, we tried everything we could think of, from "Summertime" to "Be-Bop-A-Lula."

> *Summertime, and the livin' is easy.*
> *Fish are jumpin'*
> *And the cotton is high.*
> *Your daddy's rich*
> *And your mama's good lookin'.*
> *So hush little baby,*
> *Don't you cry.*
> —GEORGE GERSHWIN, "SUMMERTIME"

In November of 1962, I was seventeen years old and starting to write instrumentals on a new guitar I had gotten for my birthday from Rassy, a Gibson Les Paul Junior with a sunburst finish and a single black Gibson pickup. A real electric guitar! It was my first one. The finish was cracked a lot but I thought it looked great. It had a little case that was pretty flimsy, made of cardboard or something, but with an alligator skin–looking finish. It was not the deluxe hard-shell case that John Daniel had for his Les Paul Standard, but I was extremely happy just to have a real electric guitar, simple as it was.

Rassy and I eventually moved out of the apartment on Corydon and Hugo to 1123 Grosvenor Avenue, close to River Heights, a better neighborhood. We were about halfway up the social ladder compared to the super well-off River Heights and neighboring Tuxedo communities. I started going to high school at Kelvin High but stayed in touch with Ken. Our musical link remained strong even though he had moved as well and was now going to a different high school, Churchill High, in another part of town.

We practiced and got better. That's what I was focused on. I failed my first year at Kelvin and had to repeat grade ten. I was so distracted by music. While I was supposed to be studying, I drew little diagrams of stage setups, imagining how the equipment and amps would sound in different configurations. I was studying, but not my lessons. After two repeated grades in a row, my dad was writing letters to Rassy about my grades being bad and it was upsetting to both of us, but mostly to Rassy. She would go around the house talking about what an ass my dad was.

About that time, my grandma died and Grandpa moved in with us. He stayed in what used to be Rassy's bedroom and she converted our dining room into her new bedroom. Grandpa spent a lot of time at the club with his old pals. It was called the Carlton Club, and they used to play cards and go curling. Grandpa, W. N. "Bill" Ragland, spoke with a deep southern drawl and was very nice to us, contributing to our rent, but stayed mostly to himself. I don't remember us eating together much. Grandpa ate at the club.

There was a nightclub out on Pembina Highway called the Sugar Shack, named after a hit record of the day by Jimmy Gilmer and the Fireballs, and I remember going there to see Bill Black's Combo. Bill Black played bass with Elvis back in the day, and the guitar player in the combo had a crazy unique sound he made by banging on the strings with his comb. This is how the guitar sound with Bill Black's Combo got its percussive edge. It was very original and had a boogie bass line to it. There was also a sax, a cool smoky piano, drums, and Bill Black's electric bass in the combo. There was no singer. It was a strictly instrumental group.

When Ken and I went out to the Sugar Shack, I stood right in front of the band for hours, watching every move they made. When they played their big hit "Smokie—Part 2," it was really impressive because they sounded just like the record. Exactly like it. I had played that record over and over on the Seabreeze. Slack-jawed, I stood there watching them. There I was, this wide-eyed kid, blocking their view, gawking at them from ten feet away. They were probably looking for women in the audience.

Around March of 1961, Rassy got a job on a TV show called *Twenty Questions* and she became very happy. It was a quiz show. Rassy was pretty occupied with her new job. It took a lot of her time and she was getting into the swing of things. She had a few dates with Bill Trebilcoe, who was one of the panelists on the show, and I remember how she started wearing bright colors and looking really happy and different than she had looked in a long time. That made me happy, too. Something went amiss, though, because she reverted back to her old self after a while.

Then I remember her drinking more and more. It was not like she was drunk, but she seemingly always had something with her to drink. She was gone to the club a lot, the club being either the Niakwa Golf and Country Club or the Curling Club downtown. She would send me out in the Ensign to get her beer, after calling and making arrangements with the store. When I got there, they would carry out a case of Labatt's pilsner beer and put it in the trunk for me. All I had to do was carry it up the stairs at the back of the house from the garage when I got home. I found I had more time to myself then, and I spent a lot of it listening to records on the Seabreeze and practicing on my guitar.

Marilyn Nentwig, my girlfriend about that time, was very pretty, had a twin sister Jackie, and they were both a lot of fun to be with. Marilyn and Jackie were regulars on a TV show named *Teen Dance Party*. Besides being beautiful, they were great dancers, too. I went to a show once but I didn't dance; I was too shy for that. Marilyn liked me anyway and we had a really good time together. We were just a couple of kids growing up. I used to visit their house all the time and we would play the electric organ they had in the living room. Ken Koblun visited their home with me, too, and he would get down on the floor and play the bass pedals with his hands. We must have been quite a sight! I loved their house and family. Everything was fun and happy. The whole family was together and they were all so mellow, no fighting or bad feelings that I ever saw, always having a good time.

Marilyn helped me write down the music to one of my first songs, "I Wonder," on a sheet of paper so I could send it to myself and not open it, protecting my copyright in a basic way. The theory was that the envelope would remain unopened and the postal stamp would show the date it was mailed, proving that I wrote it and when. She wrote the notes from my singing and I wrote the chords over the words. That kind of reminds me how my mom used to edit my dad's manuscripts with him.

> *Well, I wonder who's with her tonight,*
> *And I wonder who's holdin' her tight.*
> *But there's nothin' I can say to make him go away.*
> *Well, I never cared too much anyway.*
> *I guess that I'll forget her someday.*
>
> —"I Wonder"

Marilyn and Jackie were a couple of nice girls and it was a really happy time. I hope they have grown up and are living good healthy lives. They certainly deserve to. Of course, life has a way of surprising us all.

During my first months at Kelvin, we played a couple of gigs as the Stardusters, and also as the Classics with a new player, John Gowenlock, on rhythm guitar. John had an electric guitar he had made himself. It was funky and sounded pretty darn good, but soon we broke up. I don't remember why. That was at the end of the year, just before Christmas. It was becoming clear to me that we could rock best with just two guitars, bass, and drums, like the Shadows, the Fireballs, or the Ventures. I met a drummer at school named Jack Harper, who was a friendly and funny guy, and he wanted to play with us. Jack said he had a friend, Allan Bates, at nearby Grant Park High School, and Allan played electric guitar. When I met Allan, he knew a lot of chords and was very good.

From the very beginning, I was driven to make the sound I wanted to hear. It was hard to do, but I had to tell Jim Atkin, a good guy who had stuck with the band for quite a while, that we did not need bongos and vibes. I told Linda that we were changing and didn't need piano, and I told John that we were going to become an instrumental band, so we didn't need a singer. I never liked the part of leading a band where you have to change players or lose somebody because you don't want that sound anymore, and I still don't like it, but it is key to success. You have to evolve, painful as it may be on personal levels, and the music has to come first. Always the music comes first.

I came up with the name the Squires for the new band. Jack Harper on drums, Kenny Koblun on bass, Allan Bates and myself on guitars. We started practicing at Jack Harper's house and sometimes in our apartment on the third floor of our triplex on Grosvenor, right in front of the Seabreeze. Once, we rehearsed at Lynne Hamilton's house. She was Allan Bates's girlfriend and had become a good friend of the band, petite and cute with a positive and happy feeling. Ken had a homemade bass reflex speaker cabinet he had constructed out of wood from plans he found in *Popular Science* magazine and an amp he made from a Heathkit. His bass sounded good. I still didn't have an amp. Money was tight.

The Winnipeg Piano Company, on Portage Avenue, was a big local music store where every musician in town went to hang out. Downstairs were all the amps and guitars. They had such a great variety, I would go down there to be with the equipment, dreaming. Randy Bachman went there a lot, too. Randy recalls that the scene was like little Liverpool. We had hundreds of bands right in Winnipeg and it seemed like everyone was in a band.

There was another smaller store named Ray Hamerton Music, and they carried Fender piggyback amps, which were the absolute coolest in my opinion. There was always one on display in the window. I loved those amps, but I could not afford one.

The Galaxies, one of the top three bands in town, had two Fender piggyback amps: a Showman and a Bandmaster. I can still see their complete setup in my mind with their huge double-bass drum kit and those two big Fender piggyback amps set up at River Heights Community Club. I was in absolute awe of that band's equipment.

The scene in Winnipeg was very supportive, just as Rassy had described in the little Ensign on our trip from Toronto. There were community clubs everywhere, maybe fifty of them in the city, with dances every weekend and bands playing. Young bands of kids like me were just getting started, going from community club to community club all through the city, climbing the ladder of fame, getting bigger crowds, more money, and more acclaim the harder we worked and the better we got. It was as real as it could be. What a great place to learn how things worked. Winnipeg was the rock and roll capital of Canada.

Somewhere along the line I got an amp; an Ampeg Echo Twin from the Winnipeg Piano Company. Rassy helped me with money to buy it. The amp was good, with two twelve-inch speakers, but as I soon discovered, unless I used the reverb it was just one twelve-inch speaker. The other one was only for the reverb, so the sound was not as big as I thought it was going to be. At least I had an amp, though.

We practiced and got a sound going. We were all on about the same level, although Allan Bates was better trained and knew more. He was cool and really into it. He knew a lot of jazz riffs. We played a couple of gigs, and then Jack had to drop out because he had sports and other stuff to do. Those were his priorities. Jack was always a unique guy with a lot of soul. It was like he was still in the group, even though he dropped out. He kept hanging with us.

Bates had a drummer friend at Grant Park High School whose name was Ken Smyth. Ken's dad bought him a set of drums in a pawnshop so he could play with the Squires, and the band practiced hard in his basement during January. Supportive parents like that are sure a big part of dream building. We had our first gig with Ken on drums at Riverview Community Club in south Fort Rouge. It was February 1, 1963, and I was seventeen. Ken was a stocky, athletic guy and played really well, with a good beat and positive energy. I think we made five dollars for the night, but it may have been nothing. We kept practicing, played a lot of gigs, and got solid. We were getting good.

Rassy's Ensign could hold all of the band's equipment but it was a real stretch. We tied the trunk down with ropes, leaving it partly open, and had three guys in the front and one in the back with the instruments. Sometimes, Smyth could get a car from his family and that was easier, but a lot of the time the Ensign would have to carry all of us, including our equipment. It was "packed to the gills," as Rassy used to say. We damaged the headliner once loading the car for a gig, and I felt bad telling Rassy. She didn't freak out. She was behind the band and everything we did. She was more concerned for our safety because we were all crowded into that little car.

Most of our Squires shows were nearby; local gigs within a ten- to fifteen-mile radius, at community clubs, high schools, and church dances. We started at five dollars for our first night and moved up to twenty or thirty-five bucks a night as we got better. The wooden bass reflex cabinet Ken had made to go with his Heathkit amp was too big to fit in the car. It had to be cut down and made smaller. That was sad. We all liked the sound. It stayed pretty good, though. We cut the bottom off at an angle so it could lean back just like a Fender piggyback amp would when you used its chrome legs and tilted it.

We actually started to get a little following. We would notice the same kids showing up all around town to hear us. That was pretty cool. We played all instrumentals and I was writing a lot of them. We interspersed our originals with the Ventures, the Shadows, and other popular groups' tunes. We were a raggedy lot in that little car going from gig to gig all around Winnipeg in 1963. I was still feeling that feeling in my soul when the seasons changed and fall was about to end. I was growing. The leaves were turning.

I was doing the band's booking with a lot of help from our network of friends. It was pretty grassroots; friends played a huge part. Before gigs we would get together at the Grosvenor house, and I would cook us dinner, which was mainly Kraft Macaroni & Cheese with wieners, beans, and ketchup, followed by peanut butter sandwiches.

In the wintertime, we would have to get the car going during dinner so the heater would be warmed up by the time we left and our guitars and drums would be safe from having their finishes crack. It was mighty cold! We would load up, and off we would go together to the gigs in Rassy's Ensign, while Rassy was off working the TV show.

One of our regular gigs was at Patterson's Ranch House, located at the corner of Logan and Keewatin in Winnipeg. We used to play there on weekend afternoons and take a share of the gate, which was not much money. It was a country-and-western place, as the name attests. One of the country bands, Bluegrass Bob and the Bobcats, played there often. I remember seeing a trailer with their name written on it. That name really stuck in my mind. It took a lot of nerve for us to even ask the boss if we could play there. Obviously we couldn't play there at night because we were so young and didn't play country music, but he let us play in the afternoons. Sometimes we would play for ten or fifteen people on Saturday and Sunday.

It was Saturday night
And I was just sixteen
I had a couple a dollars
Stickin' in my jeans
And I walked down to the corner
On a wintery night

It was howling and a blowing
And a-drifting snow
And my friends were waiting for me
'Cause we wanted to know
Who was playing music
Down at Patterson's Ranch House
Tonight . . .

Well they never let us in
Because we looked too young
But we hung around the doorway
Just to have some fun
Watching all those duck-tailed dudes
With their groovy chicks

With those '57 Chevys that were
Raked just right
And the "candy apple" flashing in
The bright streetlights
They were packing up the parking lot
At Patterson's Ranch House
Tonight . . .

Well everything'll be just great
Even though I don't have a date
We'll hang around and stay up late
Listening to the rockin' band

Ya know Garry has a friend inside
Who'll maybe take us out for a ride
And slip us a beer on the side
Down at Patterson's Ranch House
Tonight . . .

Well I hung around the doorway
In the freezing air
And music was the reason
We were really there
We were shaking all over
to the sound
of the new Guess Who

I saw a rocking Burton Cummings
And a young Neil Young
And no one had a clue
What they would soon become
They were just

Diggin' the music
Down at Patterson's Ranch House
Tonight . . .

Well everything will be just fine
If we can make it to the dance on time
Peeking through the cracks for a sign
Of our favorite local rocking band
And I'm stealing every lick I can
I'm gonna be a guitar man
Playing in a rocking band
Down at Patterson's Ranch House
Tonight . . .

—Baba Farid, "Patterson's
Ranch House Tonight"

It would be cold as hell when we went in there to set up in the afternoon. The dance hall was upstairs, with a large wooden floor and a stage at one end. At first, there was no one there when we played and we just played to practice, but we advertised a little with notes on the bulletin boards at other clubs and had some word of mouth. I think the most people that ever attended had to be around thirty or forty. We thought that was great! The place probably held about three hundred to four hundred.

After we finished playing, it was very intimidating going downstairs into the restaurant area to ask the boss for our share of the gate. The building was all old wood with sawdust on the floor, a very old and well-worn country-and-western bar/restaurant. Sometimes it was a long wait, sitting in a booth, waiting for him to come out. We never knew if he was giving us the right amount and there was no way to check. It was a very little amount of money, but he always gave us something. I mean, he could have given us anything he wanted and what could we have said? We were scared shitless of this guy; we were so green. I think he was a pretty cool guy to give us a shot at all. I guess he had a soft spot for kids like us. Music people and club people almost always take care of their own.

SUMMER CAME and the Squires were growing in popularity. We had a DJ from the local Winnipeg station CKRC accompanying us to some of the gigs, and our name was always on the radio. Crowds were getting bigger at the community clubs. CKRC had a recording studio and an engineer, Harry Taylor, who liked recording all of the local groups that were good. He was into it just like we were, trying to catch a break by recording a hit in the little studio. The studio had a couple of mono tape machines, so sound on sound recording was possible. Bob Bradburn, our DJ, set it up for us to go to the studio and audition for Harry, to see if he thought that he could record us. It was a huge deal. We prepared for the audition with extra practices and were really well-rehearsed.

One day, we loaded all of our equipment into the Ensign and headed downtown to the CKRC studios. When we got there, we played all of our originals. Harry Taylor listened to us, and he picked a couple of them, and said, "Let's do those two." One was called "The Sultan" and the other one was "Image in Blue." They were based on the Shadows' sound and we had them down. We made another date to come back, and prepared to record those two songs. A week later, we returned and ran through them again and again. Harry experimented moving the microphones around, trying different echo, even trying different microphones. He was quite into it. Harry, with his Buddy Holly horn-rimmed glasses and white shirt, was a very serious engineer.

CKRC studio was located on the second floor of an old multistory brick building on Carlton Street, in the heart of downtown. In fact, it was the old Winnipeg Free Press Building, where my father had gotten his first job as a journalist. I didn't know that at the time, but there I was, at 300 Carlton Street, following my dream, just a few feet from where my dad started to follow his when he was about the same age. I wish I could have called him and told him about it when I discovered it years after that session. I think it would have made an impression on him somehow, made him understand how similar we were.

When we got in the studio, Bob and Harry had an idea. They wanted to add a gong to "The Sultan" to make it sound more dynamic. I thought it was a great idea. They also wanted Bob to say the title, at the end of "Image in Blue," and they wanted the title changed to "Aurora." That took me a minute to get used to, but I did accept it. At the end of the record, Bob would say "Aurora" in deep echo. We ran through the tunes a couple of times, and the final recording date was set: July 23, 1963. That day, we came in and recorded successfully and left the building with our hearts soaring.

We were recording artists! Bob had gotten us on V Records, a label that was making its first venture into rock and roll after releasing polkas exclusively for years. We were trailblazers! "The Sultan," backed with "Aurora" as the B-side, was released as a V Records 45 rpm single four months later. I will never forget the thrill of hearing it on the radio for the first time. I was walking in the clouds!

1958 Standard Motors Ensign

few weeks after recording our single, Jack Harper and I went on a summer vacation to Falcon Lake, about one hundred miles east of Winnipeg. Jack was still one of my best friends. It was a beautiful vacation spot—a lake with boats and a swimming area, a dock, and cabins everywhere. We went in the Ensign. Rassy let us take the car and have a good time. Jack and I had brought a pup tent and enough money to buy food, which we sometimes cooked on the public grills that were available in the campgrounds. We pitched our tent and set up our little dwelling. It was cool to be there, independent and on our own.

I didn't like to go swimming because I was shy about my physical self, being really skinny and not a sports type at all, but I still had a great time. There was plenty to do. There were lots of other young people there, families with their children and people just coming for a couple of days in campers.

Nearby, there was a dump. There were always a lot of big bears there, scrounging around looking for something to eat. It was fun driving the Ensign there at night with the lights out, slowly creeping in under the moonlight, getting close, and suddenly turning on the headlights so we could see all the bears. They would all look at us, their eyes gleaming red in the reflection of the headlights.

There was a little place with a jukebox, and I would play "Four Strong Winds" by Ian & Sylvia, over and over, learning all the words and singing along. I loved that song. I had the feeling that it was about *my* life, and the music touched me deeply. I completely related to it and lived it every time I listened. It was everything to me.

> *Four strong winds that blow lonely,*
> *Seven seas that run high.*
> *All those things that don't change,*
> *Come what may,*
> *Our good times are all gone,*
> *I'm bound for movin' on,*
> *I'll look for you if I'm ever back this way . . .*
>
> — IAN TYSON, "FOUR STRONG WINDS"

There was something about how immersed I was in that song that made me realize I had to get the same quality into my own music. I started singing along, loudly if I was alone and quietly if anyone was near enough to hear me. I knew my voice was high and I could tell that I sang in a different way from real singers, but in my soul, in my heart, I knew I was really singing and it felt right.

We would sometimes go to Lynne Hamilton's family cottage, where we would hang out with all the kids who were at the lake. Lynne, as I said, was a fun girl and Allan Bates's girlfriend. One night we sang "Four Strong Winds," and I kept saying we had to do it over and over until we got it just right. I can imagine that I was really carried away with getting it right and I probably was a bit over-the-top. That was just my energy for music.

About that time, I met Pam Smith. Pam was my first love. I still remember her well. I know I always will. She was very kind and loving, funny and cool, and she was very pretty. She had a twin sister, Pat, and the two of them were really a blast to hang with. Jack, Jim, and I were always looking for them. Pam and I hung out and talked a lot. I confided in her some of my insecurities about how skinny I was and she told me it wasn't that important, stressing that there were other qualities about me that were more important. She made me feel good about myself. We got really close and eventually I gave her my Kelvin ring. We were going steady. That felt really good.

In Winnipeg, we only saw each other on weekends because she lived on the other side of town, in East Kildonan. Of course, I was playing gigs with the Squires, too, and that made my social life on the weekends different from most guys', but she stuck with me. I got to know Pam and Pat's family pretty well because I would visit them often. They were really fine people, a happy family home. It sure felt good over there.

We played every weekend, and Pam was there most of the time. It was a wonderful experience, crowding our equipment and bodies into whatever cars we could rustle up, and the time passed quickly, as the good times always do. I saw a picture of Pam a couple of years ago that Jack sent to me, and she still looked beautiful, wearing a Pendleton shirt, just the same. It feels good to think about it now and I would like to take another deep breath of that winter Winnipeg air with Pam and I, and all of those friends.

After we went back to Winnipeg, the school year started up again, and finally my big dream came true, but with a catch. With

Rassy's help and support, I bought an orange Gretsch from John Glowa, who had played with Allan and the Silvertones before Randy Bachman joined the band. My Gretsch was just like Randy's. I sold my golf clubs to raise my share of the money for the Gretsch. Rassy put in the rest. The golf clubs had meant a lot to me at one time, but not as much as my music, by any stretch of the imagination. I first showed up with this beautiful guitar in hand, my pride and joy, at a St. Mary's Catholic Youth Organization dance on September 20, 1963, with the Squires.

The underlying story of my new Gretsch is that I misled my mother Rassy about this transaction, because I wanted it so bad and it was very expensive, maybe too expensive for us to afford. She, knowing how much I wanted a new guitar, offered to pay part of the amount if I would pay her back. I had some of the money and she put in the rest, but unbeknownst to her, the guitar cost more than I had told her. I was paying more money, on the side, to John in installments for a number of months. It was only a few months of extra payments I made, but I had to fudge the books of the Squires to hide the payments I was making to John while I was making payments to Rassy, bless her heart. I still have a sick feeling about that to this day, just thinking about it. That kind of thing never goes away. It is just not right. If I had been honest I probably would have gotten the guitar anyway, and it would have been one of the happiest moments of my young musical life. Of course, my mother is gone now, and there is no way for me to tell her the truth, which we would probably have had a good laugh over. There was a life lesson there. Try to go lightly to your grave.

The Squires kept on growing and playing gigs. The pay got higher. We were playing more and more. We took a gig downtown, playing at the Cellar, a seedy club in an alleyway where druggies and undesirables mingled with night people, working girls, and musicians. The entry was down a dark stairs, off an alley, to a dim red light. A guy you could hardly see took your money, a cover charge, to get in. It was funky and dark, all brick painted black inside. We could hardly see the audience when we played. We did multiple sets a night. The place had an unfamiliar odor, probably grass, and it was really smoky. We had seen the Crescendos play there, and the Silvertones. All the bands that were good enough played the Cellar because it was the only place to play during the week. We did it for three nights and didn't get asked back. I was probably too young to be there anyway, still in high school.

During the summer of 1963, I found an advertisement in the paper for a 1948 Buick Roadmaster hearse, being sold as excess by a funeral home. I asked Rassy to help me buy it. She said she might be able to help if it wasn't too expensive. After calling the number in the paper, I got the address and made my way to it in the Ensign. When I got there, a man came out and let me through a chain-link gate, and I walked into a lot full of older cars and inspected two 1948 Buick Roadmaster hearses. They were huge, with very large back doors, and rollers for the coffins to roll in and out of the velvet-upholstered back. "Perfect for our equipment!" I exclaimed to myself.

I named the hearse Mort. I was very happy. I remember going out for a drive through River Heights, feeling the same freedom I felt on my first bike. Now I could go anywhere, and a feeling of independence was upon me like never before. Mort immediately gave the Squires an identity that set the group apart from everyone else. Soon we were playing farther and farther out of town and things were getting really good for the band. We continued playing the gigs we had played through high school, improving our sound, growing and evolving with the music, happily cruising to the gigs in Mort.

I spent a lot of time visiting at Pam's house and would practice on the big upright piano in her family room downstairs, where we would hang out. There was a great family feeling in their house that made me feel comfortable. I don't remember a lot of that in my own home. The twins' mom and dad were very happy. I could always feel the love. Music was taking over my life completely, though, and in late November of that year, 1963, I broke up with Pam. We were still friends, but my commitment to music was huge and I must have felt I was unable to spend the time with her that she deserved. I stayed in touch, and still had feelings for her, and she for me.

1948 Buick Roadmaster Flxible Hearse "Mort"

CHAPTER NINE

The year 1964 came along and with it came change. The Beatles had arrived, taking the entire world by storm. They hit Canada before they hit the States. We got their records first. We heard them singing. It became obvious that our band needed a singer as well, but none of us had ever sung in public before.

I had written some songs in my bedroom and had been singing them to myself, but no one had ever heard me. I was pretty insecure about my voice. One of the songs was titled "No" and another was titled "I Wonder." I wasn't ready to come out singing my own material, but I was thinking about singing a known song in front of people. I had still never practiced singing with a band.

The first time I sang in public was in the Kelvin High School cafeteria. At noon hour there was some sort of talent show; I am sure it wasn't just me singing. I got up in front of a bunch of students as part of some sort of lunch hour entertainment program, getting up there with a guy named Stuart Adams and someone else. Stuart was an English guy. We did two Beatles songs. I was playing guitar and I think he was, too, but I'm not sure. I was terrified. I'll never forget that feeling, "four-engined butterflies," as my dad used to say. It was obviously something I wanted to do, so I did it. We sang "Money (That's What I Want)" and "It Won't Be Long," two great Beatles tunes from their big hit album. I don't remember a positive or negative reaction. People were mostly bemused and curious. Later, I used to joke that I was serious about making music for a living because the first song I ever sang in front of people was "Money (That's What I Want)."

> *The best things in life are free*
> *But you can keep 'em for the birds and bees.*
> *Now gimme money (that's what I want)*
> *That's what I want (that's what I want)*
> *That's what I want (that's what I want), oh yeah,*
> *That's what I want.*
>
> —"Money"

Even with Beatlemania sweeping the world, I was still really into Jimmy Reed and had two or three of his albums that I listened to constantly on the Seabreeze. I loved the simplicity and honesty that oozed from every one of his songs. His voice was not amazing and his harmonica was simple and direct, while not being derivative of Brownie McGhee, who I had heard at the Fourth Dimension. Jimmy played harp with a rack—a harmonica holder—around his neck so he could play guitar at the same time, and he would hold notes for a long time, focusing on high, expressively plaintive tones. To me, he was very haunting, one of the greats, a genius original, making the most of the least, with a definitive sound in the blues.

Maybe he was just too successful for the hard core to appreciate him while he was alive. I sure did, though. We started doing some vocal tunes with the Squires, including a few Jimmy Reed songs, after my Kelvin debut as a vocalist. We got a mixed reaction at first but no one was throwing things at me.

> *Got me runnin', got me hidin',*
> *Got me run, hide, hide, runnin' anyway you want to let it roll*
> *Yeah, yeah, yeah*
> *You got me doin' what you want me*
> *So baby, why you want to let go?*
>
> — Jimmy Reed, "Baby What You Want Me to Do"

Some people would yell out "Stick to guitar playing" and stuff like that, kind of like heckling at a hockey game. We kept at it. Ken started singing a bit, trying harmonies. We had to work at that. We were not natural singers and had to practice the harmonies one part at a time. Harmony singing did not come naturally. Harmonic structure is complex to learn, especially if you have no idea what you are doing, which was my case. We spent hours and hours working, trying to find the parts, feeling for them, and coaxing them out of the chords. I learned that almost all of the harmony notes could be found in the chords, but there were also passing notes between them that I was trying hard to locate. I would find the notes, and then sing everyone's part to them; then we would try them together. Inevitably someone's part would pull someone else to the same note and we would have to stop and start again, relocating the correct notes. We kept playing all the regular places, and I was singing lead all the time. Ken and Allan Bates sang as well, background parts, like "That's what I want" and "Shake it up, baby." We were starting to get the hang of it.

We went back to CKRC to record again on April 2, 1964. "I Wonder" was among the titles. According to Ken Smyth, Harry Taylor, the CKRC engineer, thought I should give up on singing and just play guitar. There was a copy made of that recording, as well as an instrumental called "Mustang," from that session. I don't think the vocal was too bad at all when I listen today; actually, the track seemed a little tentative, sounding self-conscious.

On April 23, 1964, I got my first Fender piggyback amp, a Tremolux, from Ray Hamerton Music, and we were on the edge of our dreams, cruising around Winnipeg in Mort and playing all the gigs in town.

My formal education officially ended when I dropped out of Kelvin High School in the fall of 1964, having failed to pass grade ten after the second year trying. I never could pass French and had nightmares for a few years after, dreaming that I was still in school trying. Ken quit, too, and we both decided to become professional musicians. Mr. Fred "Hodgie" Hodgkinson was our vice principal, and he had called me into the office to try to convince me to stay in school. I told him I wanted to be a professional musician and play in clubs. He told me that was just temporary, and that I needed an education to make it through life. He gave me the best advice he could, but he didn't know how dedicated I was.

Bill Edmondson, a friend I had just met when he moved in right across the street from our house, had arrived from Montreal, where his parents had recently divorced, and he really was a rocker, but had never played in a band. Bill loved music and had gotten a set of drums because he used to play, and he wanted to join the band. He had all of the attitude in the world, and I loved playing and hanging out with him. At first, he was a bit rusty because he had not played in a while, but he played loud and rocked.

Then we added Jeff Wuckert on piano. Jeff was a great player, and we had not had a piano since Linda Fowler. Then something very important happened. We had booked our first big out-of-town road gig at the Flamingo Club in Fort William, Ontario, playing three to five sets a night in a one-week engagement. We practiced a lot and had our picture taken for publicity. The picture-taking session was arranged by Sharon, Bill's girlfriend from CKRC. To look cool, we had gotten some patent leather shoes and had outfits with ascots and pullover vests made for us by Jeff's mom. I thought we would be really ready for the big time when we hit the Flamingo Club, but we had a surprise coming.

When the time drew close for the band to go on the road to this big gig, and it was just a week before we were to leave, Jeff's family said they would not let him go with us. Jeff dropped out.

That left Bill Edmondson, Ken Koblun, and me. The gig at the Flamingo Club was already booked, and after playing around town a bit as a trio, we went ahead with the three of us, even though the photo we had sent ahead for publicity had Jeff in it. We couldn't afford to do another professional photo. On the morning of October 11, 1964, the Squires packed up Mort with all of our equipment in front of our home at 1123 Grosvenor, and with Rassy standing on the sidewalk and waving good-bye, we took off into the future.

Before leaving Winnipeg for the first time in Mort, I was probably not too aware of what a great time it really had been. Winnipeg was good to me. It was intense and not always easy, but it was my growing-up period. As Mort headed out of Winnipeg, Ken, Bill, and I were in the front seat and our equipment was well packed in Mort's spacious form. With the open road ahead, I watched

Niakwa Golf and Country Club disappear in the rearview mirror. Niakwa was the club my mother belonged to, the one she joined when we moved back to Winnipeg from Toronto, the one where I bought the clubs I sold to buy my beautiful Gretsch guitar.

Thoughts of community clubs, the Fourth Dimension, the Sugar Shack, high school dances, teen clubs, and the many friends and bandmates I had shared life with all rolled through my mind. With the open road now visible before us, it was only an hour or so before we passed Falcon Lake and I thought of meeting Pam, our special times together, the bears at the dump, and the breakup of the original Squires. "Four Strong Winds" played over in my soul as I held the wheel and drove on. Eventually the terrain became more varied, with hills and lakes everywhere. It is a beautiful country, Canada, and I hope to go back there someday and take this same trip again, viewing it through older eyes.

The hours rolled by and I started noticing how much gas we were using. Mort was not economical, as you can imagine. I began the practice of conserving fuel by turning off the motor while going downhill, and coasting. That was a bad idea and put a lot of strain on the vehicle's transmission and rear end whenever I slipped it back in gear to climb the next grade, but what did I know? Not much. I was just trying to save fuel. It was the beginning of something. Something I could never have imagined at the time. The gas price was set at 30 cents per gallon, and cruising at 8 mpg, dreaming about our future as professional musicians on the road, we added 1,153 pounds of CO_2 to the atmosphere on our trip to Fort William.

After about eight hours on the road, we eventually made it to the Fort William YMCA, an old multistory brick building downtown, where we had rooms paid for by the Flamingo Club. When we arrived, I received a Western Union telegram from my uncle Bob and aunt Merle, congratulating me on my first show, hoping it was the beginning of a long and illustrious career. Uncle Bob was a true musician at heart. Reading that telegram, I thought about my aunt and uncle and my three girl cousins, who sang like birds under his loving guidance. Penny, Marny, and Steffi were part of my growing up. My uncle Bob was a real funny guy and the girls sang around the piano and his ukulele every night. It was always great fun visiting them, and it was such a warm family scene; I couldn't get enough of it.

Uncle Bob played the heck out of both the uke and the piano, using only the black keys, which I am sure he learned years before from his mom (my granny Jean) while growing up in Flin Flon, a big northern Manitoba mining town with gravel streets and modest housing. Granny Jean was the musical force in town, the organizer of a theater group that did musicals and a regular piano player at the local bars. She was, by all reports, a honky-tonk queen. On Sundays, she visited every church in town, all the denominations, one after another, playing the pump organs.

Granny Jean's maiden name was Patterson. Her daddy was a traveling salesman who had come to town selling medicines and cures in a horse-drawn wagon. He put on a show out of the back of his wagon. There was also a preacher in the family from the Patterson side, and we have one of his Bibles in our house, one that was handed down through the generations, that my late aunt Dorothy gave to me the last time I saw her.

Putting down the Western Union telegram, I noticed there was a Bible on the nightstand of my room. I looked out the window, surveying my Fort William view. It looked older than I had expected.

A local DJ named Ray Dee from CJLX came by the Flamingo

to listen to us, and I liked him right away. Later, when I met my lifelong friend and great producer David Briggs, he reminded me very much of Ray Dee. They both had knowledge of music and an assertive leadership attitude that I found and still find essential in a producer. It takes the weight off my shoulders and lets me focus on doing my thing, singing and playing.

Back at the YMCA, I started writing more songs. They were R&B-influenced tunes with a heavy Jimmy Reed stamp on them and they fit like a glove at the Flamingo Club, or "The Flame" as it was known locally. There are some accounts of us playing through a fight that broke out one night in that first week, but I don't have any recollection of that. However, if it did happen, it is a rule to never stop playing if there is trouble in the crowd. I have always respected that rule. A crowd is nothing to screw with. When the music stops, the anger really starts. It's like fanning a fire.

Well, hello lonely woman,
Won't you take a walk with me?
I know a place where we can go
Grab a bite to eat.

Hello lonely woman,
Are you feeling all right?
Well you look just like heaven
On a clear, clear night.

—"Hello Lonely Woman"

At the CJLX studio with Ray Dee producing, we recorded two songs. Bill played so loud that Ray had to put him in an isolation booth, which was the hallway. I double-tracked my vocals. Working with Ray was really creative. He was hands-on and musical, the best help we had ever had recording in the studio to that date. My voice was never an issue with Ray. He felt that uniqueness was an advantage and a plus. It was great fun, and we were really serious about making a creative, soulful record. It was more than just being in the studio. We were creating.

> *Oh, I'm so happy I found your love*
> *And I will always thank the stars up above.*
> *I'll love you forever and idolize*
> *The way you comb your hair*
> *And your laughing eyes.*
>
> —"I'll Love You Forever"

In the end, we recorded and mixed "I'll Love You Forever" and "I Wonder." Ray liked our new "I Wonder" a lot better than the one from CKRC. He did not like that earlier track. He had opinions on things and real reasons for them. I had a lot of respect for Ray. We used echo and double-tracking, really having a rewarding time in the studio, but nothing ever came of it. We couldn't get a contract with a record company. I reasoned that my voice was just not commercial, but Ray thought differently, and we kept on going.

We stuck around town because we had a gig booked, opening for Jay and the Americans at a CJLX show at the Coliseum. It was a huge gig for us. They were big stars. While we waited in Fort William, Del Shannon came and sang somewhere. Ken, Bill, and I stood and watched from the audience, just like we used to watch the Silvertones back in Winnipeg.

Del Shannon, with a mink guitar strap over his shoulder, sang all of his hits: "Hats Off to Larry," "Runaway," and "Stranger in Town." He was really unique and interesting. Unfortunately, years later, Del committed suicide. He seemed smaller than his voice and looked very isolated and alone, but he was an amazing singer and had a very strong vibe. There was something sad about his performance, though. I couldn't put my finger on it. He seemed bigger than the gig. I sang "Stranger in Town" myself after that because I liked it so much, and we added it to the Squires' list of songs. Later, I wrote my own song titled "Stranger in Town." We practiced our new songs and waited to play the big CJLX show. I liked that feeling, being part of that big show. The crowd was huge and excited. However, Bill was really missing Sharon, and that was developing into a problem for us.

At that time, I was starting to think about going to the States. I knew that was where it was at. If we were going to make a dent, why not make it somewhere where it mattered and we would get noticed? Why not Hollywood, where the West Coast Sound was? I had noticed that the farther out of Winnipeg we got, the more excited people were to see us. We were from somewhere else. The mystery surrounding that gave us a little more freedom in our performances somehow, even if we were only fifty miles out of town. After the show at the Coliseum, we threw our stuff into the back of Mort and rolled northwest back to Winnipeg on the Trans-Canada Highway. It felt a little different this time. I kind of felt we were going in the wrong direction.

With Mort, we got around town and stayed busy, flushed with our out-of-town success. Mort was becoming our trademark, our identity as a band. The Squires and the hearse were like one.

Everywhere we went we would park right near the door and people would stand outside and look at Mort's monstrous shape, looming near the entrance to the community club, high school, or church dance where we were performing, announcing our presence. We were on a roll, but another surprise was coming.

As soon as we returned from Fort William, Bill quit the band, saying that he wanted to be with Sharon. Ken and I were alone, all that was left of the Squires, but we were not ready to quit.

The first time we were really successful on a higher level was a hootenanny night at the Fourth Dimension Club out on the edge of town. It was March 7, 1965. That night at the hootenanny, things just went right. We were in the groove with our new drummer, Al Johnson.

We must have sung pretty well, and we jammed on at the end of a few songs. The crowd really went nuts! What a great feeling! To be accepted like that and have people actually clapping and yelling after we played. We were buzzing heavily as we loaded our equipment back into Mort's cavernous form. That night was a major turning point for us; being accepted and hearing the crowd go crazy was infectious.

I started introducing more of my original tunes and singing them every night we played, along with a lot of other songs that were made popular at the time by the English groups. "I Wonder" was one of the first original songs we performed. Then there were more. A lot more.

Things were moving very fast and the band members changed like musical chairs until we settled on a trio with Bob Clark on drums and Ken Koblun, who was still with me, on bass. Bob sang and we were doing three-part harmonies. When we went back to

Fort William, we were able to make a living for a while. We met Steve Stills, who was traveling through playing the Fourth Dimension there. We had peaked and gone as far as we could go.

So I traveled on, toward Toronto, with some guys I had met, but Mort didn't make it. We broke down in a little town called Blind River. After a few months, Mort was fixed, and I picked up Mort, ready to drive into Toronto and have another shot at having a band.

After about an hour driving east, with some really ugly mechanical sounds emanating from underneath, Mort sadly limped to the side of the road near an old decrepit roadside hotel. I had to leave Mort there in the parking lot of that hotel out on the Trans-Canada Highway. I had only made it about fifty miles past Blind River. I remember hitchhiking away from there, getting a ride toward Toronto and looking back one last time at the beautiful Mortimer Hearseburg, parked forever in my mind in that hotel parking lot. The old hotel was actually just a two-story wooden house, with a makeshift addition, not as grand as you might imagine. There were some other unfortunate cars parked haphazardly around it, too. No doubt they were victims of a similar fate.

For a while I made up this whole story about how I pushed Mort over a cliff. I actually believed it myself, but it was all fantasy. What really happened was even worse. Abandonment. Dreams die hard. That old funeral coach/rock and roll delivery truck full of memories took a lot of me with it. It was so great, and it has never faded from my mind. I think I'll take that one with me.

We've been through some things together
With trunks of memories still to come

We found things to do in stormy weather
Long may you run.
Long may you run. Long may you run.
Although these changes have come
With your chrome heart shinin' in the sun
Long may you run.

—"Long May You Run"

Daddy, seeing me through new eyes when I arrived in Toronto, had learned firsthand how dedicated I was to being a musician. Helping us, he found a place to rehearse in the lobby of the Poor Alex Theatre just off Bloor Street, near Yorkville Village. Kenny and I began practicing there with a guy named Geordie McDonald on drums. We had connected with Jim Ackroyd from the Galaxies back in Winnipeg, who had also come to Toronto to seek his musical fortune, and he was singing with us for a while, and playing guitar. We were starting to sound pretty good. We did a new song of mine called "Casting Me Away from You" and were thinking of calling ourselves the Castaways. We practiced every day for hours and hours. We got good and just needed an audience.

We used to laugh and play
Games together.
We found things to do
In stormy weather.
But now I find
You're leaving me behind.
Casting me away from you.

—"Casting Me Away from You"

I was trying to get something going for us with a manager, Marty Onrot. He had some ideas for us and wanted to call us Four to Go. I didn't like that name at all. Marty brought in a couple of club owners who we played for in the Poor Alex lobby, but no one would hire us. Those solitary auditions were not like playing in front of people. With no energy from the crowd to feed off of, it was sterile and uncomfortable, not musical. It was not like the Squires, who had played at a hootenanny. That is what we should have done. Nothing happened. Shortly after that, Marty told me I should give up the band and just write songs that other people could sing. I hated that idea and did not take his advice.

There was a street near Yorkville Village in Toronto that I used to walk on a lot. On that street was an old garage repair shop and in front of the building I noticed a 1947 Buick Roadmaster convertible. It was black with a white top and red leather interior. Overall, it was pretty worn-out, but you could still see the beauty of the lines. I looked at it every time I walked by because it had all the same features as Mort, except of course Mort was taller and longer and was a hearse. That old Buick Roadmaster convertible cost me seventy-five dollars and I don't know if I ever completely paid for it. Buying it was kind of a dreamer's move on my part, but if I could find another one today in nice original shape, I would probably still get it. That's how addicted I am to 1947 and 1948 Buicks. I have a soft spot in my heart. I remember driving it down Yorkville one night, feeling pretty cool. It was a beautiful old convertible. It smoked a lot, and a few days later it stopped running. I abandoned it on a street off of Yorkville and don't know what happened to it after that. Sad things I tend to forget.

Around that time, I was feeling lost and bent out of shape. I had

no place to go and wasn't eating very well. Everything was changing and seemed to be careening out of my control, when I was res-
cued by an old friend, Bunny Stuart. I stayed at his house with him
and his dad and mom, near Old Orchard Grove, where I used to
live. With little money to my name, I found care and support there
at Bunny's home.

1953 Pontiac Hearse

The part of my life spent with Mort was gone and the Squires were over. I had to do something. I had met a bass player named Bruce Palmer, a thin guy I met in Yorkville Village, the hip part of Toronto, where the music scene was flourishing. Bruce got me in his band, the Mynah Birds with a guy named Ricky James Matthews. We were great but we didn't last long. After getting a big break and going down to Motown in Detroit to record, things fell apart and our record never materialized, but our next move was big and life changing.

When we returned to Toronto late one night, Bruce and I met in a little club called the Cellar, on Avenue Road near Yorkville, to plan what we would do next. We decided together to go to LA and follow our dreams. To get there, we would sell the group's equipment and buy a 1953 Pontiac hearse I had found in the paper. It was just outside of Toronto, and when we went out there to see it, we bought it right away and drove it home. This hearse was not quite as big and deluxe as Mort, which was a top-of-the-line model. It had less trim and extra chrome and was just not as magnificent without all the cool velvet inside, but it still suited our needs and drove really well. I still had my Manitoba driver's license and we gathered a few friends to take the trip with us; a folk singer named Tannis Neiman and her friend Janine, plus one other girl who wanted to go, and a guy named Mike. The girls had some weed and a little money. We left the next day, never considering how John Craig Eaton, the Mynah Birds' financial backer, would feel about us selling all of the equipment he had purchased for us.

We were just an old funeral coach full of stoned hippies heading southwest to Hollywood, California, where the music scene was vibrant and the West Coast Sound was on fire. The trip was exhausting. We traveled Route 66 day and night. I don't remember much about where we stopped or where we slept, although we stayed a few days in Albuquerque and left three people there: Janine, Tannis, and Mike.

That trip, making about 10 mpg in the hearse, added about 4,900 pounds of CO_2 to the atmosphere, but I didn't have a care in the world. Finally, we arrived in Hollywood on April 1, 1966, exiting on Sunset Boulevard, and immediately started trying to find 77 Sunset Strip. Of course, there is no such address. It was just a TV show. We ended up at the end of Sunset and the Pacific Coast Highway, where we parked by the beach and walked barefoot out onto the sand and put our feet in the Pacific Ocean. As we looked back through the foggy mist to the evening traffic on Highway 1, I felt strongly in my heart that we had really accomplished something. We had made it to the Pacific Ocean and California, home of the West Coast Sound. This is where the Beach Boys had come from, the Byrds, the Mamas & the Papas, and so many others. We had made it.

The hearse was still running well and feeling great. There was a certain leather smell that I liked and the dashboard had beautiful chrome parts on it. All in all, it was a wonderful vehicle and had served us well.

We found my old friend from Fort William, Steve Stills, in Hollywood just as we were leaving to go to San Francisco, so we stayed in LA and started again right where we left off. We had always wanted to play together. Bruce and I joined Steve and his friend Richie Furay. We added a Canadian drummer, Dewey Martin, and formed Buffalo Springfield. Needing a manager, we drove the Pontiac hearse down Sunset and met with some business guys. Things seemed to go fine; of course, I had no way of knowing what they were really thinking, but it felt good.

After that meeting, on the way back up Sunset, there was a huge crash under the hearse. The driveshaft had fallen out and was dragging on the road. Pushing the old hearse slowly over to the side, we parked it. Somehow we got it towed to a garage near Highland Avenue, but I had no money to get it fixed. That was the last time I ever saw it. Somewhere in the cosmos there is a 1953 Pontiac hearse with Ontario plates and no driveshaft. Some bolts probably fell out of the universal joint and it could have been fixed easily, but I didn't know anything then. It was gone. Out of reach for a broke hippie.

1954 Packard Ambulance-Hearse

WE EVENTUALLY SIGNED with Greene and Stone, two guys from New York who had something to do with Sonny & Cher. They became our managers. There was a chap named Chesley Millikin from Australia who we met through one of Greene and Stone's secretaries, Joy, a pretty, black-haired girl who kept her distance from us, to keep her job. The most interesting thing I recall about Chesley, along with his accent, was his mode of transportation. He owned a 1954 Packard ambulance-hearse combination, a rare bird if ever there was one. To me, it was the logical successor to Mort and the Pontiac, continuing in the great tradition that began in the Squires. It was silver in color, kind of metallic, with a siren built into the roof above the windshield, but the siren did not work.

I decided I had to have that vehicle. With what little cash I had collected from the first Springfield gigs we got at the Whisky a Go Go, I purchased that Packard from Chesley as a reward for the success I was having and I started driving it around Hollywood. Of course, since I had no papers and no legal right to be in the USA, I had no driver's license. That made me very nervous every time I drove the Packard, but I hoped that I would eventually get my papers because Greene and Stone had already told me they had a lawyer with connections.

We continued playing the Whisky a Go Go, opening for a lot of bands, including the Gentrys and the Grass Roots. Eventually, toward the end of our six-week run, we got billing on the marquee outside, and this was a major event for us. Greene and Stone had signed us to Atlantic Records, under the ATCO label, and we were beginning to get a following at the Whisky. We even had our own groupies. Two friendly Italians who ran the Whisky—Elmer Valentine, the manager, and Mario, the doorman—took us under their wing and watched out for us, steering us away from trouble now and then. Trouble was everywhere in the form of drug dealers, bad actors of all kinds, and opportunists, and we were as green as you could be. This was a remarkable time of growth, recording in the studio during the day, making our first *Buffalo Springfield* LP, and playing the Whisky at night.

> *Do I have to come right out and say it?*
> *Tell you that you look so fine?*
> *Do I have to come right out and ask you*
> *To be mine?*
> *If it was a game I could play it,*
> *Trying to make it, but I'm losing time.*
> *I got to bring you in,*
> *You're overworking my mind.*
>
> *Indecision is crowding me;*
> *I have no room to spare,*
> *And I can't believe she'd care.*
> *Like a dream, she has taken me,*
> *And now I don't know where*
> *And a part of me is scared,*
> *The part of me I shared*
> *Once before.*
>
> —"Do I Have to Come Right Out and Say It"

Every night after the shows at the Whisky we would go to Ben Frank's, a nearby diner on Sunset that had a big night scene, and get a bite to eat. Groupies would follow us there and we were easily available. We were young and foolish, not knowing what we were getting into. It was like a feeding frenzy. I had never seen so many girls. It was mind-blowing. We all were learning a lot of new things and getting a few new diseases along the way. What an education for a naive Canadian boy.

One night, we were at Ben Frank's and this cute girl with way too much perfume and makeup came up to our booth and asked if she could sit with us. I said sure, and she slipped in the booth beside me, placing her hand between my legs. What a sensation. I had never had anything like that happen before. Of course, I immediately took her to the parking lot to show her the back of my silver Packard ambulance-hearse combo.

I didn't have that fantastic Packard ambulance-hearse for very long and I don't remember what happened to it. It probably developed a problem that I could not afford to repair. I imagine I left it parked somewhere. There was never a registration, insurance, or anything legal like that to deal with. It was cool to drive and have wheels again, but it was a relatively short-lived experience, sort of like the 1947 Buick Roadmaster convertible I had in Canada and left on a side street when it developed problems that I could not afford to have fixed.

About that time, something very important happened. I found a Gretsch Chet Atkins horseshoe model like the one I had had in the Squires. It was in the possession of a musician who had fallen on hard times, much like I had when I sold mine in Toronto, a year or so before. He was living in an apartment building on Melrose Avenue. When we arrived there, Stills and I, the place had a seedy quality to it and was uncomfortable just to be in. People there did not look healthy. Some junkies appeared to be living in the hallways, looking up at us as they sat on the floor, like we might have something for them. We visited for just a few minutes, and for a small amount of cash I was able to get my second Gretsch. It even had the white case just like my original one. That guitar had my old sound, the sound I played in the Buffalo Springfield.

THE SPRINGFIELD had been living at the Hollywood Center Motel, located right on Sunset Boulevard near Highland, all of us together in an old two-story wooden house overlooking the pool at the back of the property. As we got a bit more money, I found another place to live. Some girls I knew from the Whisky, Donna and Vicki, turned me on to it. Donna and Vicki were protective, like gang girls, and warned me about some of the bad girls who were out trolling for us; the ones who were using hard drugs and were potentially dangerous. Soon I was all settled into my new hippie home, at the Commodore Gardens apartments in Hollywood, smoking grass and writing songs for our first LP.

Turn me up or turn me down,
Turn me off or turn me 'round.
I wish I could have met you
In a place where we both belonged,
But if crying and holding on
And flying on the ground is wrong,
Then I'm sorry to let you down,
But you're from my side of town
And I'll miss you.

—"FLYING ON THE GROUND IS WRONG"

A lot of times, after a night's playing, I got a ride back from the Whisky with Donna and Vicki. Often we would go to the International House of Pancakes on Sunset late at night. At three a.m., the lights were bright and the place was full of people, a lot of whom had been at the Whisky. We enjoyed hanging out together and talking about the show that night or whatever was happening with other musicians in Hollywood. I would usually have pancakes like the ones my dad used to make for me on Brock Road after my paper route. Donna and Vicki would move in if any of the girls they considered dangerous would get too close to us. They were like sisters to me.

After about a month or so, I got in big trouble with the manager at the Commodore Gardens for tacking up grass mats on the walls. They wanted to charge me for damaging the building and I didn't have enough money to pay them, so one night I stealthily departed with all my worldly possessions, including my guitars and my fringe jackets, and left the grass mats behind. Upon close inspection, I'm afraid my early history would be riddled with incidents like that. I was not a very reliable tenant.

1957 Corvette

When I moved into Laurel Canyon, I had to find a new car. Even though I didn't have it anymore, I knew that the Packard ambulance-hearse combo could never have made it up those canyon roads; I was sure of that.

The Springfield played a few more local college and high school gigs in Hollywood with the Byrds on weekends, and then returned to the Whisky for a ten-day run. Greene and Stone continued managing us, and Buffalo Springfield was picked up by the William Morris Agency when an agent named John Hartmann saw us at a club called the Cinnamon Cinder in San Diego.

We played a lot of gigs in clubs during June and July. Momentum was picking up. On July 25, 1966, we got our biggest gig yet: opening for the Rolling Stones at the Hollywood Bowl. Although we were never close enough to the Stones to meet them and didn't hang around to hear them, we were noticed at the Bowl by Nick Vanoff, producer of the *Hollywood Palace* TV show. He hired us for a future appearance. In November, our first LP record, *Buffalo Springfield*, was released.

With a big TV show booked, the advance from Atlantic Records, and our first record released, I decided to reward myself again and purchased a 1957 Corvette for $1,250. Metallic bronze, with a really cool and powerful, throaty sound, that Corvette was the first sexy and fast car I owned, and it felt amazing to drive it. I loved its beautiful design, wheels, and classic instrument panel, even though it smelled of gasoline most of the time.

This tradition of rewarding myself has continued for many years and, in fact, is still very much in practice today. I love my cars, and to me there is nothing like the feeling of accomplishing something and being rewarded. It completes the experience. Over the years, automobiles of all kinds marked different goals and achievements reached on my journey through life. The evolution of that has changed and grown into refining existing cars. Making them better and better is my reward now.

LAUREL CANYON was where a lot of the musicians I knew lived. Many of them were in successful bands. I rented a cabin way up at the top of Ridpath Avenue near Utica Drive, high in the canyon in a secluded area. My 1957 Corvette had no trouble getting up that steep, curvy road leading to my little knotty-pine cabin in the eucalyptus trees, and it felt great to have my own vehicle again. On my way up there, occasionally I used to see beautiful Michelle Phillips from the Mamas & the Papas in her yard, and I always looked for her whenever I passed that house. I never got to meet her, though. She was one of those girls you loved from a distance but knew you could never touch.

I met a singer at the Whisky whose name was Freddy Brechtel. Freddy was a lead singer without a band, looking for one. He was a little like Sky Saxon without the Seeds or Mick Jagger without the Stones. He was kind of lost. We were good friends and spent a lot of days cruising around in the Corvette.

Once, we went all the way out on the Pacific Coast Highway just to experience the coast vibe and go to Malibu. Exploring, we drove all over the coastal mountains with the Corvette's throaty sound echoing off the canyon walls. Eventually we stopped at a place called the Malibu Inn, a restaurant-bar entertainment place with a giant jukebox console that played movies of musical performances. It was called Electronovision, and I had never seen one before. There were a lot of songs on it from the *T.A.M.I. Show*, which was a big rock and roll show that had been filmed in 1964 at the Santa Monica Civic Auditorium as an American International Pictures release. James Brown, the Rolling Stones, the Beach Boys, the Supremes, Marvin Gaye, Lesley Gore, Chuck Berry, Smokey Robinson and the Miracles, and several other headline acts, along with great dancers, appeared in this most amazing and revolutionary music film. I stood there transfixed, watching all of these acts on Electronovision, while pouring quarters into the machine. I had never seen anything like it. I could watch it over and over again. The sound was stereo and great. I spent an hour right there, marveling at the way this machine had used technology to marry different art forms and make them accessible. Eventually we drove back to Hollywood, but my mind had been blown by what I had seen and I couldn't forget it. That was 1966.

MY 1957 CORVETTE was an LA car and I was feeling very Californian, as only a Canadian could. The wind blowing in my hair, driving down Sunset Boulevard. I was a very happening guy in my own mind, flush with the success of Buffalo Springfield, and all of twenty-one years old, just eight months after I had arrived in California with Bruce.

My twenty-first birthday, in 1966, was notable because that was the night the Sunset Strip riots began. The first big disturbance happened at a place called Pandora's Box, a club located at Sunset and Crescent Heights Boulevard. About this time, locals were upset at all the hippies hanging out on the streets around the clubs. The flower children, as they were sometimes called, were seen as a nuisance, just loitering around, and a ten p.m. curfew was imposed.

The flower children loved the clubs and the rock music and, feeling that Sunset Boulevard was theirs, they were pissed. They didn't want to go home at ten p.m. Young people freaked out at having their civil rights violated, flyers were circulated urging people to stand for their rights, and they did, and it got ugly.

The riot that happened there was mostly because a popular radio station, big with rock music lovers, had announced a rally that night at the club in the center of the action on the strip, Pandora's Box, giving the location on the air, Sunset and Crescent Heights Boulevard. Sure enough, when about a thousand flower children, hippies, and others showed up, the cops went nuts on them when the ten p.m. curfew passed and the flower children went crazy. The friction continued until the end of the sixties, but it was most intense in 1966 and 1967.

About the same time as Stephen Stills was writing his song "For What It's Worth" as a reaction to the riots, I was traveling down Sunset with Freddy Brechtel in my 1957 Corvette, doing nothing obviously illegal, and I was pulled over by the sheriff, who demanded to see my nonexistent license. I tried to fake that I didn't have it with me, but I was taken straight to jail.

> *There's something happening here.*
> *What it is ain't exactly clear.*
> *There's a man with a gun over there,*
> *Tellin' me that I got to beware.*
> *I think it's time we stop, hey, what's that sound?*
> *Everybody look what's going down.*
>
> —"For What It's Worth"

Those were some edgy times. Stephen's song nailed it. We sang his song and recorded it. It became our biggest hit. It was real. We had a message and connected with the people. That's the way it started for us. Stephen and I and many others wrote songs after that about anything topical that happened, commenting on our times, following the lead of the protest singers of the past: Seeger, Dylan, Guthrie, Ochs, just to name a few.

Buffalo Springfield was booked on the Johnny Carson show and I didn't want to do it. I felt very strongly at the time that we should be all about the music. To my way of thinking, *The Tonight Show* was just some jive Hollywood entertainment show that had nothing to do with either us or our audience. It was irrelevant to what we were singing about. I quit the band with no conversation or anything. Johnny Carson never happened, and other shows like it were off my list. I suppose I could have made that point better by talking about it with Steve instead of by quitting the band, but I was not mature enough then for that.

Consequently, at some point I lost the Corvette because I wasn't playing and couldn't make the payments. The car was repossessed. That was a lesson I have not forgotten, and since that time I don't think I've ever done anything other than pay cash for a car.

Of course, I rejoined the band after a short time and we were back on the road again. Buffalo Springfield continued to play a lot of California and West Coast shows, becoming weekend warriors (bands that go out and play on weekends and then return home during the week), as well as doing some extended tours in the east.

On March 22, 1967, we played the Crystal Ballroom in Portland, Oregon. At that point we were playing some very wild shows and the band was starting to stretch out on Steve's classic song "Bluebird," pushing and pulling it to its limit with psychedelic, string-bending, distortion-ridden, molten, and crashing jams, culminating with me breaking all the strings on my Gretsch and Dewey crashing the hell out of his drums, while Stephen played his ass off. The crowds were going absolutely apeshit while Bruce and Richie kept the groove going. That was the Buffalo Springfield that never was heard on record.

We would be all sweaty and jacked after one of those sets, and that night in Portland when we hit the dressing room, something went way wrong. Stephen and Bruce and I got into a big fight over something and I was out of my mind. Not high, just crazed. I took my beautiful orange Gretsch and crashed it over a chair, breaking the back of the body wide open. I had too much energy and didn't know what the hell to do with it. Things like that may be why I got a reputation as being an angry guy, I don't know. I could also be funny and lighthearted, but I was sure out of control at times.

Back then, a brand-new Gretsch like mine came from the factory with a soft leather pad on the back to prevent the wood from getting scratched by belt buckles, so I got the guitar fixed and patched, and covered the damage with one of those pads. I still play it today.

The shows we did with that band were among the very best I have ever played. Buffalo Springfield took it to the limit for the first time in my life, and there is something special about the very first time you do anything. We were on the edge, exploring, and the crowds were eating us up. Unfortunately, the world never really got to see Buffalo Springfield. No good recording exists of the original live band and no film shows what that band really could do and did. That is why the name always evokes a bittersweet feeling among those who saw it at its peak. That broken guitar crashing into that chair may have been an early sign of the frustration and sense of missed chances associated with the band that the remaining members still feel today. It's really an incomplete story. It was truly too good to last.

1948 Continental "Abraham"

CHAPTER TWELVE

In late 1967, living in Laurel Canyon during the fading times of Buffalo Springfield, I had just purchased an old bronze 1948 Continental. It was a unique Continental design, had a perfect Bedford cord interior, and was in magnificent shape. I named it Abraham in honor of Abraham Lincoln.

I had recently returned to the group after another leave of absence. This time, I had missed the Monterey Pop Festival because I really had no interest in being part of it. Looking back, I was fairly unreasonable, selfish, and hard to get along with, but I believed those gigs had nothing to do with who we were. I didn't like playing on big bills with other bands.

During my time out of the band, I had arranged and recorded some songs with Jack Nitzsche, orchestrations that were a huge departure from my work with the Springfield. I was happy to be back in the band because Stephen and I really enjoyed playing together, and I think we were both beginning to recognize the blessings of our friendship in a new way.

I had brought "Expecting to Fly," an orchestration that Jack and I had done together, to our second LP project, *Buffalo Springfield Again*. Stephen and I had been in the studio producing "Rock & Roll Woman" and "Hung Upside Down," two great songs of his. That period was one of the best for us, working together, trying to make a really fine record. After having tried to do things separately, we were beginning to realize all the benefits of working together.

> *Someday I will be free,*
> *And there'll be times, you just wait.*
> *I will come to you, see,*
> *What I'll bring you when I get straight,*
> *Oh it's too late.*
> *And I'm hung upside down.*
>
> —"Hung Upside Down"

> *I tried so hard to stand*
> *As I stumbled and fell to the ground*
> *So hard to laugh as I fumbled*
> *And reached for the love I'd found*
> *Knowing it was gone.*
>
> —"Expecting to Fly"

After the LP's release, we were in a good groove and had been playing quite a bit, supporting the Beach Boys and headlining a lot of local California gigs of our own, but our moment may have passed us by. Bruce Palmer had recently been deported back to Canada for drug possession and the group was not the same without his magic bass playing. Stephen and I loved playing with Bruce, who had been on the record we had just made, but now he was gone. So many things had gone wrong, and the band struggled to get back to the groove of those first days. That was the real deal; those early days at the Whisky and on the road. That was Buffalo Springfield at its peak.

One evening, Abraham was rolling along the Pacific Coast Highway with Stephen and I on our way to a gig at the Earl Warren Showgrounds in Santa Barbara. It was January 6, 1968, and we had known each other three years. We shared a liking for big American cars and were having a fine time, enjoying the smooth, luxurious ride of the old classic Lincoln Continental. The Pacific Coast Highway was perfect cruising for Abraham, whose big V12 engine, built for the open road, could easily overheat when stuck in slow traffic.

A few months later, I was growing as a musician and writing so many songs that I needed my own outlet. I had outgrown the band, or at least was unable to reconcile how to divide my interests between myself and the band's. It was hard to decide where a song should go: on my solo LP or a new Buffalo Springfield record? Stephen had much the same situation and was moving toward other outlets, too, so eventually the band just broke up, not having reached the commercial success we knew we were capable of. Richie had a lot of songs of his own and had started a band called Poco, which was making waves in country rock.

I still think Buffalo Springfield might still be together today if we had only gotten started in the right direction with a great producer like Barry Friedman, Tom Dowd, or Paul Rothchild. However, we ended up with Greene and Stone, two managers who wanted to be producers. They had no idea what to do with us. We may actually have been the first band they produced.

When I moved to Topanga Canyon and bought my own house

on Skyline Trail, I was forced to park Abraham down below the house because the road was so steep. Tom Wilkes, the art director for A&M Records, lived with his wife, Lynne, down at the bottom of Skyline Trail, about two hundred yards below my house, almost straight down. They let me park Abraham outside their place in a turnaround. Abe was very heavy, and even with a giant, gas-guzzling twelve-cylinder engine, the Continental could not make it up the grade to my house. Abraham was designed for the open road, cruising along between gas stations in the bountiful luxury and excess of the times.

This situation couldn't last forever, so soon I sold Abraham to a happy new owner rather than leave it parked at the bottom of the hill all the time. A couple of years later, Tom Wilkes created the cover for *Harvest*, one of my most successful recordings.

1964 Mini Cooper S "The Norge"

n 1967, near the end of Buffalo Springfield's short life, I purchased a Mini Cooper S, a car that was speedy, popular, and trendy. This marked the first time that I owned two cars at once: Abraham, the big Continental, and my new Mini Cooper. While I was on the road with the Buffalo, I had the Mini painted bright white and the windows blackened so you couldn't see inside. I had a new black-vinyl interior installed, and when we returned from the road, my Mini was all ready!

It looked like a refrigerator and I referred to it as the Norge, a common brand of fridge. I felt very cool in the Norge, no pun intended. Buffalo Springfield was about as big as it ever got in those days. I was zipping around Hollywood in it, and it easily made it up the hill to my little Laurel Canyon cabin. I drove the Mini to many of our local gigs.

After the Buffalo broke up, I was getting ready to start my solo career and Elliot Roberts was my manager. He managed Joni

Mitchell, and for a short time at the end of Buffalo Springfield, he was managing us. I had fired him from managing the Springfield because I thought he was not paying enough attention to us. It was very petty on my part. We were on the road. I was sick with the flu and needed something, and Elliot was out playing golf. It was a ridiculous reason to fire him. That didn't stop me. I was pretty crazy and really self-centered at the time. Be that as it may, it happened. Then, when the group split, I tried to get Elliot to manage *me* right away. Elliot, it must be said, is one of the funniest people on the planet. He was able to spout one-liners at uncanny moments and blow anybody's mind. He was so much fun! What a great friend and cohort he was then and still is today.

When I moved to Topanga Canyon to escape the city, my life was changing fast. So was the look of my car. I had the Mini's wheel wells flared out and got big wide wheels and tires, and I painted it gray primer. It was not going to be the Norge anymore. It was to become a badass Mini.

One day, while I was having those changes made, I was walking down Topanga Canyon Boulevard, going for breakfast at a little café run by a pretty lady, Susan Acevedo. A couple of guys in an old military personnel carrier picked me up and gave me a ride. One of the guys in that giant vehicle was David Briggs, who was to become my friend for life and my unparalleled record producer.

Briggs was always vague about his upbringing. He had grown up in Wyoming with his aunt and left at a young age to seek his fortune in LA with his friend Kirby. He must have been in his teens. His talent for drawing music out of me was uncanny. He knew just what to say and when to say it. No one ever knew my muse the way Briggs did. We were brothers. His vocabulary was astounding. I don't know where the hell he got it, but he was always coming up with the most eloquent descriptions of things, and yet he could be crass and crude at the same time. Sometimes he was downright rude to people, but he had a way of escaping at the last minute when he had pissed off someone twice his size. Briggs was a man of many, many talents and I was lucky to have known him and share so much of my life with him, making so many records.

Elliot had gotten me a great contract as a solo artist with Reprise Records, and I was living in my new Topanga house, purchased with my record company advance for signing as a solo artist. Briggs and I had been hanging out, going over my new songs, and were ready to start recording my first solo album. At that time, I had fallen in love with Susan Acevedo. We were married in a small service with some friends in the house, so it was a whole new era for me.

I had come into possession of a puppy named Winnipeg, a white German shepherd with little brown-gold tips on his ears. Winnipeg was from a pet shop on Topanga Canyon Boulevard about a mile below where I lived. He was a good dog, pictured on my *Everybody Knows This Is Nowhere* LP cover and on the inside as well. Originally, that cover picture had been taken for my first record by a photographer Reprise had hired. I liked a painting that local Topanga artist Roland Diehl had done for my self-titled solo debut better, so we waited to use the photo with Winnipeg. Inside the foldout are pictures of my beautiful wife Susan and I, Briggs, Crazy Horse with Billy Talbot, Ralph Molina, and Danny Whitten, and Winnipeg. I really miss records with their big covers and inside sleeves.

Winnipeg was a friendly little guy when I got him, and I have a lasting image of him licking my nose to wake me up while I was asleep on the carpeted floor of my new house. Often I got very sleepy from Dilantin and phenobarbital, the medications I was taking to control seizures. Those two medications taken together were enough to knock me on my ass. So there I was, conked out on the carpet, waking up with this little puppy licking my nose and barking at me.

One day Winnipeg and I were on a little trip in Abraham, traveling on Saddle Peak, a narrow road above the coast in the mountains above Topanga Canyon. We had gone there to scope out a house that Briggs was renting. When we arrived at David's new place, I left Winnipeg in the car because David's dogs, Hannibal and Attila, a pair of German shorthairs, were not friendly with other dogs. After I visited with David for a while, I went back to the car and noticed that Winnipeg had eaten part of Abraham's perfect Bedford cord interior. Bad dog. But what did he know? He was just a puppy. I was just learning about dogs and he was just learning about cars.

About six months later, when Crazy Horse had finished *Everybody Knows This Is Nowhere*, I was practicing with CSN, just after the huge success of *Crosby, Stills & Nash*, their first album. Stills had come out to the house in Topanga and asked me if I wanted to join the group. CSN wanted to go on the road, and Stills, as well as Atlantic Records president Ahmet Ertegun, wanted to get Stephen and I playing together again to make CSN a little more suited for live performances. Ahmet always enjoyed our interplay, recognizing it as a big part of the Springfield sound.

CSN had its own sound and I wondered how my singing would fit in with theirs. Three-part harmony is pretty basic, but four-part is more complex. We did find ways to do it, though. It was a real experience for me to sing with such good singers and they taught me a lot. David and Graham are pitch-perfect. Stephen and I are a bit looser. When we were on, it was real good, and we were on a lot.

I loved singing with Stephen. It was fun singing with them all. What a sound.

Every day I would drive the Mini, with its superwide tires, blacked-out windows, and dust-covered gray-primer paint job, directly to CSNY rehearsal at Stephen's house without one traffic light or freeway. I hardly ever saw another car. I had my own way of getting there. It was a dusty old ridge road that was rarely used by anyone and ran along the top of the mountains separating the San Fernando Valley from the beach cities. The view was incredible. There were no signs and no rules. I would fly along in my Mini, listening to Frank Zappa and the Mothers of Invention blasting on my 8-track. That was a way cool outfit, the Mothers. The road went on for about twelve straight miles of dirt and dust before it became Mulholland Drive at the San Diego Freeway.

At that point I would hit the pavement and cross over the freeway, continuing on Mulholland, just flying along. It was a very exciting drive. For me, though, the best part was the twelve miles of dirt road coming out of Topanga. I never saw anybody on that road and I flew along, raising a cloud of dust that must have been visible from miles away. The road was just clay dust. In the winter, it was impassable. That was a great drive. The stealth road warrior Mini just tore that road up.

Some mornings I'd go in real early and record with Crazy Horse at Sunset Sound from ten to one and then go to Stephen's for practice with CSN. At those sessions with Crazy Horse, we cut "Oh, Lonesome Me" and "I Believe in You," both tracks I used on my next album, *After the Gold Rush*.

> *Now that you've found yourself losin' your mind,*
> *Are you here again,*

Findin' that what you once thought was real
Is gone and changin'?

—"I Believe in You"

At the Topanga house, Susan, her little daughter, Tia, and I had a next-door neighbor right below us on the hillside. All I could see of his house from my deck was the top of the roof. The owner was a large guy, very loud and excitable, a gay and exuberant character. One night, Susan's company, Scuzzy Catering, was serving for a big party, as she often did. She had a bunch of pies ready to take down to the site of the party and had loaded them all carefully into the Mini, which was parked in our garage, at the bottom of a long flight of stairs. When she went back up the stairs into the house to get the last apple pies, she heard a giant crash under the house next door. The Mini had slipped out of gear and rolled down the hill, crashing directly into the supporting post for my neighbor's house and knocking it down, causing his garage to collapse on the Mini and crush it.

He came running out and was screaming at Susan, arms flailing and overemphasizing like a bad actor in a Shakespearean play. Susan had a Sicilian moment and really came back at the guy, calling him every name she could think of and making up a few new names as well. He had no idea what he had gotten into. It was very dramatic. Alex, Susan's girlfriend and partner in Scuzzy Catering, came to her aid, rescuing the pies from what was left of the Mini, right under the screaming neighbor's nose. My rockin' little Mini was totaled. Gone forever.

1934 Bentley Close-coupled Coupe Mulliner

After the sale of Abraham, one of the first things I did was buy a black and silver 1934 Bentley close-coupled coupe, body by Mulliner, from an old gentleman in Glendale, who smiled happily as I drove away, seeing that I loved his fine old car so much. Everything about it was old; the seats were really old leather, the paint was cracked but original. It was really fine. It smelled aged and great, just like old leather should. This car was in exactly the kind of condition I looked for in later years when I began to appreciate the beauty and irreplaceable quality of originality.

David Briggs and I were making our first record together. It was my first solo LP. Two young guys on a mission, we were working on our masterpiece. Day in and day out, Briggs and I drove the old Bentley between Topanga and Hollywood—where Briggs was recording at Wally Heider Studios, T.T.G. Recording, Sunwest, Universal, United Audio, and Gold Star Recording—and always returned to Topanga late at night. Briggs and I drove on 101, flying through the night on our way back after a long session in the studio.

The car had right-hand drive, and on the driver's side there was a lever in the door that you could pull back or push forward, instantly opening or closing the window at lightning speed. I mean really fast! Slam! This was a lethal weapon, capable of severing a finger very easily. If someone tried to reach in and get you in the driver's seat, you had some real security and protection in that feature/weapon. But that was not the only feature this magnificent car possessed. It had an exhaust cutout lever on the floor as well. This feature was wild, to say the least. To save fuel and add power, it was possible to cut out the muffler completely by pulling the lever, thereby opening up the exhaust to run straight, without a muffler to impede the flow. When that was done, the car became *very* loud and went a bit faster. So that was exactly what Briggs and I experienced every night, cruising along the 101 freeway, talking about the record, what we would do tomorrow, what was good, what needed to be done again, everything, all while this spirited Bentley flew down the road, creating its amazing sound, faithfully carrying us to our destination. How throaty it was! What a sensation. Those were some of the best moments I can ever remember having in a car. The spirit of that automobile was undeniable. There was no problem getting this car up into my garage on Skyline Trail. It had a four-speed stick transmission on the floor and plenty of power to easily access the garage under complete control at a nice slow speed in first gear. That Bentley close-coupled Mulliner coupe was an incredible feat of engineering, flying down the road with the engine's throttle wide open.

SOON AFTER we finished our first record, when I had not yet married Susan, I had to go on the road to do some solo gigs up in

Canada to promote it. I was booked up there at some coffeehouses—Le Hibou in Ottawa and the Riverboat back on Yorkville Avenue in Toronto. I left Winnipeg at the Topanga house with a friend to care for him.

While I was in Toronto, I stayed in an apartment that was right across the road from Bob's Hobby Shop, where I had bought my first Lionel train. I had a one-week stand at the Riverboat, and Bruce Palmer came by a couple of nights to see what I was doing. One night my dad came by, too, and visited with me for a while in the dressing room, catching up on how things were going. I think he was really starting to believe I was doing what I was meant to do, and he was curious. I played a lot of songs from my first LP that night, as well as some Buffalo Springfield songs.

> *When the dream came,*
> *I held my breath with my eyes closed.*
> *I went insane,*
> *Like a smoke ring day when the wind blows.*
> *Now I won't be back 'til later on,*
> *If I do come back at all,*
> *But you know me,*
> *And I miss you now.*
>
> —"ON THE WAY HOME"

I really looked forward to getting home and seeing Winnipeg, but that didn't work out. When I returned to the house, there was no friend and no dog. I never did find out what happened. I was very young and made a lot of poor judgments about caring for things, particularly living things. Experience was not yet my friend.

While we were making the record *Everybody Knows This Is No-*

where, I was driving the Bentley up one of the steep Topanga hills, climbing toward my house, and as I entered a curve there was a pop in the rear end and I suddenly lost traction. The motor would turn but the wheels would not. I soon learned that a spider gear had failed in the rear end assembly. Fixing it would not be a problem.

At this time I made a *very* large mistake and decided that I should restore the car completely. I had it delivered to a place in Santa Monica called Prestige Motors. It sat there for a very long time. I figured I would go back in a few months and it would be restored, completely cherry. On my first visit back to check on the progress I knew I had made a big mistake. The car was pretty well dismantled. The interior was out and part of a new one that had none of the patina of the old one was in its place. The exterior paint had been damaged and stripped. Bumpers and magnificent headlights were out being re-chromed. Nothing was finished. The chrome had been fine and did not need any work at all and the new chrome that had been done was not nearly the same quality as the original.

Original. That is when it dawned on me that I had destroyed what I loved so much by trying to "make it better." I had gone way too far and ruined a perfect car. That car was never the same. When I moved up north I had it shipped to the ranch, unfinished. I didn't get to drive that 1934 Bentley close-coupled coupe again, but it was perhaps the finest car I had ever driven.

Forty years passed. The beauty and irreplaceable quality of originality lived on.

By 2010, album sales had really slowed down. Time had passed and the record business was plummeting. There was almost nothing left of what I used to feel, sitting with my friends, listening for hours to our favorite artists on analog vinyl (sometimes the same song ten times in a row), feeling the rush of emotions every time. Some people say one thing, some say another, but I think the terrible quality that record companies have settled for to sell music on the Internet effectively removed all that was good in the listening experience, except for the lyrics, beat, and melody. There was almost no way to *feel* the soul in the sound the way we used to. I missed the sound.

I had to make adjustments in my personal life to make up for the loss of income and sell the part of the ranch that housed my car collection. I had to choose which cars I would keep. In 2010, I sold the Bentley to someone who would try to bring it back. I didn't want to sell it, but I was done. It was too painful, remembering what the car used to be like. Many cars were sold in what I call the big purge of 2010. It was difficult, yet it somehow lightened my load and I didn't mind too much. I got used to it. Freeing it was, the big purge.

I planned on building a smaller place, which would be less than one-quarter the size of the original barn, to house my cars on the part of the ranch that we kept. I had a great structure built by local builder John Dixon, who earlier had reinvented our house with me by adding on to the original in a massive expansion project we now call Shakey Heights. John built a small car barn for me and I call it Feelgood's. Today, Feelgood's is my office and holds about six cars and many old amplifiers from my recordings and tours over the years—beautiful things built to make music. A lot of my favorite things in the world are in there.

I focused on the cars that really had a human and enduring lifetime connection with me and I kept those. Those cars hold some of my favorite thoughts, feelings, and memories, my moments of bliss. They are things of metal, but they harbor part of my soul.

1951 Willys Jeepster

B ack in Topanga Canyon in 1968, Susan Acevedo had a restaurant named the Canyon Country Kitchen. I quickly fell in love with her. One morning, before we were married, I was enjoying a "one eye" breakfast at the Canyon Kitchen, looking at Susan. I was reading "445 Collector's Cars" in the *LA Times* want ads. I usually didn't bother with the headlines unless something was happening of interest, and Susan was by far the most interesting thing happening.

When I saw that Santa Ana Motors had a 1951 Willys Jeepster for sale for $750, it gave me an excited feeling, and I was interested in looking at it right away. The trip to Santa Ana took a couple of hours, and I went with my friend Danny Tucker, so that if I bought the car, I could drive it home immediately. Danny was a happy-go-lucky guy who I always enjoyed being around. He was an actor, a friend of Briggs, and a great conversationalist. Danny had helped me move into my new house the day the deal closed, and we had become good friends.

The 1948 through 1951 Willys Overland Jeepster was an open phaeton, slightly reminiscent of the designs from the twenties and thirties. When we got to Santa Ana Motors, the faded yellow and black Jeepster convertible was visible in the front of the lot and I knew immediately that I wanted it. When I did drive it, I found it to be a pretty good runner, needing nothing. Its convertible top was a little raggedy, and the gearshift linkage was funky, making it so that you had to almost go into reverse to get to second gear from first, doing a maneuver that kind of reset the position of the linkage and allowed second gear to be accessed. I looked at that as a theft deterrent. If you didn't know that little secret there was no way you could steal the car. You would be stuck in first gear.

Aside from that quirky feature, the car was pretty straightforward. Things were well-worn, including the knobs and the chrome on the dash, which was very spotty and well-aged, but the car itself was a real beauty, soulful and open like a desert cruiser. Its jeep pedigree shone through as I stood back and surveyed my latest purchase. On the highway driving back to Topanga, I discovered the overdrive, which allowed a top speed of about sixty to sixty-five miles per hour when it was engaged. Without the OD engaged, the car was very sure-footed and the low gear ratio would make it perfect for the back roads of Topanga that I loved to traverse, so I was a very happy camper.

IN LATE SUMMER OF 1969, July or August, I released my second LP, *Everybody Knows This Is Nowhere*, playing with Crazy Horse for the first time, the beginning of the most fruitful musical relationship of my life. Crazy Horse is the easiest band for me to fall into a groove with. There is something about the beat of that band, Ralph Molina's sensitivity to what I play and his knowing where I am about to go with the beat. About then, there was a screenplay in the works by Herb Berman and my friend Dean Stockwell, both Topanga dwellers and people I had met through Susan. Their story was set in the canyon and very loosely revolved around an artist carrying a tree from the ocean up through the canyon. An earthquake and tidal wave also played big parts, with the wave rushing up the canyon right to the edge of the little village. There was a lot more to it than that, with some characters who transcended the moment and carried some messages. Universal executives came to my house with Dean one day. Dean wanted them to meet me because I had written a loose soundtrack based on what I had read in the treatment. I think since my records were selling well that Dean thought the executives should know I was doing the soundtrack. Every bit helps when you are trying to get a movie supported. The title was *After the Gold Rush*. The screenplay was a very artistic endeavor, probably too far out there for the Universal executives, and the film was never completed, but I was influenced by it. I made the record.

Briggs and I took a lot of rides in the Jeepster on the back roads of Topanga, listening to cassettes together, checking the mixes, and I took a lot of rides alone. During the *After the Gold Rush* sessions, I had just purchased a pound of Panama Red from someone in the canyon. A joint of Panama Red and a Jeepster ride made a really fine combination, and we experienced that often in those days, traveling to the tops of the mountains on old roads to stop there and just look at the beauty of California through our young eyes, our vision heightened and sensitized by the good weed.

Dreams abounded as life rushed by.

Well, I dreamed I saw the knights in armor comin'
Sayin' something about a queen.
There were peasants singin' and drummers drummin'
And the archer split the tree.
There was a fanfare blowin' to the sun
That floated on the breeze.
Look at Mother Nature on the run
In the 1970s.

—"After the Gold Rush"

We were living our dream—making our music, conquering our goals, and celebrating every victory with the relish only a young soul can fleetingly know. We were truly there, on top of those mountains, rolling through those valleys with the women, love, and the songs we were singing, and that was just the beginning. The records Briggs and I made together are testimony to the love and pain, to the joy and sorrow, of coming of age.

I was so engrossed in my music and art that I lost track of Susan and the sensitivity it took to protect our love. I must have been too young to hold on to her because soon she was gone and we were over. The success and fame wore on her, and on us, it was a strain on our young marriage. It buckled and fell.

We went our separate ways. I was young and accepted change easily. I felt the need to move on, north to the trees and the rolling hills I had seen from the jet plane windows while flying over San Francisco's golden peninsula as the summer ended and the green grass turned to wheat straw. I purchased my ranch up there and moved out of our Topanga house while the escrow passed, waiting for that September day when I could finally move to the North

Country and the ranch I would call home for decades more to come. The future was much bigger than the past.

> *When the winter rains come pourin' down*
> *On that new home of mine*
> *Will you think of me*
> *And wonder if I'm fine?*
> *Will your restless heart come back to mine*
> *On a journey through the past?*
> *Will I still be in your eyes*
> *And on your mind?*
>
> —"JOURNEY THROUGH THE PAST"

Finally the escrow completion date arrived and it was time to move north. Johnny Barbata, our CSNY drummer and the former drummer for the Turtles, rode north with me. Following us were Bruce Berry and Guillermo Giachetti, two of CSNY's roadies, in Bruce's old 1958 Caddy limo.

It was summer's end. Raging wildfires burned on both sides of the freeway.

Johnny and I drove along in the Jeepster, loaded with my guitars and gold records. We headed north on 101, out of LA's San Fernando Valley. We left that crowded valley behind, climbing up the long grade that would eventually peak and take us to the coast, then through Santa Barbara, past the Earl Warren Showgrounds where Buffalo Springfield had played so many times, on through San Luis Obispo, north to San Jose, and, eventually, to the ranch.

Traveling in the Jeepster was freeing; our hearts were eager with expectation as a new chapter began for all of us. Johnny was looking for a place to buy near the ranch, talking about it as he beat on his knees with a pair of drumsticks, and the other guys were going to check out the area as well, looking for places to settle. Briggs was planning to come up to try to find a house. It was a monumental transition happening in the blink of an eye.

The Jeepster fairly flew along the road at about sixty miles per hour for nine or ten hours, burning about twenty-six gallons of gasoline. The sun had already set when we arrived at the ranch. The smells and sounds were so refreshing. The air was crisp and clean. We were in the country, far from the city. It was much less populated than Topanga. We didn't know we had just put 520 pounds of CO_2 into the atmosphere, laying a few more bricks in the foundation of global warming.

We slept in sleeping bags on the floor of the little ranch house, and I was already talking about the walls coming down and the fireplaces I would build. I wanted to use redwood planking like my old house in Topanga had. Our lives were so full, and now we had moved to an area unknown to us, full of promise and disappointment, both in healthy amounts. A lot of discovery lay before us: love, hard drugs, more money than ever before, responsibilities of parenthood, more fame, and even more fame.

When we awoke, the sounds of hundreds of red-winged blackbirds greeted us from the little lake in front of the cabin. We needed food. Looking in the Yellow Pages, Johnny found a health food market that was located in Palo Alto, a town on the other side of the hill, near Stanford University. It was located on California Avenue and was in a big building shaped like a Quonset hut. NEW AGE NATURAL FOODS said the sign as we pulled the Jeepster into the side parking lot.

Inside there was a newspaper called the *Whole Earth Catalog*. We picked one up and walked the aisles, which were crowded with Earth Mamas. These beautiful and wholesome-looking young women were everywhere, a different breed than the hippie girls I had met in Hollywood back when I first arrived in the Pontiac hearse. It was hard to believe that was only a few years before. Johnny stood, amazed, looking at the selections of granola in bins at the end of one of the aisles. Coffee beans and hand grinders were for sale in another area. Fresh fruit and vegetables were abundant. This was the healthiest store I had ever seen, not that I was in the habit of looking for health food.

In the parking lot, we put the top down, sat in the car stealthily smoking a joint, and watched for a few minutes as Earth Mamas came and went. This place became a regular trip for us in the first few months. We got all of our food there except for bacon. For some reason I couldn't understand, they had no bacon. We stocked up on supplies and one day went to an antique store, where I bought an ancient refrigerator that had a round compressor on top. It looked like something out of a science fiction movie and we got it delivered to the ranch. The narrow forest roads were too scary for the delivery service, so we had to lead them in with the Jeepster.

I have always loved narrow roads, and the roads around the ranch were perfect cliffside one-laners, winding through the serene beauty of the redwoods. I would spend hours just driving around, learning the roads—where they went, how passable, how quiet they were—and I was in love with my new home.

The first day I arrived at the ranch, the foreman, Louis Avila, and his wife, Clara, were living in a little house about two hundred yards away from the modest main house I lived in. A lake with geese and ducks, fish and frogs, and always red-winged blackbirds lay between my small house and theirs. Reeds surrounded the water. It was so beautiful, and every day I would walk down a little path from my house to a couple of huge redwoods right by the shore, sit down, and have morning coffee.

Those legions of red-winged blackbirds sang to me in a loud chorus every morning and sunset. Sometimes I would sit there and toke on a joint at the end of the day, waiting for another song to come to me. The songs loved it there and came constantly, and on my birthday, I wrote a song for Louis.

> *Old man look at my life,*
> *Twenty-four and there's so much more.*
> *Live alone in a paradise that makes me think of two.*
> *Love lost, such a cost,*
> *Give me things that don't get lost,*
> *Like a coin that won't get tossed, rolling home to you.*
>
> —"Old Man"

I had gotten another pound of Panama Red somewhere and it was great weed. Pure bliss. There was a great dirt road, perfect for the Jeepster, I used often to get down to a grocery store from the hill. I always looked forward to the drive. I would light up a joint and get behind the wheel. The road was dusty as could be and we traveled it often, the Jeepster and me. As the years passed, it was closed off and paved, becoming a private road with an electric gate, but I knew the code. Eventually a security car patrolled it and I was not allowed to drive on it anymore. It was kind of symbolic of the growth that was taking off in the area.

The country roads were getting paved over and what used to be wild was tame and private. Things were changing again, and I was starting to feel that it wasn't for the better. Something else died with that dusty dirt road.

Slippin' and a slidin'
And playin' domino.
Leftin' and then rightin'
It's not a crime, you know.
You got to tell your story
Boy, before it's time to go.
Are you ready for the country?
Because it's time to go.

—"Are You Ready for the Country?"

CHAPTER SIXTEEN

As I settled in at Broken Arrow Ranch and continued exploring the area, I discovered a little place up on the hill called Alex's, where I eventually found the next love of my life, Pegi Morton. A fellow Canadian, Alex Reid, had started a restaurant-bar and had a couple of local ladies working for him, making tip money. He was just getting started. If the ladies didn't make enough in tips, Alex would give them a little money. The restaurant was mostly used by locals and was just starting to draw folks who weren't from the mountain itself. I visited occasionally and that's where I first saw Pegi. She was in her late teens. Her incredibly blue eyes and blond hair would have gotten anyone's attention. She was the hostess at Alex's and the main attraction for me.

One evening while I was eating at Alex's, I asked her for pepper and she looked directly in my eyes and said, "Sure, it rips through your system and takes seven years to digest." I was pretty captivated and interested in her by then and tried in vain one night to get her to come down and check out my new hot tub at the ranch. She said,

"No thanks." That was the beginning of a four-year courtship that lingered off and on. One Halloween there was a party at Alex's and Pegi came as Wonder Woman. I thought she was. Pegi and I were married in 1978 at my sea-level house in Malibu, in a private ceremony with a few close friends.

As all of this was taking place, the ranch continued to develop. The Jeepster was always there with the family, sort of a local resident. There were a few assorted ranch equipment barns. One of these barns was made into my first car barn, which held about four or five cars. After I married Pegi and our son Ben Young was born, it was converted into a gym and train barn where I built a large train layout. Ben used to travel over there in his bassinet on the Jeepster's front seat with me. I would put him on the train table and talk to him as I laid track and built scenery out of stumps and moss from the forest.

Paul Williamson, nicknamed "Wog," was a local guy from Pescadero, a nearby fishing town. His family was an old respected coastside family. Paul became a good friend, and he started to take care of my cars in the seventies. Wog found Jon McKeig and introduced me to him after an accident damaged one of my cars around 1975, and I hired Jon to do some bodywork.

Jon was a master body- and paint-man from Scotts Valley, another nearby town. He worked with metal like no one I had ever seen. He would put stress on a piece of bent metal by pulling on it with a counterweight and watch it straighten for a week, then adjust the stress until it was perfectly straight, letting time do the work. Metal seemed to move in his hands while time stood still. One day after a few years, he came to me and said he would like to work for me. So, in the mid-eighties, I hired Jon McKeig to take care of my car collection. I loved Jon's work and thought perhaps he could manage the restorations of the vehicles that needed it and touch up the ones that didn't. That was my plan. Jon was a veteran of the Vietnam War and was always there to help our family any way he could. The way he was with our children, especially Ben Young, showed his true colors, and Pegi and I both love Jon very much. He was one of the kindest people I have ever known.

Paul had brought him in and now he took over Paul's job, but Paul kept driving my tour bus. He was a great guy to have on the road. We had a lot of fun, and he was a safe driver. Wog continued being my good friend and drove my bus on the tours I did in the eighties, and there were a lot of them.

At one point I had to store all of my cars down in Pescadero near Paul's house because I didn't have enough space on the ranch to hold them. Unfortunately, extensive damage happened to some of them down there when moths got into the interiors, resulting in the use of mothballs, further ruining many of the cars by making them smell bad. I felt bad that I was responsible for the damage. I really needed a good place for them to live. It was not enough to have the cars if I couldn't take care of them.

The ranch grew again with another parcel in 1980, by some 1,200 acres, and after cruising over the expanded ranch in the Jeepster, I found a perfect location to erect a big prefab metal building to house my collection of clunkers and classics. There were a lot of them because I never sold anything.

Finally my cars would have a place to live.

With cars, collecting and obsession walk a similar path. There is a fine line between the two and I was close to it. I was beginning to wonder about myself, but luckily for me, the feeling passed.

I quickly found a musical use for the big car barn. I had to break it in. I love new spaces to play music. Initially it had a gravel floor and a great big sound, so before I had concrete poured, which would be better for the cars but would ruin the sound, I had Larry Cragg, my super-talented guitar technician and amp specialist, come and set up my amp rig there.

With Old Black and Gold, my two Les Paul Gibson guitars that I used the most with Crazy Horse, I was ready to begin. Larry had set up my full-stage rig—a Fender Deluxe amp, a Magnatone amp, and a Baldwin Exterminator amp—along with my custom foot pedal made by Sal Trentino (the electronics) and Johnny Foster (the woodwork). Johnny was Tim Foster's brother. Tim was my tour production manager.

Sal Trentino was a master guru of electronics, designing, tuning, and repairing tube amps, among many other talents. He was a legend with the musicians in the area. He kept Carlos Santana and many other guitarists from Bay Area bands sounding good. Both he and Larry Cragg came from Prune Music in Mill Valley, one of West Coast rock and roll's legendary spots. It took a lot of talented people to create my big, creamy, distorted sound. I told Sal what I wanted and he built the innards of the pedal board for me.

Larry showed up on the ranch one day in early 1990 in his 1970s Camaro SS, one of his many muscle cars, and set me up in the car barn with all of my equipment, after which I started arriving each day at around ten a.m. in the Jeepster. At that point, the car barn was just a huge empty building, save for a few cars. I would plug in Old Black, fire up my amps and a joint, and start playing and writing. That is where I wrote *Ragged Glory*, maybe one of Crazy Horse's favorite studio albums.

> *Well, I saw an old man, walkin' in my place*
> *When he looked at me, I thought I saw my face*

His words were kind, but his eyes were wild
He said, "I got a load to love, but I want one more child"
There's a mansion on the hill
Psychedelic music fills the air
Peace and love live there still
In that Mansion on the Hill.

—"Mansion on the Hill"

The setup stayed there for about a month, undisturbed except for my daily comings and goings. I was in a groove writing, and soon I was recording *Ragged Glory* in the big wooden white barn located on the courtyard of the old ranch house. This area was the center of the original Bella Vista Rancho, which was more than two thousand acres in its prime. The courtyard had a beautiful fountain that flowed depending on the state of the water source for the ranch. If there was a water problem, a break in a pipe, the fountain would not flow. After a big storm, it would gush, sending water into the air. When the foreman walked out in the morning, the first thing he would see was that fountain. That's the way it worked back in the day.

Under the direction of Briggs, we had converted the inside of the white barn into a studio we called "Plywood Analog" because of its plywood construction and analog equipment. We had a rented recording truck that we parked outside in the courtyard. Recording trucks were common at that time, full of great-sounding analog gear. Briggs was in the truck with John Hanlon engineering. The Jeepster and all the other cars would be parked around in the courtyard as we recorded, like they were listening and waiting. After a few weeks we had completed the album.

Ragged Glory is the only record we have ever made where we played the whole running order twice a day, never listening to play-backs and always taking notes on how the music felt. At the end of the recording stage, when we sensed we had played all of the songs well, we read the notes and reviewed the tapes. It is often true that the initial reaction to a performance is the most valuable and that postanalysis can be tedious and unproductive.

After construction on the car barn was finished, we brought all the cars up from Pescadero, the three moth-eaten ones included, and stored them on the ranch. It was great to finally see them all in one place. What an amazing collection it was! That was the moment when I really started to see how many cars I had accumulated. I noticed again that things had gotten a bit out of control and that I was obsessed. I had too many cars that needed extensive work and I knew I could never afford the money or time to fix them all. I had some guilt about the moth-eaten ones, and I got a few of them repaired.

Knowing that I loved cars and rewarded myself by buying them, I felt there was something good that would come out of it. The cars were beginning to talk to me, to tell me things about themselves: their problems, the damage they caused. I started thinking a lot about the damage they caused.

Jon McKeig worked continuously on the building for a number of years and made it a beautiful place to service, display, and restore cars. I loved the space he created, but we didn't have the staff to take care of all of the cars, and money was becoming more and more scarce as things changed in the music world and consequently in my private life.

I think I gave Jon more organizing, bookwork, and overseeing responsibility than I should have, and he was unable to focus on what he did best. I now know I could have enabled Jon to be more productive if I had handled things differently. It takes a lifetime to learn some things.

One of the jobs Jon took on was restoring the Jeepster. We had defined our own restoration process. Our idea was to make it look old but get it into perfect condition: retaining its age in the bumpers and dashboard and staying with the original materials while blending the new paint colors to look faded yet new. Jon took his work very seriously. It was during this project that I saw Jon's genius and how his demons manifested in his problems with completion. Jon spent many years searching for parts, straightening and painting, rubbing and filling, painting and rubbing. The Jeepster felt like a baby's skin, soft as it could be. The edges were smooth as silk and the colors were faded to perfection. It was a masterpiece to behold. When it was completed, the Jeepster was a work of art; a restoration that all of my other restorations would have to live up to. It took more than ten years to complete. I loved it and still do.

The Jeepster was mechanically restored by Bruce Ferrario, a man committed to excellence and probably Jon's counterpart in the mechanical field. If I had only known Bruce earlier in life, the completion of so many more projects would have been possible. You live and learn. I found Bruce through Roy Brizio of Brizio Street Rods, and I had found Roy when Larry Johnson, my partner in filmmaking, mentioned his shop, having noticed it on his way to an editing suite we worked in nearby in South San Francisco.

In 2012, the finished Jeepster was parked in the place of honor, my garage under our house. I hope it has many more miles with my family, my dogs, and me. Having been around for so much of my life, that 1951 Willys Jeepster occupies a special place in my soul and is just like an old friend.

Recently, in 2013, I met Ben Young up on the mountain and we enjoyed a dinner together at the Mountain House, the restaurant-bar where I had met his mother some forty years before. This night, Pegi was out on the road playing a club tour with her band, the Survivors. Pulling the old Jeepster up in front of that place, with the heater blasting welcomed warmth, I felt the passage of life and how fleeting it really is. In a silent prayer to the Great Spirit, I asked to be worthy of more time. There was still so much to do.

1947 Buick Roadmaster Estate Wagon

Before moving to the North Country in 1970, I lived for a while at the Chateau Marmont, a gracious old hotel in Hollywood that looks down over Sunset Boulevard. Ahmet Ertegun, president of Atlantic while the Buffalo Springfield was recording for the company, always stayed at the Chateau. I met him there a few times and liked the old place with its Spanish architecture. When I moved out of my Topanga house and into the Chateau as the escrow cleared on my new ranch up north, I spent a lot of that time hanging out with Gary Burden, the art director and co-creator of my album covers, at his studio in Hollywood. Gary's artistic nature and supportive friendship accompanied and guided me as I made a transition to my new life, away from Hollywood and the fast-moving scene there.

Time rolled gently by at the Chateau Marmont. One summer morning I was outside on the patio, taking in the ambience of Sunset Boulevard as traffic passed below, reading section 445, collector's cars, in the paper. I saw an old 1947 Buick Roadmaster Estate

Wagon for sale. I called up the number and Gary and I went to see it in the parking lot of the Roosevelt Hotel in Hollywood. This ramshackle hotel was full of old movie stars and filmmakers who had already seen their big time in the spotlight and were more or less on the skids. What a bunch of characters. The owner of the Buick was a porn-film producer. He had painted the Estate Wagon navy blue with a regular brush on the outside, and similarly applied construction-orange paint completely covered the beautiful wood interior. The old Buick ran well, though, with its smooth Dynaflow automatic transmission. It was very soulful and reminded me of Mort. Of course, the dash and instruments were identical.

I have a big soft spot in my heart for that vintage of Buick. I would still find it hard to turn one down if it was presented to me, even today, particularly a convertible. The owner wanted $750 for it, so I gave the man his money and we drove the old baby over to Gary's studio and started to remove the paint with some wire brushes and paint remover. That didn't last long. It was hard work and we were not that energetic. Smoking grass, dreaming, writing songs, and creating album covers was more our speed at the time.

In Hollywood, I found an auto restoration place on Melrose Avenue named Coachcraft. There was an old German master craftsman in there, Rudy Stoesel, who ran the shop. He had a couple of Rolls-Royce woodies, called shooting brakes, under restoration. When Rudy saw my Buick Roadmaster Estate Wagon, he said, "Why do you want me to work on that piece of shit?" I was sold! He was the guy. His puffy face looked up at me with a near sneer. He showed me how the metal panels would never line up perfectly because it was American made and the car companies here never got anything right.

I knew different. It would line up if Rudy restored it. I said, "Rudy, I want *you* to do it."

Over the next year or so I went back to Hollywood regularly to check the progress on the Buick Estate Wagon and Rudy would abuse me for spending all that money on "a piece of shit." He showed me how I screwed up. "You fucked up the registration plate with your stupid wire brushes. I can't do anything about that stupidity," he said, waving his finger at me. Then he showed me the original color, dune beige, and the original interior material, Bedford cord. It was beautiful. He purchased another car for parts, again because mine was "a piece of shit." About a year and many dollars later, he finished the car and it was flawless. I picked it up and drove it to the ranch. It had the wrong gear ratio on the rear end, so the top speed was compromised, but I didn't want to take it back to Rudy and Coachcraft. It looked too cool. I would get that ratio changed up north.

By mid-1971, I was living with Carrie Snodgress on the ranch. Her brother John was around, living in the neighborhood, and he had a dog whose name was Tobias. Tobias was a hound, and as a memory to take with me, he scratched the back hatch of the Estate Wagon with his paws trying to get in. He loved to ride in cars. That mark is still there. I don't hold it against him. It's just cars and dogs.

Yet another dog left his mark on the 1947 Buick Roadmaster Estate Wagon. His name was Elvis, a great hound dog I got from Pegi in the early eighties. When I first saw Elvis, he was in a cardboard box under the Christmas tree, his little head popping up over the edge. He was beautiful.

What a soulful dog he was. Elvis was a Tennessee bluetick hound and a fine example of one, already with a good howl even as a puppy. Ben Keith had found Elvis for Pegi in Tennessee. I had first met Ben while I was in Nashville doing *The Johnny Cash Show*. We went into the studio there to record some of the new songs I had written. Ben became my lifelong friend and played steel guitar on those sessions, making one of my most popular albums ever, *Harvest*. He played and sang with me on every record that had steel or slide guitar from then on, and even more that didn't, because Ben could play *anything*. He was playing with me right up until the day he died on Broken Arrow Ranch in 2010. Ben Keith was one of my very best friends and perhaps the greatest musician I have ever played with.

I had Elvis for many years. Elvis was a good boy most of the time but not all the time. Once he had a little sore on his tummy and it leaked out some while he was in the Roadmaster Estate Wagon's backseat, where he loved to ride. There is still that little stain there on the backseat. I'm keeping that the way it is. It's just a little stain, and it reminds me of him.

1944 Military Jeep "The Blue Jeep"

he Lazy Double L ranch, so named by its owners, Long and
Lewis, employed Louis and Clara Avila as caretakers. Louis
and Clara were each about sixty years old and Louis had a very leath-
ery face from being out in the sun working the land his whole life.
His hair was full and white and he talked slowly in a friendly way.
Clara, his wife of about forty years, was a very nice, soft-spoken lady.
They were very much in love and lived in a little house about two
hundred yards from my cabin, just on the other side of the beautiful
little lake. They were there the day I first saw the place.

Louis took me around the Double L that day in a 1944 military
jeep, painted blue and very faded. On the front of the jeep there was
a burlap sack that was tied with ropes and covered the whole flat
surface of the hood. The purpose of this was so that Snip, Louis's
dog, a little Australian shepherd cross, could ride up there and not
slip off while the jeep traversed the rough hills and fields of the
beautiful cattle ranch. It gave Snip's feet a good purchase.

Whenever Louis wanted to move his cows, he would just take

Snip down and aim her at the right cows, whereupon the little dog would take off nipping at the feet of the bovines, moving them toward whatever area Louis pointed to. Louis, Snip, and I drove all around the breathtaking property together. It was summer and I knew I wanted the place. The price was right and I was ready. I had just had two big hits in a row with my records *Everybody Knows This Is Nowhere* and *After the Gold Rush* and was flush with cash. When I purchased the ranch, the blue jeep was part of the deal and Louis and Clara stayed on as caretakers.

Louis stood a little off-center due to an injury he sustained while walking through a field one day when he stepped in a deep hole and put his back out. He never got it fixed. He just soldiered on. His manner was always casual, country.

My dog at that time, Filmore, was a white German shepherd pup, just like Winnipeg. I got him right after I moved to the ranch. Those were some happy times, driving all around discovering my new ranch, getting to know every acre in that old jeep with Filmore running alongside.

> *My army jeep is still alive*
> *Got locking hubs and four-wheel drive*
> *Ain't got no radio,*
> *Ain't got no mag wheels*
> *Ain't got no digital clock*
> *Ain't got no clock.*
>
> —"Motor City"

Filmore definitely did not like riding in cars. He would instantly get carsick. It only took one look at that forlorn face of his to see that he was about to throw up all over the seat. Filmore went with me on a lot of walks in the morning. I liked to carry a cup of coffee in one hand and I would place it on a fence post when I was done so I could pick it up on the way back. Usually Filmore and I went back a different way, so there were a lot of fence posts with coffee cups on top of them.

We both loved our morning walks, a great tradition between man and dog. When I left to go on the solo acoustic tour through Canada in January 1971, I had to leave Filmore behind with Louis and Clara, but something went amiss. When I got back from the tour, Filmore was gone. I vowed that would never happen again. Later, when I got a bus, I planned to take my dogs with me everywhere, and I did.

It was the late seventies when Ben Young was born, and he was diagnosed with cerebral palsy at the age of six months and Pegi and I were trying everything to help. Ben Young was a quadriplegic.

Pegi and I were living on the ranch and had enrolled Ben in a development program designed by the Institutes for the Achievement of Human Potential in Philadelphia. The program we were on was an intense one, with no rest, and round-the-clock patterning every day. We did the program with Ben and his volunteer patterners for eighteen months, seven days a week, approximately fourteen hours a day.

At the end of every day, Ben's reward was a blue jeep ride with Mom and Dad. Sometimes it was sunset. Sometimes it was dark, but we still went on a ride together and told Ben Young what a great job he had done and how we were so happy with his progress. He loves the blue jeep rides with us to this day, and so do we. They are always a very special family time. Ben certainly has earned as many as he wants. The phrase "blue jeep ride" is very meaningful to us.

For the love of man,
Who could understand
What goes on
What is right
And what is wrong,
Why the angels cry
And the heavens sigh,
When a child is
Born to live,
But not like you and I?

—"For the Love of Man"

Today the blue jeep is in the barn where it has been since the first day I came to the ranch and met Louis and Clara. It has been mechanically restored by Bruce Ferrario and is in excellent shape. It has never been painted and still has the old blue color I love, but it has faded slightly during the years of service to our family.

1951 Jeep Overland Pickup Truck

When I started to live on the ranch in September of 1970, I realized I should have a pickup truck to lug things around. I wanted an old one and thought maybe a jeep would be good, and when I found one in the local paper, it was at American Auto Works, down the hill in San Carlos, a little town on the peninsula.

It was about forty-five minutes to San Carlos on one-lane roads that wound their way through the redwood canyons from the ranch to the flatlands of the peninsula. Every route I chose was always based on avoiding other cars or traffic lights until the last possible moment. Sitting inside of my old cars while I was driving on these roads, it was easy to lose track of who I was and what year it was. After driving for a while and not seeing anyone, it became the year of the car. I was generally not in a hurry, especially back in those days, when time was on my side.

The redwoods are still like church to me, good for the soul, I love driving along surrounded by their grace while the sun streaks through like God-rays.

We went lookin' for faith on the forest floor,
And it showed up everywhere,
In the sun and the water and the falling leaves,
The falling leaves of time.

—"You're My Girl"

It was on one of those routes that I drove the Jeepster, making my way down gradually toward the hustle and bustle of San Carlos. I think Johnny Barbata was with me so he could drive the Jeepster back to the ranch if I bought the pickup. Soon, we arrived at the place where the car was located.

The 1951 Jeep Overland pickup was a faded blue, with some of the original orange paint showing through where parts of the blue second-generation paint had worn, but the body was in pretty good solid shape. Being a jeep, it wasn't big, but it had a Chevy 327 engine in it, replacing the original four-cylinder, and was very powerful, but not mellow as when it was first built. That was a surprise, and a bit against my grain, but I bought it anyway and marveled at the radical acceleration it possessed.

The jeep was a fun truck to drive and after test-driving it to La Honda, I took it home and parked it by the house. Now I had my own pickup in the driveway, but after a while the rough ride bothered my back more and more and I drove the truck less and less.

That December, music reentered my life. I did a three-day stand at the Cellar Door in Washington, DC. When I was back home at the ranch for a few days after DC, I got inside the jeep pickup. I turned the key and it fired right up, but when I went to put it in gear and I tried to raise my foot to put it down on the clutch, nothing happened. My leg would not rise and I couldn't lift my foot up to the pedal.

This had happened one time in Topanga, and I went to a chiropractor Susan referred me to. He was able to fix me up with a couple of adjustments. I had been working with a hoe, cleaning weeds outside the house and preparing for a little garden. Perhaps I had been repeating the same move with the hoe repeatedly. Possibly I was even hoeing obsessively and manically!

Now, thinking back to the day before, I remember that I had strained myself lifting some very large pieces of walnut for the walls in the dining room. I was lifting and reaching to hold the heavy slabs in place. I really didn't know my own strength or how little strength I actually had, so I would try anything. I was young, not knowing that my body could be broken. I ended up in the hospital and spent a week in traction before I was released in a brace I had to wear until I was healed.

Eventually the 1951 jeep pickup was parked in my old junkyard, where cars were left and almost never used. It's kind of a sad place, but it's also a monument. Years passed. I would drive by, seeing it there, parked among other cars past their time of service. Most of the cars and trucks that arrived there never made it out, and that pickup is still there, forty years later.

1955 Chrysler Imperial Sedan "Blue"

CHAPTER TWENTY

Just after moving to the North Country while exploring the area near my new ranch, I found one of the most interesting places: the meeting of Highways 92 and 101. A tall temporary overpass made of wood like an old train trestle was located at the intersection. While crossing it, I could see a junkyard full of old cars. My favorite kind of junkyard. It was called Henry's Auto Dismantling.

"I'm gonna have to take your wallet, son," said Henry when I walked up to him and asked if I could look around. Henry needed that for security because he felt there were so many valuable parts in his yard. He needed to know no one was stealing anything.

"Any of these cars work?" I asked.

"Just those ones over there," he replied, pointing in the direction of a row of fifties classics in pretty rough shape.

There was an old turquoise 1958 Continental convertible, a very intriguing design that caught my eye for a second, very wild looking, but it was pretty beat-up. Next to it was a 1953 or 1954 Nash, not looking too good. Then there was a 1953 Lincoln Capri that looked pretty nice, and a good-looking 1955 Chrysler Imperial sedan. I stopped right there, remembering the same car parked outside a house on the main street of Omemee. It was, of course, brand-new then, when I was nine or ten years old in late 1955.

Although this Imperial wasn't new anymore, it seemed like it was to me. Strangely, it made me feel younger, remembering my boyhood. The taillights were beautiful, standing on their little posts. What a radical design, I thought to myself. There was a speck of blood on the front seat, but it wasn't a big one. I wondered what that could have been from. An accident? Something else?

The interior looked pretty good really, aside from that little speck. A little worn here and there but it had a nice color and a shiny thread woven through it. The car was blue, a two-tone with a cream top. When I got behind the wheel, I saw the dashboard was clean. No broken lenses were visible and the paint was good throughout the whole interior. There were no missing parts that I could see. Inside and out, the car was complete.

I asked Henry if I could start it up. He went back into his little office, a small one-room building surrounded by car parts and tires, with bumpers and chrome pieces leaning all over the outside of it. When he came back out he had a set of keys jingling in his hand.

"I think these are the ones," he said.

I took them and went back to the Imperial, gave it a turn, and it cranked slowly but didn't start. But it was talking to me. It was ready. I pumped the accelerator and tried it again. The old Imperial came to life. She started up with a wheeze and a cough and then settled into a nice, even purring sound.

The next day, two weeks before my twenty-fifth birthday in 1970, I went back and bought the car for a couple of hundred bucks.

Driving it back to the ranch I noticed a few things wrong with it, but it ran nicely and I was feeling good, although on the steep hill entering the ranch I could sense that the brakes were worn out. I got that fixed, changed the oil and other liquids, filled it up with gas at thirty-six cents a gallon, and parked it in the driveway next to my house. The price of gas was cheap in 1970, but for the Imperial, the cost in CO_2 to the atmosphere was high at nineteen miles per gallon. Every nineteen miles, the luxurious, top-of-the-line Imperial emitted 19.5 pounds of CO_2 for an average of one pound per mile. I loved my new car and drove it everywhere, mostly leaving the Jeepster at the ranch except for back-road trips to the grocery store in Woodside, California.

A few months later, when I had returned from a Canadian tour and was taking Carrie to see the ranch, the Imperial and I were descending the long grade for the first time together. I was feeling so good about this place I had found to live. On the way down the grade, Carrie named that 1955 Imperial "Blue." Blue, a stately and cool lady, took us to a lot of good places, cruising on those redwood roads, maybe smoking a joint and taking it easy in a smooth-riding, big and comfortable luxury car. Blue was transporting us to another time.

Will I see you give more than I can take?
Will I only harvest some?
As the days fly past will we lose our grasp,
Or fuse it in the sun?

—"Harvest"

Later in life, Blue's time finally started to run out as she gathered mechanical issues and sat unused. Nothing hurts a car more than being ignored and left behind. They don't all make it to restoration, and Blue, after an extended stay in the ranch junkyard, was finally recycled.

One fine summer day I went back to Henry's.

"I'm gonna have to hold on to your wallet, son," Henry said again.

Inside, Henry's office was very clean, in marked contrast to the outside of his office. Henry's shirt was clean and pressed. He had a twinkle in his eye. I decided right then that Henry was a real character. He spoke with a deep voice in an accent I couldn't quite place. His glasses were sparkling clean. He kind of looked like the filling station attendant in one of those old gasoline commercials I remembered from *Hockey Night in Canada*, the Esso service attendant giving away place settings with each fill-up, plates or silverware.

Walletless, I walked around behind Henry's office through an area I had not spent much time in before, to a long lane of cars from the fifties. Seeing an old Nash, I thought about that company, American Motors. It didn't last too long. American Motors was almost gone by the beginning of the sixties. Their cars just didn't look as cool as the big three manufacturers, GM, Ford, and Chrysler. Style, power, and appeal were extremely important.

People identified with the image of their cars. GM and Ford remained the strong survivors. Chrysler was always number three, with advanced styling and new features blazing the way. That history was all on display in Henry's Auto Dismantling. Lane after lane of designs, reflecting the changing times of America. I was fascinated by it all. It was truly a museum. That's what I saw: a car gallery. Others saw a pile of junk. I saw memories, history, pieces of people's lives left behind to gather rust and ruin, plants growing right through them as they waited in line. *For what?* I asked myself. Mostly, though, I just thought about the personal stories and dreams behind each one of those cars, and I wondered about the people who designed them.

If I was a junk man
Selling you cars,
Washing your windows
And shining your stars,
Thinking your mind was
My own in a dream,
What would you wonder,
And how would it seem?

—"Words"

The sun was getting low as I walked back to get my wallet. I stopped by the office and glanced at the line of "running" cars, the ones that might run with just a little bit of attention. There was still an empty space where the Imperial had been. It left a void. Just down the row was a white 1953 Lincoln Capri looking at me. I looked back at it.

It was the second look; that is the one that got me. This was a beautiful car with red and black tuck-and-roll leather seats and one small place where the leather was torn, lots of chrome and stainless trim inside and out, and just a little corrosion. This was a hot-looking car. I checked out all of the trim pieces. They were almost all there. There was a knight's head with a chevron. It was repeated in several places. I counted three or four. One of them was perfect.

I noticed the fiftieth-anniversary badge in the dashboard, commemorating fifty years of the Ford Motor Company. A lot of pride had gone into this car. The styling was smooth and graceful, understated actually, compared to what was coming in the years ahead. This was a captured moment in time. This 1953 Lincoln Capri had been painted white somewhere along the line, but close inspection revealed a two-tone red and black original finish underneath. I went to see Henry, who told me it wouldn't start without a new battery but he would put one in the next day if I wanted to come back and hear it run. I was excited and told him I would be back in the morning.

I drove home and thought about it some more. I was starting to accumulate a lot of cars. The driveway was getting full. The cars were all inexpensive and I thought they had more to give, more of life to live. They were not done with their service. The next morning I returned to Henry's Auto Dismantling and we started up the Lincoln. It ran really well, sounding strong. I paid Henry for it in cash. We did the paperwork. It felt right.

I drove the Capri onto Highway 92 and across the wooden overpass toward home. It had a really throaty-sounding muffler, glasspacks like a hot rod. Cool. Brakes were good, too.

So it went. I had the old yellow and black Jeepster I had driven from LA, the Chrysler Imperial, the Lincoln Capri, and a pickup truck. Those were my cars. They were all old, but if one broke down I still could use another one while I got it fixed. I loved the old ones. They felt right to me. That was the way I looked at it. There was no reason to get a new car, even though I could afford one. I loved driving these old story-ridden cars on the redwood back roads of the Santa Cruz Mountains. They reinforced a feeling of being lost in time, a place I was comfortable. The year of the car.

I started collecting a lot of parts for the Capri, mostly trim parts that were missing or broken, like plastic knight's heads with chevrons and some stainless trim. After visiting a few junkyards, I had collected a complete set and had it all laid out on towels on a workbench in an old barn. I felt very good about this collection of perfect trim and was planning on painting the Capri its original colors and using the parts to make it perfect. After that, all that would be left to do was fix a little leatherwork on the driver's-side front seat. It was tuck and roll so it would be easy to replace only the worn parts with new leather, but I kept on driving it as it was.

Soon I discovered the real reason that the Capri had found its way to Henry's Auto Dismantling. The car had an electrical problem that was very evasive. Everything would suddenly just shut down. I would be driving along and the car would die and coast to the side of the road. Dead. The engine would not turn over. The lights wouldn't work. Everything electric was nonfunctional. After a while, it would start to work again and everything would be fine. The problem was hard to find because there was nothing wrong most of the time. I tried to get it fixed, had many parts replaced, but the problem stayed. Several times the car went to the shop for repairs. An electrical specialty shop worked on it and was unable to find the problem. It was very frustrating because the car was great when it ran.

Finally the problem was solved even though no one knew exactly what it was. A lot of things had been done at once, so we didn't

1953 Lincoln Capri

know what fixed it. It cost me a lot more to fix that problem than what I had given Henry for the car.

On September 8, 1972, after we had been living together for almost a year, Carrie and I had a child, Zeke Young. He was a beautiful baby boy. We brought Zeke home from the hospital in the Capri. After a few days he started sleeping in a handmade crib that one of our local carpenter friends, Larry Christiani, had built for us as a gift out of eucalyptus. It was an intricate crib that hung from leather straps and springs on the frame, which allowed us to rock it gently. During his first year, little Zeke grew quickly and was a happy boy, with a beautiful smile and blond hair. He was beginning to explore and soon was walking.

The fragility of our short courtship and our young child soon started to reveal that Carrie and I didn't know each other very well and had not anticipated what it would be like to actually share a home. We started getting along poorly and eventually we had a bad breakup, rooted in my continuing dedication to music, my time away from home, our infidelities, and our inexperience raising a child. The love had been intense but it was not strong enough to survive. We separated in early 1974. I remember thinking to myself that I would never do that again, and that if I did remarry, it would be for a long time and the kids would stay with their parents, come hell or high water.

At the time, CSNY was considering recording again, and the band was just beginning, feeling it out. Crosby had a song called "Homeward Through the Haze." It was very dark. I did not realize then that David was freebasing cocaine. We were trying to get something going, but the magic wasn't coming to us the way it used to, although it was still there like a fog out on the ocean that didn't come in to the land. Graham was doing everything he could to make it happen. I admired his strength and conviction for the band.

I was driving the Capri every day from the ranch to Sausalito, where the Record Plant Studio was, enjoying the ride, but the sessions were not going well. One day, about halfway to Sausalito, I just turned the Capri around and went home to the ranch. I called the guys.

"Let's try again later," I think was my basic message.

I know this was probably not the right thing to do, but I thought it was right for the music. It is not easy making these moves, but they have to be made when the music is at stake. That's how I felt.

> *Another flower child goes to seed*
> *In an ether-filled room of meat hooks.*
> *It's so ugly.*
>
> —"Hippie Dream"

One day, a while later, I was driving through the redwoods and the Capri's engine made a strange sound and stopped. It would not start. I parked it by the side of the road and one of my friends, Jimmy Delucca, who drove one of CSNY's road trucks, volunteered to tow it back to the ranch. I gave him directions. On the way there, he got a little lost and took a different route that involved a steep hill. He lost control of the car while towing it down that grade and it rolled off the road into a tree and suffered a lot of damage.

Things went downhill from there. I was able to find another front end, but it wasn't exactly the same; it was from 1954, not '53, and the chrome design and bumpers were different. I thought I wouldn't be happy 'til I got the original 1953 fiftieth-anniversary parts and made it right. It never happened. A dream unfulfilled. The 1953 Lincoln Capri missed its moment. Time was flying and so was I.

Eventually I had the engine rebuilt, solving the original problems. Louis and Clara left the ranch after a while and went to live in Modesto, where they had old friends, and Louis passed away a few years later. Clara lived a long life and came back to visit the ranch one or two more times over the next ten years or so, just to see the place where she used to live with Louis. We spent some good time with her when she visited Broken Arrow. Louis and Clara always called the ranch "God's Country." Even though she is gone now, too, and another generation has passed, I can still see her walking by the lake and up the roads in the mist of morning, getting her exercise.

Why are you growin' up so fast
My boy?
Oh, you'd better take your time.
Why are you growin' up so fast
My son?

Almost time to live your dream
My boy.
Oh, you'd better take your time.
Almost time to make some plans
My son.

Vacation gone, school is out,
Summer ends year in year out.

Oh, you'd better take your time
My boy.

I thought we had just begun.
Why are you growin' up so fast
My son?

Vacation gone, school is out,
Summer ends year in year out.

Why are you growin' up so fast
My boy?

Why are you growin' up so fast
My son?

—"My Boy"

Citroën Deux Chevaux

In the summer of 1971, exiting an elevator onto the mid-floor of a gray parking garage in downtown New York City, I could feel a sense of urgency or apprehension among those who were accompanying me. In the corner, almost hidden by a big car, was a French Citroën Deux Chevaux, a very small car easily memorable as Inspector Clouseau's vehicle of choice (if you have ever seen a Peter Sellers movie about the inspector). My friends, including Carrie and her brother and someone else, were looking at the car with me, but they said they did not want to go near it until it was sold to me officially, even though I had already paid for it.

There was something odd about the whole thing. Why did they not wish to be close to the car, and what or who was it they kept looking around for in the garage? Eventually I came to understand that something was in the car, having been shipped from Europe and then moved and stored in this downtown garage. Something was inside the car but it wasn't visible by just looking at it.

I learned after questioning them for a while that the car was a courier of sorts, with a hidden cargo perhaps in the quarter panels, and it may have been the subject of surveillance, perhaps even when we were there. I had purchased the car, but I couldn't have it until Carrie's brother was officially the owner and gave it to me, and this curious situation was making me suspicious as I felt trepidation in my fellow travelers.

A few weeks later the car was delivered at the ranch, shipped from New York. It turned out to be a really fun car to drive, just right for the ranch and the back roads, no matter how rough they were. This car with its small engine was really quite unique and required a mix of oil and gasoline to run.

I looked thoroughly at all of the side panels and every other place that could have hidden anything but could not find a trace of tampering. There was certainly nothing obvious to me. There was always an air of mystery about the car's story, though, and somehow I think there was a clue that I missed. Perhaps something Inspector Clouseau might have noticed with his keen eye.

I enjoyed the car immensely, driving it around the ranch and even up on the hill to Alice's restaurant a few times. Top speed was about forty miles an hour. There was a seat that was kind of a rubber sling hanging between metal arms, very funky but quite comfortable, actually. It even had a sunroof that rolled back. The gearshift was in the dashboard where it could be moved in and out with a lever that had a large ball on the end to hold on to while changing gears.

Eventually something went wrong with this car and I sold it because I couldn't find anyone who knew how to work on it. The folks who bought it had been looking for one for a long time and were very happy to get it.

I was starting to be known as a guy who loved old cars. In the fall of 1971, I was buying cars left and right. Half of them didn't run very well, but they were all unique looking and defined a style. The price of gas was thirty-six cents a gallon.

Around 1972, I bought another car in LA. I don't know what the heck got into me. I think I have a disease. Anyway, it was a 1950 Packard Clipper and the only positive thing about it was that it had a great hood ornament, a beautiful bird with its wings spread out. It looked like the front of an old ship or something. It was a normal sedan, like the ones my dad bought when I was a kid, with nothing special about it. It wasn't a hardtop convertible or a ragtop. It wasn't a wagon. This car smoked so badly that I was unable to drive it in public, even in LA. Even then, smog was becoming a big problem and this car had so much smoke coming out of it that even I would not drive it. Somehow I got it back to the ranch and put it into the junkyard in case I ever needed parts.

Eventually I did use the hood ornament on another Packard, a woodie station wagon. The 1950 Clipper sedan was ultimately

1950 Packard Clipper Sedan

scrapped. What was I thinking? Moves like that made me start to wonder about my habitual buying of cars and my values in general. This one set me back five hundred bucks. Was there a deeper meaning? Some inadequacy I was trying to cover up? But this is a book about cars, so I won't go into that.

Sometime in late 1972, I located a 1948 Packard woodie in a remote suburb of LA. I found this fine example in many parts at a garage. I picked it up for five hundred dollars, feeling I had a rare find at a steal of a price. There was something special, almost supernatural, about this Packard woodie.

I was already the proud owner of a Buick Roadmaster Estate Wagon, yet this particular woodie was very appealing to me because of its exceptional style. It was very round, making it look like an old R. Crumb cartoon, with a distinct "Keep on Truckin'" appearance. I loved its back end, a wooden door all curvy and round. It was amazing to me how those designers came up with ideas. I imagined them staying up half the night, working on their fabulous creations. It seems like they just picked them out of the air. Whimsical and free, the postwar era produced an art form all its own. The big V8s that powered these creations rolled along emitting a pound or more of CO_2 into the atmosphere with every stylish mile, over country, through cities, states, and provinces across North America.

Back at the ranch, I had made the acquaintance of a man living on the peninsula who went by the name of Spokely Wheeler. Spokely was a round-faced, red-haired, wire-rimmed-glasses type of guy who was a mechanic. He always wore mechanic's coveralls and he worked out of his own house and garage, specializing in 1940s Chrysler products, a great many of which surrounded his house and spilled out onto the street where he lived. I recognized him as a real character and liked him immediately upon our meeting.

Although I was hesitant to do much in the way of restoration after my previous failures, I asked Spokely if he could restore my new Packard woodie. We discussed how far he could go with the work and exactly what it would entail. In the end, Spokely Wheeler did an admirable job upgrading the upholstery to a vinyl that was very period-appropriate and worked well with the Packard. The woodwork detail was done by Spokely's own hand, and included a musical note and a broken arrow he had inlaid nicely. It was a very soulful restoration, and I completely loved the finished product.

I WAS LIVING in Santa Cruz in the late seventies, escaping reality and playing with a band known as the Ducks, not a normal band. Ducks members were Bob Mosley, from Moby Grape—a group I had known since the early Springfield days—on bass, and Jeff Blackburn, from Blackburn & Snow—another San Francisco sixties band; I was on guitar; and Johnny Craviotto, now one of the greatest makers of custom drum sets in the world, was on drums. All Ducks sang.

According to legend, the story behind the Pussinger Curse goes like this:

A group of ducks crossed the street by the harbor every day, waddling in a line from the lagoon on one side of the street to the harbor on the other side. There, peaceful waters lapped on the many hulls of local pleasure craft. One day the ducks were dutifully following their leader, Master Mallard, across the pavement, when Pussinger, a local surfer in a hurry, came flying wildly down the street in his car and ran over the ducks, injuring several of them and killing one right on the spot. Master Mallard, in an uncontrolled moment of anger, placed a terrible curse over the city, since known as the Pussinger Curse. It became local knowledge that the only way the curse could be lifted was through a Nuclear Quack, a giant "Quack-In" of unsurpassed and as yet unknown magnitude and volume.

The Ducks were not able to play outside of the city of Santa Cruz until the Pussinger Curse was lifted.

In an effort to lift the curse, the Ducks played all over the city in small clubs for fans who purchased duck calls from every hunting outlet in the Bay Area and brought them to Duck appearances to attempt a Quack-In. Some audience members simply made a loud quacking sound with their own voices. Until the curse was lifted, Ducks performances couldn't be announced ahead of time.

The Duckmobile, the Ducks' 1950 Packard woodie, could be seen late in the afternoon outside of any club where the Ducks were to play that evening. That was the only indication that an appearance was imminent. Through word of mouth, every appearance of the Ducks drew great crowds overflowing onto the streets and often a Nuclear Quack was attempted by the audience coming together and quacking as one. The Quacks grew increasingly loud and long, but the curse was never lifted and the Ducks were never heard outside of the city limits.

1948 Packard Woodie Station Wagon "Duckmobile"

One fateful night, a beautiful winged bird, the hood ornament of the Duckmobile, was ripped from its hood, right outside a club where the Ducks were playing. The Ducks never recovered. That sad event broke their spirit. Since that sorry criminal act was committed, Santa Cruz, California, Surf City, has long suffered from transients, homelessness, street crime, an active drug trade, and some well-known unsafe areas where the Pussinger Curse still remains particularly strong to this day. Santa Cruz is now considered one of the most crime-ridden towns in all of America.

1947 Buick Roadmaster Sedanet (Fastback) "Black Queen"

CHAPTER TWENTY-TWO

I n November of 1972, Zeke Young was two months old, the ranch was full of new life, and I was ready for a new car. Spokely Wheeler had just made a visit home to Idaho to see his relatives, and when he returned to California he told me he had found a 1947 Buick Roadmaster fastback in a church parking lot with a FOR SALE sign on it. The car was priced at $650 and Spokely thought it was a great deal. He described it as a low-mileage, original car, period, end of story.

I was always looking for Buicks that reminded me of Mort, and this model was identical in the controls and dashboard, very familiar to me, just as the 1947 convertible I had bought and abandoned in Toronto years before had been. Excited, I asked Spokely to please go back to Idaho and pick it up.

A few days later, he arrived at the ranch with the Roadmaster and it was everything he described. A beautiful rich black, it had lines that were very sleek and it drove like a dream. I took it down to LA and back to try it out and it was a perfect ride, no problem anywhere, except a little squeak that I could hear on the redwood roads around the ranch, something in the hood release.

Eventually I noticed some small flaws in the paint on the hood, which was otherwise mirror perfect. There were some ripples that almost looked like water. I grew fond of them. In 1973, I took the car down to LA to record an album called *Tonight's the Night*. It had been a rough year with the losses of Danny Whitten, the Crazy Horse guitarist and singer, and Bruce Berry, our CSNY roadie, both to drugs. These two deaths touched me deeply, and the music we made down in LA at the Studio Instrument Rentals rehearsal hall was kind of a wake.

Briggs rented a lot of recording equipment from Wally Heider, including a sixteen-track tape machine, some outboard gear, microphones, and a tube recording console called the Green Board. Beginning at about midnight, we drank a lot of tequila while recording, going until the wee hours of the morning. Among our occasional guests for these late-night sessions were Joni Mitchell and Mel Brooks. After the sessions we would jump in the Buick, named the "Black Queen" by Briggs, and drive down Santa Monica Boulevard to the Sunset Marquis Hotel sometime before dawn. Night after night, that's what we did until *Tonight's the Night* was recorded.

The Black Queen sat for years in my car barn, still with beautiful lines that no one could ever take away from her, but a little worn-out and not looking as great as some of my other cars Jon had worked on. Briggs always used to ask me, "Why don't you fix up the Black Queen?" I didn't want to ruin it. It looked perfect to me; a time capsule of good memories. After Briggs died, I reconsidered and fixed her up in his honor. Jon put in a beautiful black-and-white Indian blanket design in her interior with a black headliner. It had a comforting, cared-for, and loved feeling inside. David was right. She was a whole lot better.

The Queen rolled through my life as I recorded albums and played tours. She was there with me when we opened the Roxy in LA with our premiere performance of *Tonight's the Night*. She took me between the ranch and my home in Malibu as I flew back and forth on my beloved Pacific Coast Highway, avoiding constricted and impersonal air travel. The Black Queen, one of my all-time favorites, will always be with me, after being such an integral part of my life and writing in the 1970s. For me, the Black Queen defines a place where life, music, and machines come together. Now she has a permanent stall in Feelgood's Garage.

1954 Cadillac Limousine "Pearl"

CHAPTER TWENTY-THREE

The year 1974 was very tumultuous in my world. I had broken up with Zeke's mother, Carrie, creating a void between Zeke and I. This was the heaviest weight I had ever experienced as a result of any of my decisions, and I was doing a lot of second-guessing about it, but I still felt I was doing the right thing. I saw Zeke on the weekends at first, as these things usually go. There were some very reflective and sad moments as I weighed the consequences.

My life became a bit more erratic. I had moved down to Malibu and was renting a house on Broad Beach Road, near Zuma Beach, and had been hanging out with Rick Danko of the Band, who had become a friend. We spent a lot of time at a place called Shangri-La, a ranch estate house that the Band had made into a studio. It was located about five hundred yards inland from the Pacific Coast Highway, opposite Zuma Beach, and was a great place to play music. A lot of musicians were up there at times, and I enjoyed being able to have a studio so close to where I lived. That's where I met Levon Helm and he told me about his friend Johnny Tyson from Arkansas. Johnny's family company, Tyson Foods, used to fill our Shangri-La freezer with Cornish game hens. They were easy to cook. Many times, gangs of musicians were there enjoying these dinners. One night, Dylan came by and I played him a couple of new songs, "Hitchhiker" and "Cortez the Killer." When he heard "Hitchhiker," a confessional about the progressive history of drugs I had taken through my life, he told me, "That's honest." That moment still crosses my mind. It makes me laugh every time I think of it because Bob's humor is so wry. I think it was his way of saying kindly that the song was not very inventive as far as creating a story goes, just that I was following a history and not making up anything new. It's still funny to me, at any rate, the way he put it.

I guess you might say I was falling into the seventies Malibu lifestyle for rockers and actors. I was experimenting with cocaine, and I still smoked a lot of weed and drank my share of beer and tequila. During the week, Briggs and I often visited the new Crazy Horse Saloon, formerly the Malibu Inn, the same place where I had discovered Electronovision years earlier.

When I saw Zeke on weekends, we would go to the Topanga Country Store at Pacific Coast Highway and Topanga Canyon Boulevard to buy a sixteenth of a cord of wood for the fireplace and load it into the trunk. Zeke Young and I both loved fires. Then we would curl up in front of a roaring fire, Zeke in my arms, at the rented Broad Beach house we called home and named the Meeker Mansion in honor of its owner, Mr. Meeker.

That summer I went on the road with CSNY on a tour of baseball stadiums, promoted by Bill Graham. Before we left, we rehearsed on my outdoor stage at the ranch, right across from the studio, in a redwood grove. It simulated an outdoor stadium stage and was perfect for rehearsing the type of show we were about to do. Many times, the Jeepster or one of the other old cars would be parked right in front of the stage as we played, listening, while the rent-a-cars huddled far away from the stage.

At the ranch, while rehearsing for the tour, I wrote a new song called "Hawaiian Sunrise." It seemed like every day I had another new song. With all the changes going on in my life, I wrote songs daily, turning the changes into something. I always looked at occasions in life as inspirations for songs.

> *Pretty Maui Mama,*
> *Lying over the water*
> *With my son in your eyes,*
> *Will you hear the melody I play?*
> *It changes every day*
> *Oh, Hawaiian sunrise.*
>
> *Once when we were there*
> *We had a relaxing time,*
> *Thought we might settle down.*
> *But the music called me*
> *And my friends have*
> *Much to spread around,*
> *We move from town to town.*
> *Oh, Hawaiian sunrise.*
>
> *And in the morning when you rise,*
> *Will you look in my son's eyes?*
> *I know you do.*
>
> *Pretty Maui Mama,*
> *Lying over the water*

With the moon in your eyes.
From my hotel window in the clouds
I love you right out loud.
Oh, Hawaiian sunrise.

And in the morning when you rise,
Will you look in my son's eyes?
I know you do.

—"Hawaiian Sunrise"

We were singing so easily. It was flowing. We were all high on weed and excited. Crosby called up Peter Fonda, and we sang "Hawaiian Sunrise" for him over the phone from my cabin living room, all four of us. It was the best we ever sang it. To this day, I'm sorry we weren't recording it. That is one of the biggest lessons I have learned about recording music. "Get it while it's hot." Every song has its moment, and we let that one escape into a telephone.

Hearts and hopes were high. How could we not be soaring? Our tour was sold-out. Our records were all hits. The time was flying by. We were booked all over the USA and parts of Canada, and would eventually make our way to Wembley Stadium in London. The first show was in Seattle, and I had decided to travel from gig to gig with my friends Ranger Dave and Mazzeo. Ranger Dave was an intelligent and very interesting character who had tried oyster farming on the Pacific coast. Most of his work was done near Ano Nuevo Point between Santa Cruz and Half Moon Bay, and we talked about it quite a bit. He was fascinated with the process. Jim "Sandy" Mazzeo was an artist who I had met at a commune called Star Hill Academy that bordered Broken Arrow. We three were close friends and had a lot of great times together.

We all were going to share the driving. Zeke would be traveling with us for a lot of the tour, too, joining us along the way for some "daddy time," as Carrie used to call it. We rented a new GMC mobile home for the tour; Zeke called it the Mobil Obil. It was a fun ride. There was a bedroom in the back that was perfect for Zeke.

Leaving a few days before the first show, we drove up California Highway 1 through Oregon to Washington, having a wonderful time staying in random motels along the way. Mazzeo would make camp coffee on the motor home's stove. He was expert at making it, and just dropped the grounds into a stew pot, heated the water, and strained it out of the pot into a cup. It was the smoothest coffee I had ever had. Combined with the weed we were smoking, the trip was a real odyssey.

We had an old typewriter we started using, passing it around from person to person, letting each one write a continuing chapter of a story we created. It turned out to be quite a document. Eventually everyone contributed: random guests and people we didn't know from Adam. Personal thoughts were interwoven with wordplay, dreams, song lyrics gone awry, and other ramblings unclassified.

Like the old wagon trains, perhaps mobile homes are conducive to creativity and should be marketed that way. I doubt it, but ours was.

At the shows, the crowds were gigantic. Playing to thousands and thousands of people in stadiums was very different and impersonal. It was a sea of humanity, and we couldn't see many faces because the people were so far away. It really was a mixed blessing. The close, personal aspect of performing before an audience and connecting with it was missing for me. Now it was a celebration instead. The shows came up and we knocked them down. This was the biggest blowout tour I had ever been on, and I wanted to keep to myself off the beaten path; getting to the shows and playing them, but not staying in the big hotels or flying in airplanes with a huge entourage. CSNY was very famous and successful and our presence in public added a lot of pressure so I tried to skip that. Just having all of those people looking at me, and knowing I was always being watched, was overwhelming. Traveling down the highway, stopping wherever we wanted to eat, and sleeping in random motels was when we were happiest.

After a couple of shows in Seattle and Vancouver, we played Day on the Green, a concept of Bill Graham's, which was a large out-door show where people could walk around in a large zone in front of the stage or sit in seats behind that area, watching the whole scene. Flags flew. People wore colors and danced. That year was the beginning of Day on the Green. I think we were one of the first shows for Bill in Oakland. I guess these mammoth shows were the offspring of the Beatles playing at Shea Stadium crossed with Woodstock. In its infancy, the technology to run them was very experimental and I remember the huge PA system with its gigantic high-frequency horns. People in the back still said they couldn't hear very well, even with all that equipment. It was nothing com-pared to what we use today, multiple sound towers of tuned speak-ers with time delay, but the people were into the music, and it was all alive.

Some of our shows were inside arenas and a lot of those were quite good. There were a lot of drugs around and it was occasionally a little erratic, but we were getting off and giving the folks a good show. Eventually Ranger Dave, Mazzeo, and I ended up staying in some of the hotels with the whole entourage, needing to get some good rest with a comfortable room and shower. We spent a lot of time driving, and it was peaceful out on the road, the proud highway of second thoughts.

When the tour headed south, Zeke Young met us at the Albuquerque airport. Zeke's escort, Ellen Talbot, was a friend of Carrie's, and a fun-loving, creative lady whom Zeke enjoyed. She caught the next flight back to California, but it was easy to tell she wanted to stay and travel with us. No, this was boys' time. We had gotten Zeke Young a little tape cassette player in the airport as a gift. It was bright red plastic, very small, with a handle just his size, and we had equipped it with a Native American music cassette featuring Indian drums and their ancient singing. So there we were, the four of us, walking through the airport, Zeke with his Indian drums and high-pitched Indian chants echoing through the terminal as he walked along happily. Like any little guy, he loved being with the boys, and this was a real good feeling for all of us.

With lonely mountain ranges in the distance, we crossed the Southwest with its monumental landforms, open spaces, and ribbons of highway stretching across empty seabeds. Cactus families stood together and watched us roll by. The Mobil Obil was hanging in there, now with Zeke Young on board, sleeping on a little Indian blanket on the bed in the back reserved just for him.

One day, climbing out of the long valley on a two-lane, we saw an Indian encampment on the roadside, selling blankets and art. We had never passed one of those. A Native American family had set up everything so you could easily view it while approaching; jewelry, baskets, and blankets were all laid out. There were a couple of kids about Zeke's age there with the family. Zeke got excited. We opened the door and walked over to look at the offerings, which were extremely beautiful and authentic. Then all hell broke loose as

Zeke Young ran right over and bit one of the kids on the arm. All the kids started yelling and Zeke was screaming. Looking around, I saw the Native American mother walking toward me. I told her I was very sorry for what had happened. She just stared at me, unflinching. I asked her, "What would you do if your child had done what my son did?" She said she would put a knife in his mouth and tell him to bite that.

Zeke and I had a good talk about that. I tried to explain to him that hurting people was a bad thing to do. Zeke was crying out desperately for attention and I did my best with him, feeling a lot of guilt about it, feeling a responsibility for the way he was feeling and his situation in life with his brace and being different from other kids. Like the young father I was, I struggled to do the right thing and give the guidance he needed.

After several more shows and a few thousand miles, we lost the GMC. It did not make it. We all agreed it was underpowered.

Perhaps we were pushing it too hard. Perhaps we were not maintaining it well enough. The world had never seen anything like it before. It was the product of many engineering hours by countless GM employees. It was very cool-looking with three axles (two in the back, one in the front) and six tires. However, with some mechanical problems, hard-to-find tires that wore out fast from the front-wheel drive, transmission trouble, scraping and rattling, and a general feeling of unreliability, the Mobil Obil was doomed. It had to be replaced. And so it was.

With a five-day break in the tour, we made our way from Texas to Virginia, where we met a good old boy named Carl Higginbotham, a seller of buses. You might say he was a bus dealer, although he was also a boat dealer. He had an old house and barn on the lake where he had a lot of buses, some motorboats, and a big dock. Buses and boats were scattered everywhere. After checking out a few of them, we purchased an old 1957 Flxible Scenicruiser split-level motor-home conversion bus to continue our travels on the tour. It was beautiful: gold and white, with a pin-striped insignia on the side, but on its last legs. We bought it from Carl and named it "Sam Sleaze" because it looked like it had gotten lost in a time warp and had just arrived from a Vegas card game in 1957.

We had to learn how to drive a bus. It took a little doing, and we quickly realized we had to keep it off the shoulder because if we didn't, it would pull hard toward the ditch. Sam's interior was fixed up with a nice bed and sitting areas in front on multiple levels, and had a desk and a dining table. It was a very fine motor coach in its twilight and was the victim of a lot of breakdowns, which thankfully we were able to easily repair along the way. I loved Sam. Sam lasted almost the whole tour.

One night during the tour, I had a curious dream. In the dream, Mazzeo and I were working as valets, parking cars at the Brussels Hilton. We were very busy with a lot of vehicles to park. The following morning, the dream stuck with me. It was a very vivid dream, and I relayed it to Mazzeo and RD and wrote it down in our communal book. It meant something, but we were not sure what.

We continued on to Atlantic City, where we met a few girls after the show and enjoyed entertaining them in Sam Sleaze. The bus was a big hit. It had a great ambience for entertaining and most certainly had been the veteran of a lot of parties long before we came along. Sam was a fine machine and I wish we still had it today. It was very classy, in a sleazy sort of way. Eventually Sam had a breakdown that was too big for us to fix.

It happened in Ohio, well into the tour. The old Flxible finally buckled under the pressure and rolled to the side of the road in a cloud of black diesel smoke somewhere outside of Cleveland. We had to call Paul Williamson, who came out to Ohio, fixed Sam, and drove him back to California.

To replace Sam, we purchased a 1954 Cadillac limousine from a body shop in the suburbs of Cleveland for $400. We named this limo "Pearl." She had a little rust and was not in very good shape, but with some new tires and a lube job, we were up and rolling again. The motor was pretty good, if you kept oil in it. The interior was rather nice: an earth-colored cloth was on the seats and a lighter shade covered the headliner. The transmission was rough shifting from low to drive. Mazz and RD were riding in the front and I was in the back with the typewriter, entering random notes and musings on life into the communal book as we rolled along through the countryside. I guess I was about twenty-nine years old and had few cares in the world; only that I was moving.

Zeke came and went regularly. Cities and stadiums flew by. The typewriter chattered away as it was passed around. Various authors contributed chapters. Stills, myself, Mazzeo, RD, Joel Bernstein, Graham Nash, Crosby, anyone who wanted to contribute was welcome. The book was taking shape, crafted of anecdotes and not holding a thread of continuity. Little drawings in pencil by Mazzeo; Joni Mitchell added something; the road crew chimed in with stories. It was haphazardly written and no one signed their real name. They made up names or just didn't sign at all.

The old Cadillac limo rolled onto the backstage grassy area at Toronto's Varsity University football field, jam-packed with music-loving fans. The show featured the Band and Joni Mitchell as well as CSNY. I saw Danko and we said hi. Everyone was already there and we arrived only an hour before the show. Elliot Roberts and some others were pretty concerned about the reliability of our mode of transportation, but there we were, driving across the grass in our old limo with a saxophone in the rear window and the portable typewriter chattering away.

Carrie arrived with her friend Gigi to pick up Zeke and decided to travel with us to New York. We had the border crossing ahead and had been careful to smoke our weed before we reached it, all the while discussing whether to risk carrying a joint or two across the line, hidden inside some rubber alligators we had on the dashboard. We had picked them up in Tampa. The gators were hollow and the joints could just slip inside them and be invisible. They were hard to smell through rubber, but we thought it over carefully and decided not to try, especially with Zeke Young in the car.

When we arrived at the border, the guards made us leave the limo. Then we were separated and put into different rooms. Time passed. More time passed. We were busted. In a simple twist of fate, Carrie had tried to cross the border with something in Zeke's bags. I was not angry but I was not surprised, and just stood there shaking my head. I think he still had some diapers with him and although he did not use them, they were checked by the guards and we all went to jail for a few hours in Buffalo. With the help of a lawyer, we were released on bail and drove on to New York in Pearl. Zeke said his good-byes again and flew home with his mother.

In Westbury, New York, at the end of our CSNY Tour of America, Bill Graham had a big hospitality tent for us and presented us with beautiful commemorative art pieces made out of the tickets from all of our shows fanning out like the Wheel of Fortune. Bill was big on commemorating things for people, so they could always remember what they had done. He was our pioneer. Bill Graham was a very special individual, greatly responsible for shaping the way rock and roll tours are today. I like Bill a lot. He said to me once that all the big stars had bought ranches and he couldn't afford to book them anymore. He was always playing around with us, challenging us. Our US tour had ended. Leaving the hospitality tent behind, we walked by a giant ice sculpture Bill had made of the letters "CSNY" as it melted away into water and soaked into the ground.

Many years later, on October 25, 1991, Bill Graham died suddenly one foggy night. His helicopter, which he used to avoid traffic and return home after shows in the Bay Area, collided and tangled with a high-tension-wire tower, electrocuting all on board. I attended his funeral with a lot of other musicians and other people he had touched. He was truly a great man and a friend. He changed rock and roll in America, beginning with the legendary Fillmore in San Francisco and growing the music business into huge outdoor concerts, all with his personal touch. Playing for Bill was not like playing for anyone else. He made us feel like he was representing the people.

In September of 1974, the tour went on to Wembley Stadium in London, England. It was a huge show. I missed Pearl and I missed Sam. It was just not the same. I liked traveling separately and making my own way with my friends. The Wembley concert was our last live CSNY tour until the year 2000.

Thirteen years later, in 1987, Pearl would be restored to beautiful condition by Jon McKeig. It was like a brand-new limousine. The interior was very comfortable, and the divider window, which had always been cracked, now had a fine engraving of the timeless image of Pearl, an ethereal Hippie Goddess. This new artwork had successfully disguised the cracked divider window because that piece of glass had proven to be impossible to find and replace. The old limo glowed in its rebirth, now living with a new purpose and a second life.

A musical change was coming. I could feel it in my bones. I was on tour with Crazy Horse in America, playing outdoor stages, called sheds, venues that were very popular at the time. The first part of our performance was acoustic, then it went electric, but in the middle of the program there was a section of new music I was referring to privately as Blue Horse. That part of our set consisted of four new songs in a blue vein: "Big Room," "This Note's for You," "Ain't It the Truth," and "Don't Take Your Love Away from Me." We crisscrossed the nation with our tour.

When we got to Alpine Valley, an outdoor venue in the Wisconsin countryside, we went through a picket line to do that gig and I did not like it. They were protesting non-union workers working the stage and venue. I vowed this was the last time I would ever cross a picket line. We didn't know about it in advance and the place was full of people when we arrived. Bad situation. I was upset that managers and agents had not prepared me for what they knew was surely coming.

In the fall of 1987, Blue Horse, the name we had been using internally, was introduced as the Bluenotes for the first time. We had a funky and soulful horn section brought to me by Billy Talbot. It included Steve Lawrence, Claude Cailliet, Tommy Bray, Johnny Fumo, Larry Cragg (my multitalented guitar tech), and my amazingly versatile friend Ben Keith on saxophone. We played live at the Cocoanut Grove in Santa Cruz, an old ballroom right on the ocean. The Horse had slipped into a whole new thing and it felt good. It was the perfect venue for our old-style music.

I don't remember this being a great gig. Everyone was pretty high on all sorts of things. Several new songs were added with horns, including "Find Another Shoulder," "High Heels," "One Thing," and "Ain't It the Truth." Even "Hello Lonely Woman" from the Squires at the Flamingo Club days made a reappearance. The sound was not very good and we couldn't hear well, but the crowd loved it. They were pretty high, too, and I am sure that contributed to our success. There was a phenomenal ambience in that old ballroom and our music fit perfectly. By the end of the year, the Bluenotes were regularly playing clubs in the San Francisco Bay Area.

Around this time, I was high on the idea of doing a film called *The Big Room*. It was kind of a Vegas send-up, only really sleazy. I had big ideas for this, with notes outlining all the characters and the club ambience. My character was Shakey Deal and Steve Lawrence was the Big Man. Pearl and Wog had big parts. We were going to have a blast. We had a great club-owner character, old cars, babes, cigarette girls, booze, you name it. We had the songs. It was going to be a success story gone wrong.

The club would be a miniature Vegas hotel at a location formerly owned by Doris Day. It had a Caesars Palace type of entry and grand architecture, but it was small in size. Vegas in miniature. The showroom was perfect. I could see the whole thing in my mind and planned on shooting it very economically, but I could not get financing from the record company and was really disappointed. I hate it when things don't work out. When the record company wouldn't finance it and shut me down that time, I was really pissed. I had never been so limited in my creativity.

Things were going to shit with the record company and they thought I was doing the wrong things, so I was sued for playing the music I wanted to play, because they said it was "uncharacteristic of Neil Young." But the Bluenotes moved on, playing more clubs—the

Cabaret in San Jose, the Omni in Oakland—and recording on my dime until we got to the Fillmore in San Francisco on my birthday, November 12, 1987.

Then the unbelievable happened. I was at my studio on the ranch reviewing club tour recordings for an album to be called *Bluenote Café*. I had just smoked a *big* joint and was ready to listen to all the picks from the shows when I got a call from Elliot. He said the record company had dropped the lawsuit against me! I walked outside and stuck my hands in the air. I did that for several minutes before I could even speak. Really. I was so fucking happy that I almost crashed right there. Bad timing on the joint. All the old record company wanted was a "best of" album from the time we had with them. As Briggs would say, "GREATEST MISSES." There were thirteen songs. I called it *Lucky Thirteen*.

I re-signed with Reprise. It was the fourth quarter of 1987 and I could actually record in a studio. So we went back to SIR (where we had recorded *Tonight's the Night*) to try to find the feeling again.

I was having trouble with the Crazy Horse guys, Billy and Ralph, too. I love those guys, but it was not working, or maybe it really was and I couldn't see it. I probably missed it. The band was not grooving for some reason, so I started mixing it up, trying another bass player, George Whitsell, the original guitarist from the Rockets. In December we got a few good takes, "One Thing," "Midnight Blues," and "I'm Goin'," all at SIR. George was really cool, but it still didn't have that something I was looking for.

Chad Cromwell and Rick Rosas, the rhythm section from Joe Walsh whom I had seen recently at Farm Aid, had become available. I asked them to come in. When they did, they finally made the Bluenotes into a great band. A *great* band is all about the chemistry and the way the musicians relate to one another. When Billy and Ralphie did not slip into the groove with the things I wanted to do, I did what I had first learned to do in Winnipeg with the Squires. I followed the music until I found the sound. Billy and Ralph understood what that was all about as well as I did. I still play with them in Crazy Horse today.

We completed the recording of *This Note's for You*, the first Blue-notes' LP, and even did a few videos, but the video for "This Note's for You," rebelliously directed by Julien Temple, was banned from MTV, because mentioning products in songs was against MTV network policy, but we knew it was really banned because of what we were saying. Shit. What can you do? When we discovered what had happened, Elliot had fifteen hundred copies of the video made and sent them to news channels around the country. That resulted in a lot of exposure for our song and video. Our message was pretty straight-ahead.

> *Ain't singin' for Pepsi*
> *Ain't singin' for Coke*
> *I don't sing for nobody*
> *Makes me look like a joke*
> *This note's for you.*
>
> —"This Note's for You"

Ironically, although the video was banned by MTV, it also won the MTV Video of the Year in 1988 in a vote by actual viewers. It was brilliant management of a bad situation by Elliot Roberts. Some may not believe it, but I know I would never have gotten anywhere without Elliot, who is absolutely the best friend and manager ever. Friend first. He and Pegi are my best friends now.

I RETURNED to my Canadian home in 1987 for a Kelvin High School reunion as well as for a celebration of the Winnipeg music scene called "Shakin' All Over," in honor of the Guess Who's first big hit. I jammed with Randy Bachman and a bunch of other guys, and we celebrated our unique musical beginnings and the time when the community clubs were rockin' every weekend with local bands. After hanging out and playing with Randy, the Squires got together and jammed late into the night for a small crowd of beer-drinking Canadians at a little club on Main Street called the Blue Note Café. All the original members got up on the tiny stage and played together one more time. A local blues harp player, Ben Darvill, got up and jammed with us as well. He was really hot. The only thing missing was Mort parked outside.

Wog got behind the wheel of Pocahontas, my tour bus, and the Bluenotes continued traveling through the country for months, playing old auditoriums and clubs, promoting the *This Note's for You* LP, and recording *Bluenote Café*. This was a great time, with the music flowing and the big band playing night after night.

When we got back to California, a lawyer for Harold Melvin called and said that he and his Bluenotes, whose great song "If You Don't Know Me by Now" was a hit in the seventies, were suing me for ripping off their name. To me, that record is one of the best songs and recordings ever made. The soul of that performance is just great; anguish, truth, and desperation calling out from the first note. I stop what I'm doing every time it plays and listen to it. I was surprised that they were suing me, and I felt bad. I had not heard of anything from them in years and thought it would be okay to use the name. After I settled with them, I renamed the band Bluenote Café, but things were changing and we never played together again. That period was over, ending as spontaneously as it had begun. I was moving on. No reason required. Just following the muse.

All the things that we've been through
You should understand me
Like I understand you.
Now, baby, I know the difference
Between right and wrong
I ain't gonna do nothin'
To upset our happy home.
Oh, don't get so excited
When I come home a little late at night
'Cause we only act like children
When we argue fuss and fight.

—"If You Don't Know Me by Now"

1930 Rolls-Royce Shooting Brake "Wembley"

CHAPTER TWENTY-FOUR

At Wembley Stadium in 1974, at the end of the tour, CSNY had performed on a bill with the Band, Joni Mitchell, and Jesse Colin Young and the Youngbloods. We had just about everything we needed, probably a lot more, but the last show was a fiasco, a blown-out drug-fueled performance that stands as one of the low points for CSNY. We were all guilty. Self-indulgence and selfishness were the rule of the day. We should have fired ourselves after that and, looking back, we might have.

The day after Wembley, I was looking for a reward for my diligent efforts. As I walked through a large showroom of antique British motorcars, a 1930 Rolls-Royce shooting brake, what we in North America call a station wagon, beckoned to me. It seemed to be speaking my language. English. With huge, round headlights gazing right into me, I thought I heard the old woodie ask me if I needed a ride around Europe. I whispered yes to myself and walked toward the salesman.

A few days later, crossing the English countryside in "Wembley," our newly named 1930 Rolls-Royce shooting brake, we found ourselves in Harwich, a seaside village where we would board a car ferry to Europe. Graham Nash, his girlfriend, Callie, and Leslie Morris (Elliot's secretary at the time, and later Larry Johnson's wife and the mother of Ben and Hannah Johnson) had joined us, and were traveling in a second car with Joel Bernstein, our official photographer and friend. There was a small amusement park in Harwich and we went in and looked around, finding a room full of clocks that was very photogenic. Joel took a series of photographs, one of which was later used in the *Tonight's the Night* album foldout.

In Essex, we stayed the night in a hotel while waiting for the morning ferry. I was still driving with RD (Ranger Dave) and Mazzeo, who had been with me for the whole tour, and we did our best beatnik-lifestyle interpretation. Finally, after crossing the channel in miserable weather and traveling along a gray freeway for a few hours, we arrived in Amsterdam.

Coming down from the big tour, we went out in the evenings and partied quite a bit. One night I will never forget: We went to a place called the Paradiso. I smoked a lot of hashish from a big joint being passed around and got extremely high. My condition was complicated by the fact that the hash was blended with a strong tobacco that made me very dizzy. I think that might have been the most stoned I have ever been. I was not high, having a great time with everything accentuated by the good weed. I was stoned, just trying to maintain well enough to get home before I crashed face-first into the sidewalk.

Walking back to the hotel, my feet would lift off of the ground quite easily but I was having trouble setting them back down to earth. RD helped me along and back to my room, where he stayed with me for several hours until I had come down enough to actually go to sleep. Every time I laid down, the room would begin to spin wildly and it would take a few minutes after I sat up again for it to stop circling.

Our little party walked around Amsterdam for a few days, exploring different areas. We eventually found a great hotel, the Memphis. While we were leaving the hotel, I saw a party of people that included a beautiful young lady. So striking was she that I walked right up to her and introduced myself without a shred of my usual shyness. Her name was Melody. She was from England, and we arranged a way to connect sometime. I wrote down her number and address on a notepad and put it in my coat pocket.

During our stay in Amsterdam, we spent most of the days looking for a barge to rent or buy so that we could live in it on one of the canals that ran through the city. No one wanted to give us one. I don't think we looked right. We never had a chance. The amount of money didn't seem to matter. We struck out completely.

We also had to have Wembley repaired twice. It was becoming rather obvious that the old Rolls was not in the pristine mechanical condition the salesman in London claimed it was in.

Amsterdam was beautiful in the fall, and we loved walking in the city looking in the shops and museums, so Wembley's repairs were not much of a burden on our activities. Back at the Memphis, I was writing all the time. Every day a new song, a new melody, or further ramblings in the meandering, free-form typewritten book appeared as if by preordainment.

After staying at the Memphis for a couple of weeks, we finally grew tired of visiting museums, talking poetry, and planning fictitious events, like taking Wembley to Africa.

Graham and Callie had elected to leave for California, but the rest of us wanted to continue on, looking for some sun. Pressing on with our European vacation, we attempted to drive across Europe, heading toward Spain and the elusive sun, ignoring the fact that it was October already. Our first day on the road concluded in Belgium, where we left the grayness and foreign signs of the freeway to head toward the big city for the night. It was there that Wembley, at 9 miles to the gallon and putting 975 pounds of CO_2 into the atmosphere, finally gave up and wheezed to a stop right in front of the Brussels Hilton Hotel, where valets stood shaking their heads. We had motored about 450 miles since London. Ranger Dave and Mazzeo stayed with the car and arranged to ship it back to America.

I soon returned to Malibu and my new life as a single man who only saw his kid on weekends. I had finally played out all of the possibilities, successfully delayed the inevitable, and looked reality in the eye unselfishly for the first time in a very long stretch.

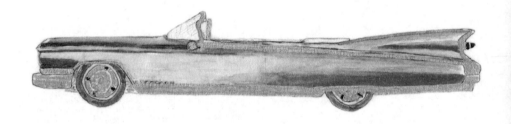

1959 Cadillac Eldorado Biarritz "Nanu the Lovesick Moose"

CHAPTER TWENTY-FIVE

The old Caddy was on a corner lot in a small neighborhood, the kind with little flags and a small shack in the middle of all of the cars. It stood out like a lighthouse on the shoreline. I liked what I saw and bought it for $2,500, which I felt was a real steal. It was a guzzler, but the price of gas was only thirty-nine cents a gallon, so that didn't matter much. A Chicago car, this 1959 Eldorado Biarritz convertible had a little rust from the salt on the roads in winter, but it was all there, solid and original with a black-leather interior, bucket seats, stainless-steel trim, and all the options. It had been painted metallic blue somewhere along the line, decidedly not the original color.

About that time, I called Crazy Horse and asked Billy, Ralph, and Poncho to come to Chicago, where I was visiting with Carrie after her mother's death, to record at the Chess Records Studio. I had located it in the phone book and booked studio time. I needed something to do and a reason to disengage from Carrie's dad's house. Poncho Sampedro was new in the group and we had only jammed once in Echo Park at Billy's house, so I thought getting the band to Chicago would be a great way to feel it out in the studio. I called Nashville and asked Ben Keith to come up as well. I had a new song I had written called "Changing Highways." The guys soon arrived and we checked into a hotel downtown.

We got together the night before the sessions so Poncho had a chance to learn the songs with us. He remembers that I was playing the songs and he would say, "Hey, Ben, you try the guitar," then he'd smoke some weed and dig the song. Poncho thought we were just hangin' out, didn't see that we were woodshedding for the sessions so he would know the songs when we got into the studio. It didn't matter, though. We got it down. Poncho's laid-back attitude is a big part of who we are today as a band.

We arrived at Chess, and Tim Mulligan, who has been with me since the seventies, when he came to the ranch with Gigi, one of Carrie's best friends from Chicago, was already setting up. The Chess studio was a place where all the blues legends had played, and I admit to having been a little intimidated. I liked the funkiness of the place. The monitors were not true and you had to compensate for that in the mixes, but the local engineers knew exactly how to do that. No high-tech solutions here, just local knowledge, born of years and years of recording. I was reminded of my times at Hitsville U.S.A., recording the Mynah Birds with Rick James for Motown back in 1965. It was that kind of place, although we were not at 2120 South Michigan Avenue, where Chess started and the real beginnings of the Chess legend were. In the mid-sixties, Chess had relocated to a much larger building at 320 East 21st Street, the label's final Chicago home. That is where we recorded, but we were still feeling the vibe. We were soaking up Chess's history and using it ourselves, feeling the legendary bluesmen we knew had recorded there.

The sessions went well and we got a funky take of "Changing Highways," which is still unreleased today. We were there for two or three days. I loved recording wherever I was and whenever I could. That's how we did it best. Crazy Horse returned to LA as Ben and I drove the metallic-blue 1959 Cadillac Eldorado Biarritz convertible south down the highway, relaxing in a pair of leather bucket seats as the world flew by, south to Nashville and the rest of my new life.

> *We're changing highways*
> *In heavy traffic.*
> *I see the lights change*
> *to something graphic,*
> *And is this your exit too?*
>
> —"CHANGING HIGHWAYS"

This was the car I had dreamed of owning ever since high school in Winnipeg, since the Flamingo Club, since forever. When we arrived in Nashville, we went right into the studio and started recording. At the time, Nashville was the right place for these songs. We had a lot of great musicians in the studio, because Ben knew everybody. None of it could have happened without Ben Keith.

We set up at Quadrafonic Sound on Sixteenth Avenue, with Elliot Mazer at the board. Quad was a little studio, built in a house, like many studios in Nashville, with an intimate feel and sound. It was a favorite among singer-songwriters like myself. The first day there, we recorded with Kenny Buttrey on drums, Tim Drummond on bass, Ben Keith on steel, and me on acoustic guitar. These musicians were known as the Stray Gators on the *Harvest* album and were all soulful, first-class players. Drummond had played with James Brown, Conway Twitty, and others. Ben had played with Patsy Cline, Hawkshaw Hawkins, and many more. Buttrey had given his beat to Roy Orbison, the Everly Brothers, and countless country artists and hits. I was fortunate to be in their company.

We recorded a song called "Frozen Man," which I had written in Amsterdam.

> *When anger has closed the door,*
> *My eyes go blind and I can only see inside,*
> *And I drown myself some more.*
> *Cool water is what I need*
> *And time and space*
> *To help me understand,*
> *But it's alright.*
> *Who could live inside this frozen man?*
>
> —"FROZEN MAN"

Kenny had other sessions booked, so he had to leave after the first one. A couple of days after, we returned to the studio with one of the greatest musicians of our time on drums: Levon Helm of the Band.

> *Far from the sparkling blue waters,*
> *Where the fish and the canvases play,*
> *And the waves are as calm as my father*
> *And the daughters are dancing all day.*
>
> —"DAUGHTERS"

Later the same day, we recorded a song that used a few of the favorite expressions that Carrie's mom loved to say.

> *I'd like to take a chance*
> *But shit Mary I can't dance*
> *So here's lookin' up your old address*
> *Ollie what a mess*
> *We got to take the rest and Try.*
> *And I Try to wash my hands*
> *And I Try to make amends*
> *And I Try to count my friends.*
>
> —"TRY"

But time was running out, so we recorded just one more with Levon before he had to go.

> *Up and down the old homestead,*
> *The naked rider gallops through his head*
> *And although the moon isn't full*
> *He still feels the pull.*
>
> —"THE OLD HOMESTEAD"

After one of the takes, Levon looked at me and asked, "What's happening with the groove there?" He had noticed that I was holding back while he was pushing on, and it was creating a rub. I said, "I think we're going too fast, so I was holding us back." He looked at me with that look, those two eyes of his, and drawled, "Don't do that. Don't fight the groove." I'll never forget that. Those are the moments where you learn. You never know when they are coming.

Levon had some gigs and moved on, and the next day it was our good fortune to have the great Karl Himmel in town—the man who put down a big groove for JJ Cale—and Tim Drummond on bass. We put down a lot of songs. I decided to call the album *Homegrown*. It was completed and is still unreleased because I was making so many records at that time and there wasn't enough time to release them all. One of the last songs I did was with Karl, Tim Drummond, and Ben, with Emmylou Harris and Ben singing harmony. It was called "Star of Bethlehem."

Christmas was approaching and we had to get back to California so two-year-old Zeke could come to the ranch and celebrate with us. It was a strange little family, made up of a bunch of big guys and this little kid, Zeke Young. Zeke held his own with the boys. Mazzeo and Ranger Dave helped me decorate, and we set up a tree in the White House. It was big, and we had lots of gifts. Some of the cheesy Gemco decorations we got at the last minute are still around our tree today and bring back beautiful memories of those times every Christmas. They are nowhere near as fine as the ones Pegi and I have collected, and somewhere along the line I lost the illuminated string of Pinocchio bells that my mom had had, the same ones we put around our trees back in Canada, but the memories sure are deep and meaningful.

All your dreams and your lovers won't protect you.
They're only passing through you in the end.
They'll leave you stripped of all that they can get to,
And wait for you to come back again.
Yet still a light is shining,
From that lamp on down the hall.

Maybe the Star of Bethlehem
Wasn't a star at all.

—"Star of Bethlehem"

When we left Nashville, the 1959 Eldorado convertible stayed behind with Long Grain. The plan was that he was going to drive it out to California after the New Year, which he did, adding 3,900 pounds of CO_2 to the atmosphere at 10 mpg. Ben drove the 1959 Eldorado convertible about two thousand miles.

I really think *Homegrown* was one of my best albums, and I hope it gets out there in its original form someday. That's how I will always remember it. Although *Homegrown* was not released, some of those original songs have already surfaced on subsequent albums over the years. A total of about thirteen or fourteen songs were recorded, including some more that Ben and I did in LA in January of 1975.

As 1975 arrived, I was living between the ranch and a rented house on Broad Beach Road. I liked Malibu and the beach walks with a cup of coffee every morning, as well as the abundance of friends down there. The blue Eldorado convertible was in the driveway. Briggs was living in a house nearby at Point Dume, just south of Zuma. Poncho was living on the Coast Highway farther south about halfway to Topanga. Billy and Ralph still lived in town, in Echo Park, an hour or so away.

Life was very good to us. We had a lot to do, youth on our side, money, homes at the beach, and every day was full. Briggs named the Eldorado "Nanu the Lovesick Moose." There was little pressure on us. Music was always flowing. I did a lot of driving between the ranch and Broad Beach and was looking to buy a house in the area instead of renting. We would go out at night in Nanu, drinking beer and Mexican coffee (coffee and tequila), which was Briggs's drink of choice. Sometimes we would go to the Crazy Horse Saloon and party, having a great time, then return to Briggs's house in Dume, where we had set up a studio with the Green Board and a tape machine. Then we would record deep into the night, rocking our brains out.

> *I have seen you in the movies,*
> *And in those magazines at night,*
> *I saw you on the barstool*
> *When you held that glass so tight.*
> *I saw you in my nightmares and I'll see you in my*
>   *dreams,*
> *But I might live a thousand years before I know what that*
>   *means.*
>
> —"Barstool Blues"

So back and forth we would go in Nanu the Lovesick Moose, up and down the Pacific Coast Highway. During the summer of 1975, Crazy Horse and I wrote and recorded furiously and often. I did not write in different ways on purpose; rather, I wrote naturally, and only in retrospect can I even notice the difference in styles:

> *There were songs living in the past:*
> *Aurora Borealis, the icy sky at night*
> *Paddles cut the water in a long and endless flight,*

From the white man to the fields of green
And the homeland we've never seen.

—"Pocahontas"

I was not only writing personally:

I'm making another delivery
of chemicals and sacred roots.
I'll hold what you have to give me
but I'll use what I have to use.
The lasers are in the lab.
The old man is dressed in white clothes.
Everybody says he's mad,
but no one knows the things that he knows.

—"Sedan Delivery"

There were songs that traveled around. I seemed to be in a lot of places at the same time:

He came dancing across the water with his galleons and guns,
Looking for the new world and that palace in the sun.
On the shore lay Montezuma with his coca leaves and pearls,
In his halls he often wandered with the secrets of the worlds.

—"Cortez the Killer"

There was searching:

I see the light of a thousand lamps
Burning in your eyes.

Still I have to stay away
From you to stay alive.

—"Born to Run"

I was a bird:

And though these wings have turned to stone,
I can fly. Fly away.
Watch me fly above the city, like a shadow on the sky.

—"Dangerbird"

I was rooted in the past, like I really was there:

Look out mama there's a white boat comin' up the river,
With a big red beacon and a flag and a man on the rail.
I think you better call John, 'cause it don't look like they're here
to deliver the mail.

—"Powderfinger"

Every once in a while I was direct:

I saw you in a Mercedes-Benz
Practicing self-defense.
You got it pretty good I guess.
I couldn't see your eyes.

—"Stupid Girl"

Our setup in Brigg's Dume garage was tight and comfortable. The Green Board was right down the hall, out of sight of the control room, which was a rec room bar. There was no video monitor.

Briggs just listened and talked to us. One night, we were recording late and Rod Stewart showed up with Britt Ekland in tow. He wanted to know if we had any songs. We played "Powderfinger" for him. Another day, Dylan came by in the late morning and played with us, just making up something on the spot, a three-chord blues thing. That's what it was like recording *Zuma*. I can't bring it back. The blue Eldorado is gone now and I think it had a lot to do with that music. It's like when you get old; there's nothing you can do about it. When someone asked Dylan about it in an interview, he said, "I can't help it." There is a time when things bloom and if you are lucky, things bloom more than once. But they don't bloom forever, and eventually they just live and soak up the sun.

> *When somebody is haunting your mind,*
> *Look in my eyes. Let me hide you*
> *From yourself and all your old friends.*
> *Every good thing comes to an end.*
>
> —"Drive Back"

Eventually I found a little house about a mile and a half north of where I was renting. I discovered it when I was walking along the beach in the morning, which I loved to do with a cup of coffee.

It was the most charming beach house I had ever seen, like a fairy tale. I purchased it and parked Nanu the Lovesick Moose right in front, tucked under the bougainvillea vines and flowers. Those flowers were my mother's favorite, although she never visited the house. As with everything else at the time, I was very fortunate. I was only feet from the sand and had two miles of beach to walk on with no houses.

Nanu, however, was not as fortunate. One day, leaving the ranch,

Nanu was involved in an accident that caused a lot of damage to her body. Driving up the hill, climbing out of Broken Arrow Ranch, Nanu was hit in the side by a little Volkswagen. Coincidentally, strangely and sadly, after this accident, my new songs changed and became more introspective and less wide-open and far-reaching than they had been in the months before. A spell was broken. The music changed.

> *Lookin' for a love that's right for me,*
> *I don't know how long it's gonna be,*
> *But I hope I treat her kind and don't mess with her mind*
> *When she starts to see the darker side of me.*
>
> —"Lookin' for a Love"

I don't want to stop talking about this car, but there is only a sad story left to tell, or maybe a real story, I am not sure. The fact is, the 1959 Eldorado is still not fixed. When the accident happened I decided to get it completely restored to museum quality and hired Jon McKeig to work on it. It is still in a warehouse in pieces, many of them painted, and the car is not as prepared for completion as it should be. It is unfinished. Unresolved. I haven't given up on it, but a lot of things have changed. The unfinished cars mean something. They represent broken dreams, lost loves, and abandoned ideas. This is the sad part. Dealing with that reality is something everyone has to do. I had to bring it up.

1941 Lincoln Zephyr Coupe

While living in Zuma at the Meeker Mansion on Broad Beach Road, I discovered a place in Santa Monica that was selling old cars called Automotive Classics. I stopped by one day and didn't see much. Then I remembered Old Time Cars was still open on La Cienega Boulevard in LA. Having some time on my hands, I drove by just to see what was happening. I had seen a lot of cool cars there in the past.

On the drive I thought about Zeke, as I often did. I was missing him a lot; Carrie had called to tell me about a big seizure he'd had, his first, which had scared us all. Having talked to his doctor, I was wondering about cerebral palsy for the first time, not knowing much about it, and was worried. Also, in talking to his mom I found out that he was doing poorly in school, misbehaving and getting into trouble and having problems with the other kids.

Living in Malibu I was close to Carrie's house in Hollywood and could go to see him, but I wasn't comfortable going there. The people who were there with Carrie were impressed with me and seemed to be hiding something; they were just too nervous around me. I looked forward to weekends when I could be one-on-one with Zeke. He liked that, too. Soon Carrie and Zeke had moved to Santa Barbara to a beach house they had found through Larry Johnson. About then, I noticed Old Time Cars, passing it just across the street.

In the front window, visible as I drove by, was a giant three-window coupe on display, an old Lincoln Zephyr, and being a Lincoln of that vintage, I knew it was powered by a V12. I had to stop and ask about it. There was nothing else in there that interested me at all; the place had slowed down a lot since it had opened and not much was happening. A salesman walked up and I asked to see the V12 engine. He told me it had been replaced by a big V8, which was a lot more reliable. I was disappointed. The car was beautiful. "It's too bad it doesn't have all of its original equipment. Maybe I could find a V12 and put it back in. How much is it?" I asked. He gave me an amount and I looked at the car for a while and craftily offered him less. We arrived at a price and I went back the next day and picked it up for way too much money.

Driving it home, I noticed that I was a bit uncomfortable in the seat, which had been reupholstered and had a back that was too upright. I knew it wasn't originally like that. Looking down at the mechanics of the seat, I saw an oversized bolt that was definitely not original. Easy enough to fix, I thought to myself.

I drove it out to the beach and picked up Jeanne Field, an old friend of mine who was part of the crew I had met while filming CSNY in New York, with the cinematographer David Myers, and Larry. Larry always called Jeanne "Miss Field" in those days. Miss Field and I were going out to Santa Barbara to see where Zeke was living now in Larry's old house. It had been hard for me to understand the directions Carrie gave me to get there. They had seemed vague. Since it was Larry's house, Miss Field already knew right where it was and it only took about an hour to drive there from Malibu. When we arrived, the place was empty. We waited around for a while but no one came.

The Zephyr rode fairly well along 101 on the way home, with its big bastard V8 rumbling along, out of place. That weekend, I returned and drove Zeke Young back to Broad Beach, and showed him how to play airplane as we cruised along California Highway 1, heading south. I loved those times with little three- or four-year-old Zeke. He was so full of love. We talked about his problems at school, and he didn't have much to say, preferring to play airplane. I waited, and eventually he opened up and talked about it. It wasn't much but it was a beginning.

We got into it a little more at bedtime. Then he fell asleep. I stayed there, watching him for a minute or two, wondering at the beauty of his little face, then lit a fire in the fireplace and played my guitar before going to bed. Before I did, I went out and got the little plastic tricycle he had brought with him, called a Hot Trax or something like that. We had left it in the trunk of the Lincoln. I wanted him to see his Hot Trax in the living room when he got up.

I kept this car a long time. It was always wonderful to look at with its huge trunk, although I never found the V12 to bring it back to the original. The big Zephyr coupe spent its last years with me in the car gallery, a beautiful piece of art, not moving too much. It was a sad day when I had to give it up in the big purge in 2010, but for one who has had such good fortune, who am I to complain?

1975 Dodge Power Wagon Crew Cab Long-bed Pickup
"Stretch Armstrong"

CHAPTER TWENTY-SEVEN

My sea-level house in Malibu was truly a unique little place, and I loved it. I was the luckiest man on earth just to be able to spend time there, let alone own it, a piece of paradise. I thought I would be there for a very long time. When I first moved there, Zeke and I both slept on the top floor. Zeke lived in the back bedroom that looked out onto the small patio behind the house. He had bunk beds. My bedroom looked out at the ocean, and I had placed the bed right up against the window so I could just look up and see the ocean. There was a public access stairway that went down from the cliff top just to the north side of the house through evergreens so people could get to the beach. That stairway was barely visible from the house.

I had a dog named Art who lived there with me. We all shared many great walks on the beach. He was a very smart dog and I enjoyed his company. A medium-sized Australian shepherd–cocker spaniel cross, he really listened and seemed to know instinctively what I was up to all the time. I had Art from the time that he was a puppy. This was a wonderful and simple time in my life. Zeke Young would visit me often, and we have a few memories of that time, both good and not so good.

Zeke's spirit, as always, was great. He was positive no matter what, and he was a great inspiration to me. Both my sons, Zeke and Ben, have CP, or something like it. Ben Young is a quadriplegic and a truly amazing young man. Zeke Young, as I've said, is an inspiration, and of course I have my talented and beautifully artistic daughter, Amber Young, who has a habit of showing me many things. I love them all dearly. My children have all taught me many lessons. Some of the most important ones are listening and caring. I am still working on them, and it may take me a lifetime to get them right.

One day Zeke and I went to Orange County together and bought a brand-new 1975 Dodge Power Wagon crew cab long-bed pickup truck. He loved it. Zeke was only about three years old at that time, and he talked about trucks nonstop for the whole month. If he wasn't talking about trucks, he was singing his favorite song by Linda Ronstadt, "It's So Easy," over and over. Just the one line, "It's so easy to fall in love, It's so easy to fall in love, It's so easy to fall in love, It's so easy to fall in love." He was a lot like me, getting something in his head and not letting go of it. It was about that time that we named the truck "Stretch Armstrong."

For the next few years we traveled back and forth between the ranch and Malibu in Stretch, approximately an eight-hour drive, releasing about 550 to 650 pounds of CO_2 into the atmosphere each time. It was a trip we always enjoyed, and we made it many times.

One such trip on a summer day, Zeke was stretched out on the front seat, sleeping on my lap, on Highway 5. We were climbing the grapevine grade on our way to Malibu in one-hundred-degree heat.

Zeke got really thirsty, and we stopped for a drink. He drank the whole Coke or Pepsi without stopping and asked me for another one immediately, which I got for him. Then he was jacked out of his mind. Even I could see that that was not a good drink for him to have too many of. As a father, I tried my best but didn't always get it right.

A TENNESSEE BLUETICK HOUND, sometimes called a coonhound, Elvis was a good dog, and I took him with me everywhere I could. Of course, being a hound, he was hard to manage and took off whenever he saw anything to chase. He was never scared to jump out of a moving vehicle if he saw a deer. One time, he jumped out of the back of Stretch Armstrong before we put the Alaskan camper in it, and actually slid along the road on his chin before he started running, just so he could chase a deer. He took off into the hills. I had to wait for him to come back. He always came back to wherever I was. All I had to do was wait, but sometimes I had to wait a long time. I was not going to lose Elvis. Hounds are very independent. I sent him to training school and he learned some good things there, but he never forgot who he was.

> *King went a-runnin' after deer.*
> *Wasn't scared of jumpin'*
> *Off the truck in high gear.*
> *King went a-sniffin'*
> *And he would go.*
> *Was the best old hound dog*
> *I ever did know.*
>
> —"OLD KING"

In 1973, I had done a tour called Time Fades Away, my first big tour of indoor stadiums and arenas, where I sang really loud (without modern stage monitors) just so I could hear myself onstage. My throat was damaged. I had developed nodes on my vocal cords, making it a bit painful to sing and almost impossible to sing quietly with any degree of control.

Over the following year I had gone through periods of voice rest to try to get the nodes to go away. That had worked for a while, but by 1975, I realized I had to have surgery. It was performed in LA by Dr. Ed Cantor, who had treated many singers and was a world-renowned specialist. I drove Stretch down from the ranch in October, and Dr. Cantor successfully removed the nodes. After the surgery, doctor's orders were that I had to be silent for two weeks, after which I was not to sing for two more weeks. One month later, Crazy Horse was at the ranch, recording and playing locally in what we called the Northern California Coastal Bar Tour.

This was one of the best times for the Horse, traveling around Northern California in Stretch Armstrong and the Alaskan camper, playing in small bars, writing songs and recording them at the ranch.

Crazy Horse traveled to all the shows in Stretch, driven by Steve Antoine. I used the Alaskan camper to change in, because I was always drenched after we played. Steve was an easygoing, friendly, and soulful guy from Cleveland who we had met while we were playing at a little club called La Cave in the late sixties when Danny Whitten was still in the band. That was before our first Crazy Horse album, *Everybody Knows This Is Nowhere*, was made. Danny was our original guitarist and singer before he tragically died in 1972 of a drug overdose. So years later, when Poncho joined the band, we had Steve Antoine drive Stretch during the Coastal Bar Tour, and it felt good to have old friends around who understood where we had been and why we were still together. One article was written about a show at the Marshall Tavern, and it showed up in a newspaper in Anchorage, Alaska, so you can see what publicity hounds we were at the time. They got the tour name, Northern California Coastal Bar Tour, wrong. They actually made up their own name, disregarding ours. Any publicity is good publicity:

Taking a cue from Bob Dylan, Neil Young and Crazy Horse have done a dozen or so unannounced shows around Northern California since December. But unlike Dylan's Rolling Thunder Review, Neil has played for free and stuck to obscure clubs like the Inn of the Beginning in Cotati and the Marshall Tavern in seaside Marshall (population 50). One of our correspondents made the 30-mile trip from San Francisco to Marshall. His report: We went over hills, through fog and rain. As we rounded a bend we found ourselves entering and leaving Marshall. We parked in the mud outside of town and walked halfway through town (five houses) to the bar. The doors were open. Nobody was collecting money. It was warm and dry inside and everybody was drinking. The place had a capacity of 100, but it wasn't full.

Young and Crazy Horse stepped out of their back room and descended the staircase to the stage. Young broke into "Down by the River," then continued with things from his new album, Zuma. "Don't Cry No Tears" brought the crowd to an orgasm as the mixer cranked the volume.

Neil came back to play a double encore of "Take Me to the Country" and their anthem, "Southern Man." His voice was still as strong and clear as ever.

During this time, one song we recorded at the ranch was called "Look Out for My Love." We were having a lot of trouble getting it right and time was dragging on. It was four or five in the morning and we were still going at it. Probably cocaine was keeping us going when we should have given up. It was during the introduction to the song that the door to the studio playing room opened and Ellen Talbot, Johnny's wife, danced slowly in and pulled down her jeans, showing us all her ass. Well, that was the take! It woke us up and we finally got it.

> *There's a lot to learn,*
> *For wasting time.*
> *There's a heart that burns.*
> *There's an open mind.*
> *Look out for my love,*
> *It's in your neighborhood.*
> *I know things are gonna change,*
> *But I can't say bad or good.*
>
> —"Look Out for My Love"

One of the best Northern California Coastal Bar Tour shows we did was in a club called the Catalyst located in Santa Cruz. We drove Stretch Armstrong and his Alaskan camper down the Coast Highway to Surf City, as it was called. Santa Cruz then was a hippie haven, full of young people having a good time. Surfers smoked garfong, rode the waves, and cruised their woodies around town. It really was that way back then, and that's the way I always want to remember it. It's part of my Canadian dream fulfilled. I always wanted to see Surf City, and that's what I saw.

Many of our friends from the mountain were part of the Coastal Bar Tour. Taylor Phelps was a co-owner of the Tunitas Creek Ranch with Jim Russell. Taylor was talented and enterprising and above all a real character, loved by all. He was with us a lot, selling T-shirts specially designed by talented mountain artist Becky Holland, whom I loved and who was always a great spirit to be around. Becky's unique and beautiful paintings depicted the Redwood Mountains, where we all lived. She sold her art all over the world and showed it in the mountain folk art section of the annual art fair at the firehouse. These and many other friends traveled with us on our local adventure.

When we played the original Catalyst, a famous Santa Cruz club, it was in an old building with a high ceiling. That building was later destroyed in the great earthquake of 1982. The night we appeared, it was packed. We took an intermission and Taylor Phelps got up onstage and started selling Becky's Northern California Coastal Bar Tour T-shirts. The crowd booed him so loudly that we were all killing ourselves laughing. This crowd didn't want to see anyone selling anything! They came to hear music and hang out. Taylor was a natural salesman and he couldn't imagine why selling anything could be so negative. He stood his ground for quite a while there onstage with his T-shirts, a box full of them on the floor, until he finally gave up. It was a hilarious moment for all of us who loved Taylor, our own P. T. Barnum.

The true highlight, though, came halfway through our next set as we did "Like a Hurricane." I remember looking out into the crowd, and it was a dense crowd, with the aroma and fog of weed hanging over it, and all I could see was one girl standing there. She seemed to be floating; her beautiful light blond hair set her apart as she moved to the music in another world from everyone else. She had a light around her, a glowing haziness that set her apart like a queen among peasants, a goddess among mortals. Her clothes were a different color than anything else in the room and she stood out so completely, dancing and floating while not moving at all, a slow-motion masterpiece of a painting.

AFTER NEW YEAR'S, in early 1976, I drove Stretch Armstrong south to the beach with Zeke, taking him home to his mother, again traveling Interstate 5 through the San Joaquin Valley. Our trip distance was about 380 miles. We got approximately 18 mpg in Stretch. Gasoline was priced at 57 cents per gallon, and during the journey we deposited about 411 pounds of CO_2 into the atmosphere. A little over 97 million passenger cars were on the road in 1976, not counting trucks like ours and other vehicles.

I did a few recordings in LA around that time. One of them was just an overdubbed vocal sketch that I put on a track I had cut at the ranch with the Horse a few months earlier. I was still on voice rest when we cut it, so the song had been recorded without a vocal. The instrumental passages on this recording are some of our best Crazy Horse moments, with Poncho playing a great part on the Stringman keyboard, an amazing analog string synthesizer. It is a very emotional ride. Two months later, I overdubbed all the vocal parts at a studio called Village Recorders. Ben Keith was there at the board, helping me. I loved that track. I knew I had to finish it. The

Horse was cosmic. Those sketches are the vocals we used on the final record of "Like a Hurricane."

I was in a hurry in 1976, as I had been in the habit of writing several songs a week for months and was backlogged; too much material and not enough time in the studio. I was recording anywhere I could and moving quite fast, finishing my records very quickly. For me, it was not as important to create a technically perfect recording as it was to get the original performances and feelings of new songs on tape. Those performances usually carried the essence of the song. That was my method. Let someone else make the perfect record. I had to take care of my own songs.

Around the beginning of 1976 at Wally Heider Studios in Hollywood, we were trying to record "Powderfinger" with Crazy Horse. It was sounding really good to me and I was way into the song. Then I came completely unglued and yelled at Billy for what seemed like an endless time. We had been right in the middle of a great take and he had missed a bunch of changes. My nerves must have been totaled for some reason. I had to work on my temper with Crazy Horse and Buffalo Springfield, as I was mostly juvenile and had no patience. I'm still not completely past it now, just a little slower to react. When you open up to deliver in the studio, you have no self-control, no defenses, no point of view. That's the place to be. You're just a lightbulb with the filament exposed, no outer glass to protect you. The emotional and spiritual music comes along at just about the same time, so if something goes wrong right at that moment there is almost no way to predict what will happen. Usually I would just lose it. Today it is not very different when it happens; we just have recording more down now, and mistakes are easier to fix with technology.

One night, Mr. Briggs and I jumped into Stretch and headed for his favorite place, Indigo Ranch Studios. I spent the night there with David and recorded nine solo acoustic songs, completing a tape I called *Hitchhiker*. It was a complete piece, although I was pretty stony on it, and you can hear it in my performances. Dean Stockwell, my friend and a great actor who I later worked with on *Human Highway* as a co-director, was with us that night, sitting in the room with me as I laid down all of the songs in a row, pausing only for weed, beer, or cocaine. Briggs was in the control room, mixing live on his favorite console.

Stretch was the perfect vehicle to reach Indigo Ranch. We created a lot of music there in a very short period of time over that year or so. It was one of Briggs's and my most creative periods. That studio was way back in the hills above Malibu, past Garth Hudson's (the magical organist in the Band) house on a dirt road at the end of a canyon. We left some of our soul right there in that building when it burned down to the ground a few years later with all of David's favorite analog equipment in it. The cause of the fire remains unknown.

1941 Chrysler Highlander Coupe

Shortly before Christmas in 1975, I was down in Malibu at Automotive Classics, just to see what they had. There were a lot of cars, and many of them had been priced ridiculously high, targeting nouveau riche stars and wealthy sheikhs and others who had money to burn. The cars usually looked good but were not really that together when you looked at them closely. They were often not worth a fraction of the asking price, and the salesmen were really snooty, especially when they realized that they were dealing with an educated customer who knew the real value. This was where I found myself that day, except I had a handicap. There was a car there that I really thought was attractive and I wanted it.

It was a 1941 Chrysler Highlander coupe. The price of gas when it was made in 1941 was just nineteen cents a gallon. It was a two-seater businessman's coupe with a red-plaid interior, a giant trunk, and a cream-plastic deco that carried across the dashboard and glove compartment. The plastic had started to curl, probably because of the California heat and the age of the plastic itself. This was quite a unique car. The salesman said that the car was from Steve McQueen's collection. *Nice,* I thought. *How can he prove that, which potentially added to the value of the car?* I asked myself. But the car was very cool. It was $2,800. Too expensive for what it was, I guessed, and more expensive than most of the cars I had ever bought. I took it for a ride and it rode like a dream.

Sometime later, I got it to the ranch and decided to restore it since it was so famous. I took it to Jon McKeig in Scotts Valley near Santa Cruz. That was a flawed idea. The restoration is still incomplete today. The car is beautifully painted but not assembled. It is complete but missing a replacement for the warped and broken plastic dashboard trim parts, which continued their deterioration to the point where they were unrecognizable.

I now think that the deteriorated plastic dashboard is what stopped Jon from finishing this car. Sometimes he would just get stuck. Jon had repaired the interior upholstery brilliantly but then had stopped just short of reassembling it, perhaps stymied by the missing plastic dash parts. When Jon saw something he couldn't fix, he couldn't continue with all the things that he could do. I don't know why. It's hard to understand, but somehow I think it has to do with Vietnam.

Perhaps I should have not bought it and just left it alone and maybe someone would have fixed it up. Right now it is a struggle, a story incomplete, an empty feeling. I have to do something about it.

1950 Plymouth Special Deluxe Sedan

Back in 1974, there was a bar up on Skyline Boulevard, California Highway 35, located on the ridge above the ranch. It was called Alex's, and Pegi was working there. Alex's was the place where "I used to order just to watch her walk across the floor."

She used to work in a diner
Never saw a woman look finer
I used to order just to watch her walk across the floor
She grew up in a small town
Never put her roots down
Daddy always kept movin' so she did too
Somewhere on a desert highway
She rides a Harley-Davidson
Her long blond hair flyin' in the wind
She's been runnin' half her life
The chrome and steel she rides

Collidin' with the very air she breathes
The air she breathes.

—"Unknown Legend"

It's funny to see how a song can start out in fact and go completely to fantasy but then still be there, in the moment. "Unknown Legend," as sometimes happens, starts out with a factual reference and just goes off into a world that opens up for me once the music starts. This song was a memory that returned to me when I found its lyrics written on an old newspaper fifteen years after I had written it. Soon the melody and chords came rushing back. When I picked up Hank, my old Martin D-28 that once belonged to Hank Williams, the song flowed as if it had always been there. When I finished it and recorded it for *Harvest Moon* around 1990, Ben Keith's playing was among the most beautiful I had ever heard.

Anyway, there was a local guy who used to come into Alex's whose name was Jim Franco. Jim worked as a sanitary engineer down in the flats and got up very early in the morning to collect the garbage in San Mateo. On his route he always found interesting stuff that he sometimes would tell me about at night in the bar over a beer. One night, he was quite excited about a 1950 Plymouth Special Deluxe four-door sedan that he saw in a garage on his route and was now for sale. It had just been sitting there for many years and was in pretty good shape, perfect body with the original interior, a bit frayed. He knew it was my kind of car and he told me about it. I bought it for about eighteen hundred bucks. It was a good runner, three-speed column shift, a little rough getting into first gear just as the clutch was released, but it was really very solid aside from that idiosyncrasy. It was green, all original paint. It always started right up and I used it all the time. I know it was with us at the recording of *American Stars 'n Bars*, an album Crazy Horse made at the White House on the ranch, because we have a great old picture of Crazy Horse with the car outside.

In our recording history, especially with Crazy Horse, we used many houses as studios, moving our antique recording equipment into these homes and just playing there. As a group, we disliked the factory feeling of recording studios in Hollywood and did everything we could to make sure our music was isolated from that type of atmosphere. Our music was not a job. It was our way of life. We lived for the music, the girls, the cars, and each other. The songs chronicled our feelings, good and bad. We didn't give a shit about being perfect. All we ever wanted was the vibe, the magic, what we called the "swim" of our sound enveloping us as we poured our souls into the music. We had just finished recording *Zuma* at Briggs's house in Point Dume, down in Malibu, and we still had more to give.

Later that year, my dad came to the ranch to visit, and that time is well chronicled in his own book *Neil and Me*, a fascinating book to me at this stage of my life, which I love to read because it is like he is still here with me. At the time, I set Daddy up in the Red House up on the hill above the White House, where we had just been recording our LP, *American Stars 'n Bars*, and gave him the 1950 Plymouth Special Deluxe, and he was very comfortable with it. It was then that I was reminded of his old habit of slamming the doors of cars to make sure they were solidly closed. The Plymouth could handle it.

The White House was always used like a boardinghouse, where Crazy Horse and the crew would stay if we were doing something on or near the ranch, and about this time we were enjoying the Northern California Coastal Bar Tour. One night we had Daddy's spaghetti, with his own special sauce, which was hot enough to fog up the glasses of those who wore them or create beads of sweat on your forehead. I've written about this before but it's worth mentioning again because I can almost taste it right now. This was dynamite sauce and he cooked it a little differently each time. The spaghetti was a perfect al dente.

The Coastal Bar Tour was accomplished by a method we perfected. Not wishing for any advertising, David "RD" Cline would contact the bar owners and tell them that we would like to play in their establishments. We would ask for the open dates and tell them that we would like to play one of those dates but would not commit to a precise one. On the day of the appearance, we would show up in the late afternoon and set up, allowing for word of mouth to fill the bar or club with locals. That way, we never were committed in advance, played for the locals, and could back out at any time. It worked perfectly.

Daddy came to a lot of the shows in the Plymouth Special Deluxe. We played up and down the coast at little clubs and bars, rarely more than two or three hundred people in the crowd, sometimes less than one hundred. Johnny Talbot, Billy's brother who lived with his wife Ellen on the ranch, handled the road manager duties.

One of our best shows was in La Honda, a redwood town in the mountains near the ranch. The place we played was called the Boots and Saddle Lodge and it had a dance hall with a little stage. The bar adjoined the dance hall. It was very rustic with log walls and a beautiful stone fireplace. Daddy parked the Special Deluxe in the parking lot under the giant redwoods and we played great that night. "Country Home" was brand-new then and we played it for about twenty minutes. The Boots and Saddle burned to the ground in a suspected arson fire some years later and nothing else was ever built on the spot where it used to be. I can still see Daddy in the green Plymouth under the redwoods every time I pass by on my way to or from the coast.

> *I hate to go down to the flats*
> *'Cause I can't park on a hill*
> *Instead of getting a rolling start,*
> *I have to pay a bill.*
> *I guess I need that city life*
> *It sure has lots of style*
> *But pretty soon it wears me out*
> *And I have to think to smile.*
>
> —"COUNTRY HOME"

Daddy, quite the lady's man, enjoyed the Northern California Coastal Bar Tour immensely. His being there in the Plymouth was a big treat for both of us, one of the best. Daddy and the Horse had a great time.

The Special Deluxe has traveled many more miles with me and it still does, especially at home on the roads of Broken Arrow Ranch. With springs perfectly suited for the rough terrain, the old Plymouth is comfortable on back roads that would challenge any sedan that was not sturdy and well made. Old Chrysler products from that era are famous for being runners in the truest sense of the word. And so it has been. Up and down the old ranch roads for years upon years, vacuum wipers beating away the winter rains, big round tires handling the potholes with ease, and the trusty six-cylinder engine firing up responsively whenever asked. The Plymouth Special Deluxe has persisted.

Elvis, my soulful and friendly Tennessee bluetick hound, took up residence for ten years on a horse blanket in the backseat. As the interior slowly gave way to the constant wear and tear, blankets of one kind or another were thrown on all the seats. The old Plymouth just kept on giving, and time rolled by. When Elvis died at the vet's, where he was having an operation to remove a cancer, he was given one last ride back to the ranch on his old blanket. Although Elvis was gone, the Special Deluxe just kept on rolling on with me and my memories in it.

I was thirty-six years old and weighed about 135 pounds. I had never been a physical person, avoiding sports and exercise like the plague. I had gotten so weak in my arms and shoulders that I was having trouble lifting my guitar strap up over my head to put it on. It was a heavy guitar, but not so heavy that I should have had a problem with it. My left shoulder joint hurt a lot when I tried to lift anything above it. I was not a physical person at that point, and had no exercise routine at all. I knew I had to do something, as I was wasting away.

While in LA, recording the album I called *Landing on Water*, with Danny Kortchmar producing and Niko Bolas engineering, I had hooked up with a trainer named Frank Moran. Frank was a fitness motivation expert who worked with a lot of Hollywood pros, actors, producers, et cetera. They had to look good to do their jobs and be fit. Frank worked me out very hard and would always leave me exhausted, whereupon he would smile and say to me: "Welcome to the land of the living." Frank got me boxing. I would show up at his place in the morning and we would box in his garage. Then I would hit a punching bag. By the time I left to go to the studio to record with Niko and Danny, I was jacked out of my mind, ready to take on anything. Frank really got me going. I was into being fit. He got me started and I'm still doing it today.

After *Landing on Water* was finished, I asked Frank to fly up to the Bay Area to continue working me out so that I could keep up with the routine. In 1983, we were working out at a place in Millbrae, near the airport, called the Royal Athletic Club. Frank said I should weigh about 185. I had a lot of growing to do! He worked me out so hard that some of the guys at the gym thought he was going to kill me. There were a lot of cool old guys there: an old Italian construction guy called Big Frank whom I really liked, and another guy who was very old and had MS or something. Those were some real people and I liked it there. I would see them regularly and sometimes we hung out and talked in the parking lot when I arrived or left in the old Special Deluxe.

I noticed this young guy in the gym regularly who had a VW. He was a trainer and worked with some of the clientele. His name was Mike "Munsen" Johnson and eventually he started training with me on the days when Frank did not come up. After a while, Frank just supervised from LA, flying up once a week, but eventually the cost of him coming became too high compared to using Mike, so we started working with Frank when I was in LA and Mike when I was at the ranch in San Francisco.

That was the beginning of a long relationship. Mike "Munsen" Johnson, also known as "Abs," is still my trainer today. He goes on all my tours and we have a semitrailer that is outfitted as a gym inside so I can work out in private with my own equipment, staying in shape while on the road, because I really don't enjoy the public hotel gyms with disco music. This has helped me immensely with my music and my life. I weigh 175 now, although it is most certainly not all muscle! We still check in with Frank every once in a while. I try to work out with Mike five days a week, first thing in the morning. We are all good friends.

One summer day in the nineties, I visited the car barn to work out with Mike in a unique little gym Jon McKeig had built out of scrap and corrugated metal on the second level, overlooking the cars. It was always settling to look at the cars in the morning, remembering all of the things we had done together. Seeing the Plymouth parked down below, I decided to take it home and leave my old Jeepster there at the barn.

When I got inside, fired it up, and started moving, I heard a sound I had never heard before. It was a crackling sound, not a mechanical sound, just the sound of things rubbing together. The sound only happened when the car was moving; it was starting and stopping immediately with the car's movement. I got out and looked around. The car was clean, like it had just been detailed. I started the car moving again, seeing nothing unusual, and the sound started right up. I called Jon, who came over and stood near the car. "What is this sound?" I asked, and demonstrated it for Jon, who couldn't hear it. "Come on. Get in," I said. "I'll take you for a ride." Then he heard it. He didn't know what it was, either.

When we started going over what had happened to the car since the last time it had been driven, he remembered using a can of rubber preservative that was supposed to stop the decay of rubber right in its tracks. Thing is, it turned rubber into a hard shiny material with none of its original attributes. So all of the rubber around the doors and windows had been sprayed with this junk and now the car crackled as it was driven. A small thing to some, but not to me with my hyper-auditory sensitivity. I hated the sound. The whole car was different now that it had lost its quietness. It went on like that for years, crackling away. Atypically, I slowly learned to live with it. Maybe that happened because I was getting old and becoming more accepting. Maybe I just had other things to do and couldn't focus on it. Eventually I even started thinking it was getting quieter.

At some point, the Plymouth started to lose power. It became hard to start. I was working with a master mechanic named Bruce Ferrario whose shop, Four Star Truck and Auto Repair, had done an excellent job for me on a few other cars. He always backed up his work and was a true perfectionist, and I liked him.

I brought the Plymouth to Bruce and he made it run like a dream, plus he replaced all the rubber and got rid of the sound! The old Plymouth was back to normal, maybe even a little more responsive. I have driven it everywhere in the Bay Area, but never out of town to another city or state. I found this car to be comfortable for short trips, especially in the hills and local areas, whereas I liked to use big Cadillacs, Buicks, or Lincolns for longer trips to LA, Sacramento, or Lake Tahoe.

In spring of 2012, when Crazy Horse was rehearsing for our first tour in nine years to support our recent album, *Americana*, and our next, *Psychedelic Pill*, the Plymouth Special Deluxe was parked right in front of the stage, ready for any challenge. A new Indian blanket seat, one of the last things designed by Jon McKeig before he retired, was looking beautiful as part of the all-new interior he installed. The motor, still humming along, was now started by an improved nine-volt battery system. It had been straining with its original six-volt system. Seemingly reborn, the Special Deluxe sprung to life again at the turn of a key. The paint was worn through to rust in some areas, but the body and chrome were still nearly perfect, just as they were the day I first laid eyes on this beauty.

Driving the Plymouth home from the Redwood Digital mixing

studio one night after hearing the final mixes of *Psychedelic Pill*, I was thinking about the playback. I did a lot of work on these tracks with Johnny Hausmann and Jeff Pinn, my two engineers. Work went on for over a month to make the tracks as great as they could be. Most of the time was spent on editing the long instrumental passages, balancing the numerous vocal parts, and preserving the feeling and vibe of each song. Part of the process called for my co-producer, John Hanlon, to come in and do a final pass of all the mixes with fresh ears. Sometimes this can greatly improve the original passes.

Billy, Ralph, Poncho, and Mark Humphreys, our monitor mixer, were all there with me, listening to our choices and voicing their opinions. It was real group listening and evaluation. Briggs was there with us in spirit. In the end, we took a couple of John's re-mixes and replaced the originals I had done with John Hausmann and Jeff. There were two songs where we decided on combining my mixes with John Hanlon's and then there were three big long songs where we all felt the original mixes we had done during the month's work contained more of the original feeling of the music.

One of John's original mixes of a twenty-six minute track, "Driftin' Back," is my favorite. It had been done right after the recording. We never even wanted to try mixing it again. Another one, "Twisted Road," he had improved remarkably by rebalancing it. I was really impressed with the difference he had made. So we developed a new process and worked closely together. The band was involved in the final decisions. We were all happy that we did it together, but John Hanlon and I still missed Briggs. A day never went by when we would not think of or mention Briggs, and we talked about him all the time during those sessions.

That night after leaving the studio, I was heading home. I kept the trusty Plymouth in first gear, slowly making my way back to Pegi under a watchful July moon. We were less than one month from our thirty-fourth wedding anniversary and she was more beautiful than ever. She's now about the same age as her mother was when she died, and sometimes I can see her mother's kindness and beauty in her face. I parked right in front of the house so I could see the Plymouth from across the lake when I went for my morning walk. If I park in the right place, the picture looks perfect.

One morning, as I walked past the 1950 Plymouth Special Deluxe's trunk, I noticed the 2012 sticker on its old California license plate. Like math as a buzzing insect, a quick calculation of years flitted through me. It was over in a split second like a mosquito bite. I settled into the front seat, turned the key, and the Special Deluxe jumped to life immediately. It was a cold day and winter was decidedly arriving on the ranch. The ducks and geese were excitedly conversing about the change of seasons as they always did when the weather got their attention. Change is important to birds.

Motoring across the ranch in first and second gears, I took time to observe the beauty surrounding me and felt blessed for a moment. I was on my way to the train barn to relax and write a little. I was going to start with some Buffalo Springfield research, and seek out the date of a show we did at the Earl Warren Showgrounds in Santa Barbara. I had some memories of that experience that I wanted to get down before I forgot. Sometimes those moments are vivid and you can almost smell the air around them. Then they are gone.

When I arrived at the train barn, it was cold inside and I built a fire. There was an old potbelly stove there that used to be in my bedroom in the old cabin when I first came to the ranch. I remember buying it and placing it there on a stone hearth I had built, with a small door beside it that led to a woodshed, where I kept all my firewood. I really loved being able to just open that door and get wood to put on the fire, then jumping in bed to read or whatever. Those were good days. Except for those memories, evidence of the stove in the house is all gone; that area where it was is now part of a hallway of the big house Pegi and I built for our growing family. The old woodshed has become a bathroom.

Picking up some newspaper, I saw the sports pages celebrating the Giants' win in the World Series over the Detroit Tigers. I crunched up the paper and threw it in the potbelly, happy for the Giants because I lived in the Bay Area, but having rooted for Detroit, I felt the loss. Detroit needed a win. Detroit deserved a win but it was not this year. I will always root for Detroit to come back and win again. The people there, the working men and women, the factories, they all meant something to me, not to mention Motown and Hitsville U.S.A. I struck a match and lit the fire.

Pushing that thought from my mind, I refocused on finding the date of a show the Springfield did in Santa Barbara. Through the search engine, I found the date. But much to my surprise and amazement, every date the Buffalo Springfield ever played was in there with it! All of the shows over a two-year period were lined up with comments about some of them and a list of other groups that played with us. The room was getting warm now and the smell of smoke from redwood burning was coming into the air. I liked the smell. I recalled most of these shows, some clearly, some not, as I read the author's comments.

The most startling thing to me was the number of times on the list that I quit the group, came back, quit again and again. The other thing that really blew my mind was the number of times the author said I had epileptic seizures onstage. Pondering this, I wondered how the band had put up with me. I am sure I didn't have seizures during the performances. A seizure is a huge event, especially the kind I had earlier in my life. I thought about this long and hard. I would have remembered having a seizure. The writer was wrong or exaggerating.

The stove was putting out a little less heat, so I piled on some more wood, taking it from a pile on the other side of the potbelly. I sat down again and kept thinking, reading the list of shows and recalling some of the events. I had tremendous anxiety about having seizures and was really terrified that I would have one onstage in front of people, and remember feeling them coming on and panicking more than once. I recalled kind of going into a shell and just standing there, half playing and half maintaining. It didn't happen all the time, but when it did, it was very intense. I remembered reading about how the Springfield thought I was faking these incidents to get attention. As I thought back over it, I became very uncomfortable and hot. The potbelly was roaring and the chair was warm on the side where the stove was. I could smell the redwood smoke. I kept looking at the computer screen, scrolling through the shows, thinking about what happened, recalling some shows that we did that the website said were canceled, remembering shows we were late for. The seizure stories continued until one in Florida came along that I remembered some of. I didn't remember the others, and I'm still not sure they happened. A lot of times people just exaggerate these things when they write, to make it more interesting.

We were on tour with the Beach Boys and the Strawberry Alarm Clock. We did a lot of shows in a row, sometimes two and three in one day, leapfrogging across Florida. The show would be starting in one venue while it was ending in the last venue. We did this multiple-show schedule day after day. It was a tight schedule but we were young and the Beach Boys did it that way. They had us as an opener on more shows than anyone else by far. I think about a third of our shows over two years were with the Beach Boys. They were very supportive. So April 9, 1968, when we arrived in Daytona Beach, Florida, Rassy came to the show because she was living nearby in New Smyrna Beach, the same area where my whole family used to go when we were still together and I was young. In the show list I was reading, it said:

> Neil Young suffers an epileptic seizure during this performance. Dewey dove shirtless into the crowd and nearly caused a riot. The police shut down the show just as Young suffers his seizure. The Springfield leave him on the stage and his mother, in the audience, rushes to his aid.

I didn't remember much about it but apparently that was one of the shows where I had a lot of anxiety and kind of froze. In the show list, they called it a seizure. The guys were getting sick of me by then and just left after the show. It must have been hell for them to have me in the band. That's all I can say now. What was happening to me was real, but it wasn't a seizure. It was anxiety about having one. I would feel this sensation in my stomach, kind of a rising feeling similar to what it feels like before you throw up, and I would panic. Then I would freeze.

What a fucking bummer. I was there with Rassy and she saw what was happening. We got some food afterward and then I caught up with the tour. That was quite a time, and it was representative of what it was like for the Buffalo Springfield having me in the band for two years, coming and going like the weather.

In a while will the smile on my face turn to plaster?
Stick around while the clown who is sick does the trick of
    disaster
For the race of my head and my face is moving much faster
Is it strange I should change I don't know
Why don't you ask her?

—"Mr. Soul"

It had become very hot in the train barn and I got up to stretch, walking around the potbelly. On the opposite side of the stove there was a redwood log about two feet long leaning against the metal and it was on fire, burning away with flames and smoke! I grabbed it by a part that was not burning and shoved it inside the stove, noticing at the same time that smoke had filled the whole barn.

There was smoke everywhere and it was hovering like smog, thick smog. Looking at it hovering over the train layout, I was struck by how realistic it appeared. I wanted to take a picture of it. Then I opened up the doors and windows and turned on the two electric fans I had installed to suck smoke out to ensure Ben's lungs were protected when we had fake smoke coming out of the Lionel steam engines. About a half an hour later, the train barn was back to normal, although there was still the strong smell of redwood smoke. I kind of liked it, though.

I left that day in the Special Deluxe with my mind reeling over the Buffalo Springfield show list and the memories it evoked in me. The most intense memory was the anxiety I used to feel in crowds or crowded places where there were a lot of choices. Overstimulation is how I think I would describe it, too many decisions to make. Grocery stores and any kind of shopping with a lot of choices were particularly challenging for me during that time. Driving was an escape, but not having a license made me constantly worry about getting stopped by the cops. On the empty country roads, I would smoke weed and drive for miles. The fewer cars I saw, the better; that made it easy for me to imagine I was in another time—the time of the car I was driving. In my body, anxiety and escapism were having the battle of a lifetime, and I was writing songs, lots of songs.

A few weeks after that, I took the Plymouth with me down to Pescadero, an old fishing town near the coast that I used to visit all the time, to see my old friend Paul Williamson. I hadn't seen Wog in a long time. We had a big blowout in the eighties, somewhere in Canada. It was drug-related and we parted ways. That was all water under the bridge. Time has a way.

Paul was a great conversationalist. Always with a story and an angle, and he had been writing me, telling me he was straight. I was straight, too, so when we got together it was very mellow and we had a lot of fun reliving our glory days as we cruised south in the Special Deluxe on California Highway 1 to visit Mazzeo in Santa Cruz. Neither of us had seen Mazz in way too long, and we decided to get together with him. On a cool afternoon, the three of us met at a restaurant Mazz had recommended.

As usual, the restaurant Mazz took us to was full of beautiful women, which was fun for three old dogs like us. We spent the afternoon talking and then visited Mazz's sailboat in dry dock before heading north back to Pescadero and the ranch. Paul was very interested in seeing Pearl, the old Caddy limo he used to drive when I was in the Bluenotes, and we promised to get together and give her a look to see what kind of shape she was in in 2012.

1950 DeSoto Suburban "Hernando"

CHAPTER THIRTY

In late 1975, just after my throat surgery, I was spending a lot of time near the ranch with my friends Taylor Phelps and Jim Russell, who had a place nearby called Tunitas Creek Ranch. It was just a few miles from Broken Arrow, as the crow flies, and there were some old ranch roads that connected the two ranches easily, so I was a pretty regular visitor.

Taylor had some chickens, some pot plants, and a lot of little buildings that he was working on. The main house was a white two-story house that had been there a long time. One of the other buildings had an old DeSoto Suburban in it, a 1950 model, kind of a stretch sedan that could be used to carry lots of people somewhere. It was not a common car at any time, yet it was practical.

This DeSoto Suburban was a natural brown color, like it was used to take people to a forest retreat or something, maybe a camp. It had big roof racks for suitcases and luggage. You could envision it with stacks of old leather luggage tied onto the racks, traveling through the forest, full of people going somewhere remote. The interior was very mellow with earth-toned vinyl against cloth, and the car held about nine to twelve people easily.

This particular Suburban was really fun to cruise in, so we would generally fire up a joint or take some blow with us when we took off on a mission exploring local habitats like bars and restaurants, leaving Tunitas Creek Ranch in the late afternoon for points unknown, or at least undecided. It was in this spirit that we took off one sunny afternoon and began an outing. I was not talking because of my surgery, so was using hand signals, whistling a bit—which was probably not a good thing for my throat, either—and writing on a tablet of paper that I had. That is how I partook in the conversations, such as they were. There was a willingness to engage in anything that came along, to meet anyone, and to go anywhere that seemed interesting. Failure was not in my experience. These, then, were the best of times.

Toward the end of one night, we graduated from fine California Tunitas Creek Ranch weed to cocaine and beer. Dinner was over and it had been a good one with beautiful waitresses to look at and many friends to talk with and share stories. We were between bars on Skyline Boulevard, which ran along the very ridge of the Santa Cruz Mountains high above Redwood City, when we pulled over at Skeggs Point Scenic Lookout to park and enjoy some cocaine. The fog was rolling across the ridge, blanketing the beautiful view of the flats with its shimmering lights. There was a newspaper in the backseat with me and I picked up a felt-tip marker, one of my favorite writing tools, and scratched out a few words.

> *Once, I thought I saw you in a crowded hazy bar*
> *Dancing on the light from star to star*
> *Far across the moonbeams, I know that's who you are*

I saw your brown eyes turning once, to stars.
I am just a dreamer but you are just a dream.
You could have been anyone to me,
Before that moment you touched my lips
That perfect feeling when time just slips
Away between us, on our foggy trips.
You are like a hurricane.
There's calm in your eye
And I'm getting blown away,
To somewhere safer where the feelings stay.
I want to love you but I'm getting blown away.

—"Like a Hurricane"

Later that night when I got back to the ranch, I sat down at the electric organ I had built. It was made by combining an old antique-white painted and art-decorated ornate wooden pump organ I had received from Dean Stockwell in Topanga with a Univox String-man analog string synthesizer plugged into a Fender Deluxe amplifier from the early fifties.

The unearthly sound resonated in my little cabin for hours and hours while I uncovered the melody and chords that dwelled in those lyrics I had written in Taylor's DeSoto. Over and over I played the themes and refrains, cascading and blissfully distorted, until I could not stay awake and the sun was rising.

Early '70s Citroën Maserati

Some things I have done are outside of whatever shred of reasoning I try to live by and are at best just examples of breaks from the norm. Maybe they are my attempts at change; maybe they represent something I don't understand. I don't think it's worth looking into any further.

So let's take a look: One prime example of this would be my purchase of a mid-seventies-model Citroën Maserati, somewhat of an exotic in its day. This was a very fast and unreliable, generally overengineered and finicky car. I don't remember where I got it. Driving it was a challenge for me, a pothead. It was way too fast to be safe, and I drove it that way because I think I felt that was what was expected of me. Most of my other cars I used to just cruise around in, laid-back and trippin' along, as it were. They were big tanks; luxurious pillow rides. Not this thing. It went against the grain. It was everything I wasn't. It was the contrarian mobile.

One day in 1975, I was on California Highway 33, inland of the central coast, heading toward the San Joaquin Valley on my way to the ranch from Malibu, possibly my first trip in the Contrarian. Traveling along at about ninety miles per hour on this deserted road, smoking a joint, I felt like Steve McQueen on steroids. It was pretty safe out there, no cops; no worries.

Suddenly a Volkswagen appeared right behind me. Then it passed me. I put my foot down, accepting the challenge, feeling confident I could outrun the Bug. At about 105 miles per hour, I hit a dip on the road and the car lurched a bit, almost out of control. The Volkswagen disappeared in front of me. I accepted myself as Neil and slowed back down to about eighty.

Feeling fairly relaxed, I cruised along for a few miles until I saw the VW pulled over with the driver outside leaning on it, smoking a cigarette. He waved. I slowed down and backed up to where he was parked and got out. "Hi," he said. "Nice car." I asked him how he went so fast and he told me he had a Porsche engine and some other things in the VW. Then he told me that he drove at a track every weekend. I thought to myself how lucky I was that I had slowed down and not tried to catch this guy. I offered him some weed and he had a puff. Then I took off down the road, heading north toward the ranch at a reasonable speed, back to being myself again.

On another day up near the ranch, a few months later, the contrarian mobile made a visit to a hippie commune near the ranch called the Land. A girl I knew lived there in a teepee; her name was Starr. I had decided to visit her, to just drop in. I had never been there before and I jumped in the contrarian mobile to go for a spin and see if I could find her. She was a nice and attractive lady and had a little boy. When I got to the Land, I parked and walked down a trail toward the place where I had been directed to go by an Earth Mama, who had been staring at my car with some disdain. I felt some judgment was being made about the car. Maybe it was too expensive and flashy; not in harmony with the Land. I was feeling a bit uncomfortable looking around and never could find the tee-pee, so I left.

I never did gel with the Maserati and sold it very soon after that, feeling lucky to have escaped unscathed.

1985 Ford Econoline Van "Ironsides"

CHAPTER THIRTY-TWO

Ben Young was seven years old when we got his first van, around 1985. It took a long time for us to realize he needed a wheelchair. We started out with a custom stroller, but as he got bigger the chair became the obvious solution. He was too big to strap into a large seat insert. We had custom special seating made that supported him in his new chair, which was a lightweight unit that folded down. That's when we decided we needed a van, because he could stay in his chair and look out the windows as we traveled, sharing the ride with us.

He loved his new van, which had a changing table in the back so we could care for him when we were out and about. It was new for us, the wheelchair, the van, the whole lifestyle, but we adapted to it easily when we saw how much Ben liked it. Traveling in his van was one of Ben Young's favorite things to do. He would go anywhere in it with a smile on his face.

We had some special art painted on the two small windows in the roof, depicting a couple of locomotives, because Ben was into trains. There was a lift in the back that allowed us to load Ben into the van and he enjoyed that process as well. A few buttons and toggles allowed us to do the whole routine of loading and unloading electromechanically. Simply put, Ben Young loved his van.

After we started using the van and wheelchair, we couldn't believe that it had taken us so long to get one in the first place. It certainly was a lot easier on Ben and on us. We still have that Ford Econoline van, which we named Ironsides, as backup today, in case of a problem with our newer models.

All of Ben's new vans carried the same license plate as his original, MOBLBEN. Unlike the first one, the others were all Chrysler minivans. We purchased them because they came equipped with a kneeling feature. Instead of using a lift to get Ben up to a high elevation to get in the vehicle, the vehicle "kneels" down and Ben can just roll in, making it a much easier process. Each time a van was retired from its duty on the mainland, it was shipped to our house in Hawaii for a last tour.

Sometimes, while Ben Young and I were away on the road, Larry used our Sharks season tickets to take Bridge School students to the Tank to see the Sharks play hockey and share in the camaraderie and fun. Those were very special nights for everyone involved. Larry Johnson was a wonderful friend to Ben Young, Pegi, and all of the students of the Bridge School.

Each of Ben's new vans allowed room for passengers on either side of him in the backseat, making it great for going to hockey games. We put a big shark fin made of foam rubber and gaffer's tape on the top of Ben's second van to go to the games. Since Ben was nonverbal, Larry would refer to his conversations with Ben as "brain-to-braining." Ben loved it. I could tell from the look in his eyes. Sometimes that's all you need.

Sadly, Ben Young was with Larry the night that he died on one of those regular trips to the hockey game. Larry was taking Ben to see the San Jose Sharks play the Anaheim Ducks. That night, Ben's caregiver, Tony Rivera, had driven Ben in his van down to the harbor where Larry's boat was. Larry had been feeling tired a lot in the past few days, even going back to his boat for a rest in the afternoon once, but as always, Larry was ready to take Ben to the game. Larry came out and said "Hi" to Ben, sat down in the driver's seat to drive him to the game, and then just sighed one last breath and passed on into the next world. That was the end of an era on January 21, 2010. What a wonderful person Larry Johnson was. So giving. My friend for life.

Larry and I worked together over the years, starting with our first movie in 1972, *Journey Through the Past*. We founded Shakey Pictures that same year. Larry was my partner in crime and creativity. He was a friend who always gave me his opinion and collaborated with me on any idea, no matter how zany or wacky it was, and I did the same for him. When he died, we were working on a picture in which we interviewed terminal cancer victims during their end-times. It was heavy, and it was Larry's idea, unfinished.

Larry and I had also done CSNY's *Déjà Vu*, a documentary about Living with War that focused on the Iraq War and the soldiers and their families. This project was near and dear to Larry's heart, coming from a military family himself. He considered himself an army brat, having grown up on bases around the country. He was very concerned that we get it right and be respectful, while voicing our concerns about the wars through the music and picture. It was a great work, another one of Larry's big contributions.

All of my musical movies involved Larry in a primary way, even the ones I did with Jonathan Demme. *Rust Never Sleeps, Journey*

Through the Past, Human Highway, Greendale, and all the other productions I worked on were collaborations with him, and he supervised all of the production efforts. That is just part of who Larry was.

Larry can be seen as my brother, as my friend, certainly one of the best friends in my life. His relationships with the Bridge School students were genuine and heartwarming. He served on our board of directors and helped in any way he could.

1953 Buick Skylark

One day in the very early nineties, Jon McKeig told me he had made a miraculous discovery. Jon was really excited. He had gone out to a body shop in Pleasanton and in the shop, disassembled to pieces, was a total basket case. It was in restoration and had been abandoned by the Blackhawk Collection in Danville, California, one of the finest and most famous auto collections I had ever heard of. They had hundreds of cars. For some reason, this one sat in pieces, neglected for years, painted but never rubbed out, never finished, never reassembled, abandoned and forgotten. It was an original 1953 Buick Skylark. But that was not all. Under the hood on the firewall was the nameplate with the serial number on it, G1. This was the first Buick Skylark ever built!

As I have said, Jon McKeig's methods of restoration are legendary for the pace they move at and the quality we strove for. We tried to make the cars like new, yet still show their age through faded colors and slightly tarnished chrome. To those immersed in the car world, these special cars are called "survivors."

Eventually I moved the Skylark #1 to Roy Brizio's shop for restoration. Jon McKeig had a big hand in the finish and the car still had his mark, especially on the interior, although some of the mechanical parts showed the differences in approaches between Brizio and McKeig. With this survivor, I got the best of both worlds. It now stands completely finished on its spoked wheels, a rolling piece of American automotive history and the pride of General Motors, residing in Feelgood's, and ready to roll at the turn of a key.

Riding home from a practice with Crazy Horse at Shoreline Amphitheatre, preparing for a world tour in 2012, the Skylark rode like a dream. I cruised along 280 to the mountain turnoff at about seventy, as I adjusted the loose mirror with the miles flowing by. *What should we open with?* I asked myself. We needed an easy one first. One that is organized, that everyone knows. One that says "Here we are," and I mean *we.* On the mountain road, I had the brights on when I hit a curve. Another car was coming toward me. Trying to dim my lights quickly and forgetting that the big steering wheel needs to turn more to make a curve, I was suddenly blinded by the headlights of the oncoming car. I nearly crossed the yellow line. That scared the hell out of me. It struck me that someday I might not be so lucky if I did not become more careful. I was tired.

The big car glided through the forest back to the ranch slowly and almost silently after that, the big V8 purring, finally off the two-lane. I stopped at the gate and entered the keypad combination, then it slowly creaked open. Down the steep hills we descended, the Skylark and I, until we finally parked in front of the house in just the right place for a morning viewing from across the pond with my coffee. Remembering my near miss, I felt good to be alive and straight. Maybe being straight helped me; maybe not. I drove slower when I smoked weed. I mulled that over and stood there for a while, marveling at the great beauty and engineering of General Motors in 1953 basking in the light of the moon. Some things never change.

1962 Chrysler Imperial LeBaron

One day in the mid-eighties, just after Mike and I had been working out at the club, heading home in the Special Deluxe I saw a big silver-gray sixties car parked on the street in Burlingame. I stopped and checked it out.

It was a 1962 Imperial LeBaron, a huge formal sedan with a special rear window unique to that model. It featured the classic Imperial taillights, which stood distinctively on a chrome support above the rear fender. The four headlights were also very unusual, standing in sculpted coves on chrome mounts. This was a very distinctive car. The interior was worn leather, and the design of the dashboard was very advanced, reflecting a futuristic view, as was the incredible steering wheel, which, rather than being round, was a soft rectangular shape. This kind of design belonged in a museum as far as I was concerned. I see these cars as reflections of the American dream through the ages, a mirror of the culture. They are the art of their time, a mirror through which you can see the American story.

Inside the windshield on the dashboard was a small sign reading FOR SALE $750, with a phone number. I called it as soon as I got home, and purchased the car without driving it.

Turning the key, it jumped to life and lived up to its name in every respect. The car ran like a top. There was a little body rot, though, and eventually Jon McKeig cut away at the beautiful lines, creating a rectangular hole in the quarter panel. The car sat outside before I started storing it in my warehouse, and it deteriorated slightly after that. I vowed to get it back into decent shape. It's still there.

The gaping hole left by Jon was still in the car as it sat years later, sadly awaiting a rescue mission that seemed to be lost and derailed. Too bad it was so easy to cut something up and then abandon it. It should be harder. Maybe in that way things would last longer. Still, there it sat. Last time I saw it I thought to myself that someday I would repair it and bring it back to a reasonable condition. It was in better shape before I had my way with it.

There is a responsibility to a car if you buy it, and I have not been a very good owner so far with that one, but the game is not over yet. I even thought of repowering the Imperial to electric at one time, but that may be for another lifetime. Maybe, maybe not. I would love to make it live in a clean way. I always hold out hope for a miraculous success in one of my endeavors, yielding a fortune and allowing me to perform miracles. I can always use more money to employ people to do wondrous things. That is a dream I have; a series of dreams I am having. For now, this gorgeous example of American automotive design sits with the body and many parts of Nanu in a warehouse, residing with old stage sets from various tours, obsolete PA systems, monitor amplifiers, and forgotten furniture.

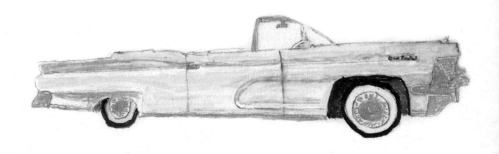

1959 Lincoln Continental Mark V Convertible

Driving on El Camino Real in the early nineties, through an area that later became famous as Silicon Valley, I saw a gas station on the corner, and as I passed I noticed a very large convertible parked at a gas pump with no one in it. Curious, I pulled into the station for a second look. As I walked toward it, the more outrageous it looked. It was the same model as the turquoise basket case I had seen at Henry's Auto Dismantling years before. I had never seen another one on the street. This one was a dark color, and it was a heavy metal monster, very heavy metal.

The vertical rear breezeway window, similar to the Mercury Turnpike Cruiser I had seen on my way home from school back when I was a kid, was rolled up and the glass was cracked. I was in awe as I looked at this convertible. There is something exciting about seeing a rare model for the first time. I walked over and looked inside.

It was not in great condition and had a dashboard that seemed to be brushed aluminum or stainless steel. "Engine turned" is the name of that metal finish, the kind you might find in an old hot rod. I looked at this car for a long while, stepping away and taking in the lines. When I got home I researched it and found it was a 1958 Lincoln Continental. The car stuck in my mind. I started learning about it. Made for three years, from 1958 to '60, with this basic body, it changed a little every year, adding here, taking away there, to give it a new look. I found that the 1959 model was probably my favorite, kind of like the Jetsons' car with angular lines accentuating the shape. The 1958 version was about two inches shorter and more rounded, kind of sculpted, and it frowned at me with a defiant grille and slanted headlights. I could not immediately decide which one I really liked best. They both had attitude.

On July 24, 1989, I found a 1959 Lincoln Continental Mark V convertible listed for sale in the newspaper. It was located somewhere off the freeway near Sacramento, and I drove out there with Paul Williamson to take a look. It was a fine day for a drive, and I was anticipating this car greatly, having only seen it before in pictures from my research.

When I first saw it I wished it was in better shape. It had imposing lines and a really well laid-out dashboard and instrument panel, in much better condition than the two I had seen previously. The steering wheel was beautiful, sculpted in a wonderful aged ivory color with a nice chrome ring and a beautiful Lincoln emblem in the center on a black background. The car was a piece of art. Its rear lights were much more graceful than the '58, sculpted and styled compared to the 1958's plain round ones. The front end looked happy, while the front end of the '58 looked sultry and a bit pissed off, or at least sad. I immersed myself in the details and got a feeling from the car. The front end of a car has a lot to say about the design, and I liked the '59 because it felt bright and optimistic.

I could easily envision Marilyn Monroe with her long scarf, sitting in that backseat with her girlfriends, wind blowing in her hair, those big dark sunglasses protecting her eyes from the breeze. This car seemed destined for greatness. It spoke to the American dream like no other car I had ever seen.

Cars always tell a story and, as you will see, this one had a lot to do with women. As I walked around the great Continental's stylish form, I could feel its history. I noticed that the convertible top had curiously been painted with a brush by a previous owner. It was white, as was the body, and the top had shrunk a little so that it did not line up perfectly with the structure that held it. This was a complicated structure, as it had to power the rear vertical window and the raising and lowering action that hid the top completely under an expansive rear deck. The Lincoln Continental was a unibody construction, not built on a frame as other cars were at the time; it was all in one piece. It had its own integral design, drawing incredible strength from its shape. All in all, it was an astounding vehicle in every respect—magnificent power, unique styling, groundbreaking mechanical design in the convertible top mechanism, and a luxuriously spacious interior.

AN UNTOLD STORY lurked in what I saw. I looked and looked at the car until I came to an inevitable question. It had an okay paint job, and there was some denting and small damage here and there, nothing big, but every panel was marred by a continuous streak of corrosion in the paint, something I had never seen before. This damage had been done purposefully. Who could have done that and why? The owner, a guy about fifty years old, could see that I had noticed this flaw and was waiting for my question.

He looked at me with deep gray-blue eyes that hid some sad memories. "My girlfriend did it," he said quietly. He revealed that she had taken a container of highly corrosive brake fluid and poured it slowly and carefully over every surface, irreparably damaging the paint wherever it landed. The damage went right down to the metal. Something must have really made her angry. Surely she knew how much he loved his car.

In an effort to make it look better, he had touched it up with a similar, although not perfectly matched, ivory paint, trying in vain to remove the malicious and hateful attack. It almost worked, and you could barely see the damage from more than twenty feet or so away from the car. He had softened the blow. From a distance, only the car's beautiful lines stood out.

"Good from far, but far from good," as the saying goes.

The combination of inflicted damage and the cracked hand-painted canvas roof gave the car a personality and a soul all its own. It was a true survivor. I took the keys, put them in the ignition, and started the engine. The Continental's monster V8, 463 cubic inches of very powerful iron, roared to life and rumbled toughly as if it anticipated a long trip, perhaps an escape.

I purchased the car right there and drove it to its new home. It was perhaps the most remarkable car I had seen, and it would play a huge part in my life. I had absolutely no idea what I was in for with that car or what a catalyst for change it would be.

RAW POWER. Cheap fuel at thirty cents a gallon. No cares about pollution in the fifties. Designs in the year 1959 were the most outrageous examples of the great American transportation dream and remain so to this day. There may be another carefree time like that in the future for America, but it will take some work.

General Motors introduced the 1959 Cadillac Eldorado, outrageous with its giant fins and taillights, chrome and stainless-steel trim, a pounding V8 with triple carburetion, leather interior, and every option imagined and some unimagined. That car was a reflection of the times, a statement.

Ford Motors answered in kind with its own flagship model, the 1959 Lincoln Continental convertible. I was now the proud owner of both of these pieces, part of American history that will surely dwell in museums forever. Freedom of expression and a feeling of world leadership in culture, whether perceived or real, shaped those days in American automotive history.

But nothing is perfect. The Cadillac Air Ride didn't work well. The Autronic Eye, a device that automatically dimmed the bright headlights when an oncoming car was approaching, was buggy. The Continental's convertible top didn't work all the time, and sometimes the mechanism destroyed itself, at great expense to the owner. The Lincoln's brakes, too, were problematic, very problematic. Living deep in the country, on the ocean side of the Santa Cruz mountain range, I had a long decline to make into my ranch on a narrow, paved road. It was steep and got steeper as it got closer to the house, so brakes were important. The brakes in my Continental had to be rebuilt several times. Weighing more than three tons, this giant convertible was a test for any brake system, and I tested it.

Once, I was out on a date with Pegi, and on the way home huge plumes of black smoke started billowing from under the car. An absolutely stunning blackness came from the undercarriage. I thought it was burning up. We had to abandon it at a gas station and call for help. It was the most smoke I had ever seen coming from a car! Pollution was becoming a big deal in California and this development was definitely not politically correct. Later, we discovered the cause was brake fluid leaking onto the exhaust line and burning under the car. The service station that had done the most recent brake job had not been very careful and had left something loose. It was a long time before I drove the car again. When I did drive it, it had brand-new brakes, which I knew from my previous experience would not last long.

A LOT OF TIME PASSED and Briggs and I, although we didn't know it at the time, made our last album together, *Sleeps with Angels*, in 1993 and '94. Jim Jarmusch, a friend and great filmmaker, made a movie called *Dead Man* in 1995 and asked me to do the soundtrack. Johnny Depp and Gary Farmer played the two main characters in this epic film about an Indian named Nobody, who was played by Farmer, and a cosmic-searching character played by Depp.

When I saw the film, it only had dialogue, and I told Jim it was a masterpiece. It was. It was a strange classic, in a world alone. It already looked like a silent-movie classic to me, the kind where someone would play live music in a theater on an organ or piano while the movie was projected, although it did have dialogue so it was not precisely a silent movie. Jim really wanted me to do the music and convinced me that it was needed.

I drove the Continental to the sessions. For my approach to the *Dead Man* project, I decided to duplicate the feeling of a musician playing music live to accompany a film in a movie theater. I rented an old stage in San Francisco from Mike Mason, a friend who I had met while filming *Human Highway* in 1980, and set up with about twenty different TV monitors in a circle around me in the middle of the room. The monitors ranged from seventy inches to seven inches in size. I set up my guitar, Old Black, my amplifier rig, and my old piano dead in the center of the room surrounded by all of the TVs. Everywhere I looked, I saw the movie. It was inescapable. When I felt like playing to it, I picked up an instrument and played live. I played Old Black, my electric guitar, solo for most of the movie, making sound effects and developing a theme called "The Wyoming Burnout" that I had written years before for a cinematic idea of my own. I developed another theme I used for one of the supporting characters. I played it all live. We recorded three passes through the whole movie without stopping. I chose to use the first half of the second pass and the second half of the first one.

That project was a huge success for me personally. Some people think it is Jim's best film, still others found it to not be. To me it is a triumph, and I am thankful just to have been included. When that was done, I got in the old Lincoln and drove home. It was a good ride, flush with a feeling of accomplishment.

Later, the time came for the movie to be released and Jim wanted a soundtrack album. Working with my friend John Hanlon, we created a *Dead Man* soundtrack, which featured the sound of the Lincoln as a vehicle moving from scene to scene, with Johnny Depp reading the poetry of William Blake, the great poet who was referenced in the story. Although there were no cars in the movie, just horses and trains, the soundtrack featured the Continental cruising through the empty back roads on a summer night with the sound of crickets at roadside as the rumbling passed by.

To get the sound, we lowered the Continental's convertible top and filled the car with microphones and recording equipment. That summer, the crickets were extremely loud, and several passages include the crickets under dialogue or Depp's recitals of Blake's poetry. With the music, dialogue, rumbling car sounds, and Johnny Depp's great readings, we weaved the web of a story for the album. The throaty sound of the Lincoln's V8 is as prominent in the film as the twentieth-century horse.

The Continental also played a part in the film *Greendale*, where all of the members in the Green family had big gas-guzzling cars. One of the characters was Jed Green. Jed's car was the Lincoln Continental convertible. One wild and rainy night, the Lincoln's windshield wipers flew off on Highway 1 at about sixty miles per hour, but that was not in the movie. We were moving the car to a new location. It was just scary as hell.

The Continental was a star, photogenic and totally unique. Jed, played by Eric Johnson, was a drug dealer who had gotten stopped by the police while driving the Continental on Highway 1. The car's big scene in *Greendale* involved Jed shooting a local cop. One of the Continental's other big scenes was Jed's arrival at the Green family's Double E Rancho. That car looked phenomenal on film, and it was a movie star, at least in my mind.

After *Greendale*, back in the car barn where I was storing my growing collection, the old Lincoln rested once more. Memories of albums I had made flooded through me as I looked at the cars I had rewarded myself with when I finished a particular album, movie, or session.

I bought my cars for their soul. They all had stories. I would sit in them and feel the stories and then write songs from those feelings. Cars carry their memories with them. To me, my cars are alive. All cars are.

1948 Buick Roadmaster Flxible Hearse "Shit Happens"

CHAPTER THIRTY-SIX

Taylor Phelps, who you have already met, died of AIDS when he was too young.

When Taylor passed away in 1995, he left me two cars: Hernando, the 1950 DeSoto Suburban that I wrote "Like a Hurricane" in, and an unnamed 1948 Buick Roadmaster hearse, exactly like Mort. Taylor had owned this hearse for about a decade and now I have it in my warehouse. It is kind of quiet, all by itself in a corner. The warehouse is the home of many things that I can't let go of yet.

I drove the hearse to Taylor's funeral after carrying his body over his ranch's old roads in a 1950s jeep truck he loved, one last time. We, some close friends of mine and Taylor's, had just taken him in his coffin up to the top of the hill that overlooked his country home, beautiful Tunitas Creek Ranch. We sat up there, smoking a joint with him. It was something that he liked to do and a place where he had loved to go. His partner, Gary, was with us. Then we slipped the coffin over the rollers into the hearse and headed for Half

Moon Bay, a little town on the coast that we had often visited together, making one last trip down the Pacific Coast Highway.

One time, Taylor and Gary had come over to the ranch and visited Shakey Heights so I could play them the title song I had written and recorded for Jonathan Demme's classic film *Philadelphia*. When they sat down on the couch, I put it on the stereo, played it through my big old Altec speakers and McIntosh amps, and listened with them. Closing my eyes, I felt the music and the song heavily. When it was over, I looked over at both of them; they were crying together in an embrace. That, and Tom Hanks's gracious mention of my song as one of the inspirations for his own performance in the film *Philadelphia*, will be meaningful to me forever, and connected my friend Taylor to the music.

Now I wonder what that hearse is doing sitting quietly there in my warehouse. Should I repair it for another ride so it is ready when it is needed? Does it need attention? Is that why I have it? Of course it is. If there is ever a situation where the hearse is required again, I want it to be ready, yet I am somehow slow in preparing, not wanting to be too ready. There is an old bumper sticker Taylor left on it, where these immortal words are written: SHIT HAPPENS.

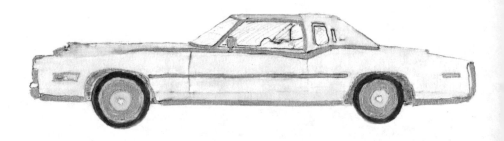

1978 Cadillac Eldorado Biarritz "Eldora" (The Pono Caddy)

n 2001, we were living in San Francisco in an apartment we had found on Green Street. It was a beautiful place to live, and our apartment had a great view of the San Francisco Bay and Alcatraz. We could see the big ocean freighters and oil tankers coming and going right from our breakfast table in the kitchen. Every apartment was a full floor. We were on the ninth, and the views were spectacular from every room. The elevator opened into a small vestibule with a door to our apartment. We had a big American flag hanging in this room, which covered the wall.

Amber was a budding artist and was in high school. The apartment's location made it a lot easier for us to drive her, compared to the ranch, which was very remote. City life was exciting to us because it was so easy to find things to do and places to go and it gave us new variety in our lives. Although I missed the ranch, it was a change I could embrace.

Our apartment had a great front room with a fireplace where I loved to curl up in an overstuffed couch with a book, the fire roaring with wood we brought from the ranch and stored in the basement. A picture of Amber in a top hat was on one of the walls.

Pegi loved the apartment. So did Amber. She had a bedroom filled with her teenage high school things and a metal bedroom set from the thirties that we had found in an antique store. Pegi and I had a lot of fun buying old rugs and furniture, and she really made it feel homey like the ranch. We would visit the ranch on weekends quite often.

I was recording an album with Crazy Horse in an old studio called Toast in the SoMa area (South of Market Street), a pretty arty neighborhood that was being overtaken by lofts and new buildings spawned by the dot-com bubble. There was a lot of new money and things were changing very fast. The studio was for sale when we were there and it looked like it wouldn't be around for long.

Everything seemed temporary, even Crazy Horse. We were not doing well in the studio. Although we had some great moments and the music was soulful, it wasn't happy or settled. It was moody and jazzy. This was where Coltrane had cut some of his early classics and we could feel it. A back door made of old metal opened out onto an alley where we used to take smoke breaks. Every night we would go to a restaurant on Market Street and eat dinner together, then go back to the studio and play some more, trying to find the magic that had always been with us.

In the middle of these sessions, we had a gig in South America called Rock in Rio. Before we left, we played a show at the Warfield Theater in San Francisco as a warm-up. It was where the Grateful Dead played a lot back in the day. There were paintings of Jerry Garcia on the side of the building where the stage door was. I felt like I was late or had missed the moment or something, just a little out of place. The history celebrated there was something I had not experienced.

We went down to Brazil's Rock in Rio and played one show and then moved on to Argentina. The crowds really loved us. Pegi and my sister, Astrid, from my dad's second marriage, were along singing with us, and we really were sounding good. Astrid had been in LA, making a couple of heavy metal records of her own. It was different to have anyone else singing with us, though, and we were a little unsettled. But overall it was great, and we rocked. When we got back from Rio and were recording at Toast again, we had new energy and recorded a song called "Gateway of Love." We did some great stuff at Toast, one called "Mr. Disappointment," and another called "Quit," but eventually I gave up and abandoned the album. Like my personal life, where I was having some serious problems with my marriage, there was just something missing. I was not happy with it, or maybe I was just generally unhappy. I don't know. It was a desolate album, very sad and unanswered. I guess you might say that I don't want to talk about it.

Toast was to be the name of the album. It felt like toast. There is a lot of soul in it. I played my guitar like an old horn, with a big fat sad sound. Ralphie, Billy, and Poncho gave it the old funky feel. It might be a gem. The ghosts of Coltrane and his musicians were everywhere at Toast. It was spiritual. Down and almost out. I missed Briggs, I knew that much, but we had Hanlon, and he was getting a great sound. It was no one's fault. There is something there and it may be a lot better than what I remember.

It is still unreleased, waiting for its huge and fat surround sound to be unleashed in an art gallery somewhere, full of paintings done by my friends. It will be a huge room with speakers in all four corners and a giant subwoofer under a big table in the very middle of the room where many glass water vessels will vibrate, creating waves moving with the bass. Beautiful women with large hats will smoke cigarettes left over from the forties and talk with angry young men about art and music. I am looking forward to it. My friends will all be there.

ALSO WITH US on Green Street was Carl, a cross of a golden retriever and a standard poodle, sometimes called a Goldendoodle. When we first got Carl in 1996 from a friend of Amber's, he was about four months old. We were living on the ranch at the time, and when we played with him on the lawn, he was always full of pep and so big! Carl could run sideways, which he would demonstrate for us every time he ran at full speed and turned to fetch something we threw. As he turned, he kept running at full speed, resulting in his astounding sideways run. That move goes down as one of the greatest in doggie history. Lovingly dubbed "Carl the Affection Hound" by Pegi, who adored him, Carl was a stunningly great-looking animal and drew praise from everyone who saw him. This was a very special dog with so much love and adventure in his eyes. We were lucky he traveled the world with us.

At the apartment on Green Street, sometimes when I took a walk on the "Poop Loop" with Carl, Amber went along with us. It was really cool taking these little walks with Amber. They were one of those beautiful low-key times we got to talk. Once, we were walking along, chatting and laughing about something, when a fabulous sight appeared right before our eyes: a giant, pale yellow Cadillac Eldorado Biarritz was parked right on the street with a

FOR SALE $2,500 sign on it! Taking a moment to admire the plush white leather interior and vinyl top, I could see that this Eldorado was in fine shape with only a little rust showing. It was a 1978 model with front-wheel drive and a giant V8.

A proud Cadillac ornament adorned the huge expanse of hood. Everything about it was deluxe. I immediately loved it. Amber loved it, too. It was an exciting and cool car. These big cars were all way out of style because of the price of gas, $1.83 per gallon, and the smog from their exhaust, but that didn't bother me one bit. Neither did the 1.6 pounds of CO_2 emitted into the atmosphere every mile traveled. This was a piece of art. We took down the phone number on the sign in the windshield and continued our walk with Carl. I called the number and made a reservation to meet the owner and check out the car.

Later, Amber and I took off to a Safeway parking lot in the middle of town, where we met the Cadillac's owner. At first, I thought it was strange we weren't going to the owner's house, but then it dawned on me that we could not have gone to the owner's house because that would not be safe for anybody. Nobody ever gave away a real home address to a complete stranger. The world certainly was different from when I was growing up in Canada.

So there we were in the Safeway parking lot. The owner was standing by the car when I walked up and said hello. He said the car ran well but didn't have the power it was supposed to have and strained on the hills, but it was reliable. I gave him the cash after driving it around the block. It felt fine to me, and I drove it back to the apartment. That Cadillac was the last gas-guzzler I bought. Amber was thrilled that I got it, and we immediately went for a ride. The next morning I drove her to school in it. It was our car. We found it together. I still take the Eldorado whenever I think I will be going somewhere with Amber: to a movie, art show, anything. I like that memory of finding it together on our walk with Carl.

Soon afterward I took it to the session at Toast and showed it to the guys. I had told them all about the yellow Caddy I had found with Amber. "It's not yellow, it's white!" said Billy. Of course, he was right. I guess my color blindness and the sunset colors made it look pale yellow to me, and it still does, kind of ivory white.

I abandoned the Toast project because it wore me out. Music can be that way. *Toast* may be great music. If it is, then it will stand the test of time. I went on to record some of those songs with Booker T. and Duck Dunn of Booker T. and the MG's, at a studio in Marin County called the Site. I drove the Eldorado up there every day and parked in the lot, probably getting about twelve miles to the gallon, passing George Lucas's Skywalker Ranch on the way. It was a cool session, playing with Booker, Duck Dunn, and Steve Potts. I could smell the fumes from the engine. It was starting to bother me that I was polluting, but I loved the car.

When Amber was about seventeen or eighteen, it was time for her to get a driver's license. We had not rushed it. She was taking her time. She felt she was not ready before then. I started giving her little driving lessons on the ranch, and of course she drove the Eldorado. Our roads are very narrow, with some steep cliffside drop-offs, and you have to really watch what you are doing. I reasoned that she would be confident in driving anything if she could drive the Caddy. Away we went, to the barn and back, practicing turning around and backing up, and eventually she drove all the way across the ranch. Over the period of a couple of weeks, she got really good.

She would move the seat up and sit up really straight behind the wheel so she could see over the hood.

She did notice that because of the size of the hood, she could sometimes not see the road. This often happened when she crested a hill. I told her to look at the side of the road out the side window and to stay close to the edge, thereby always making sure she was on the pavement. It took a little doing, but that was really a cool bonding between us. I loved every moment of it. Now she has a Prius, and I don't think she wants to drive the Caddy, but I will have to find that out. Amber is a cautious driver, very responsible.

In 2003, when I made Shakey Pictures' *Greendale* with the Upstream Multimedia crew, the 1978 Eldorado, dubbed Eldora by Jon McKeig, played a big part as Grandpa Green's car. Every morning at the ranch, I would get up before the sun and grab some coffee. Then I would jump in Eldora and drive to the coast town of Half Moon Bay, where most of the filming was done. Grandpa Green was one of the main characters, portrayed by Ben Keith, and Grandpa's car was that Eldorado Biarritz. We got some great shots of Eldora being driven by Grandpa and Grandma through Greendale and the surrounding areas. What a wonderful time of life that was, all my friends working together on something new. Sarah White was a schoolmate of Amber's and we had discovered her talent when she acted in one of the school plays. She played Sun Green, the heroine of Greendale, a young girl coming of age and finding her voice as an activist, protesting against the oil companies and a villainous anti-environment pollution-spreading corporation, POWERCO.

One day after the movie was made, we were on the road touring the Greendale stage, when Sarah took me aside. With all of the intensity of youth unbridled, she told me I was hypocritical for doing that film and having all the big trucks and buses, as well as the airplanes we used. That stuck with me. She was absolutely right. Imagine a character in my own story telling me that I was hypocritical for not practicing what I was preaching. That was a seminal moment. That young lady made a lot of sense. Very soon after, I seriously started focusing on energy solutions and using bio-fuels for my tours. That was eleven years ago. Sun Green had her first convert.

My thinking about the environment and the damage being done to it had mostly come from examples of big corporations raping the land and destroying natural things in the endless quest for oil and energy. The more I thought about it, the more obsessed I became with alternative energy. Climate change was a big idea and I began wrapping my head around it, trying to get an understanding of options for alternative energy. The more I looked, the more I learned what an immense challenge the world was facing. That's when I began dedicating myself more to the task of raising awareness, which is pretty much the only thing a celebrity can do. But I was fascinated with the technology side, too: What were the solutions? What had been tried? Why did some projects fail? And the marketing side: Why did people not get it? Why did they not understand the world's situation? Why did the media, especially TV networks, downplay and ignore the obvious so consistently, making it virtually impossible for the masses to grasp reality as far as the importance of climate change was concerned?

These were important questions. I searched every place I could find for a solution to the problem of polluting automobiles. I researched a man named Stanley Meyer who had fueled a car with water. I spent a year focused on him, trying to figure out whether that was a hoax or an amazing discovery. I visited a company named Realm Industries in California where a young man gave us a convincing demonstration and presentation about water gas. A year later, that young man was killed in an accident at Realm Industries when water gas exploded. The power contained in it was awesome, but the amount of energy that was needed to unleash it was too much. We couldn't figure it out. Realm said that they had, but they would not let anyone know because they feared the technology would fall into the wrong hands. Realm wanted to only do good with their discovery. We never could make an arrangement with them that allowed us to demonstrate their technology in a car, although they showed us a Land Rover whose engine was idling on water gas.

A man in Canada had some promising power-generating technology, but he wouldn't let us use it in an application meant for transportation. Everyone had a reason for not sharing. It was very frustrating and left us wondering whether any of these people, or others like them, actually had a solution.

I went to Australia, chasing a fuel-vaporizing concept, and got ripped off by a doctor for thousands of dollars. He told me I could use the technology and make a film about the development of it for an amount of money. I filmed for several months, and when he was done, he took my money and said the technology was his alone, that I had only paid for the right to film. There were more rip-offs and hoaxes than you could ever imagine, and I only found a few of them. I still believe that there is something undiscovered out there, and I am not the only one who feels that way. I just didn't have the endless resources to deal with these people and their eccentricities. It wore me out. I gave up on all of that pie-in-the-sky stuff after about a year and a half and started trying to focus on other methods, more accepted and demonstrable technologies that were firmly within the possibility of physics.

Then I came to know more about carbon and was blown away by the facts. I spent hours and hours reading papers on the Internet and reviewing speeches given at world conferences on biofuels. I was fascinated to learn how much I had missed, how much I had no idea about, how many people were trying to solve this riddle. I developed an insatiable curiosity about fuels and efficiency, electricity, and power storage. I said somewhere that battery technology development is my Super Bowl. That's the game I watch: the development of better batteries. I know that is the key to solar energy powering civilization. I refuse to close the door on anything forever, including nuclear power. I have faith in technology and I believe we can find solutions if we put the financial resources available behind development of secure power. A slow death through climate change is just as scary to me as a fast death. I don't want either one. We have a challenge.

So my ideas and concepts about my favorite subject, transportation, and what is both desirable and required, changed very radically in a short period of time. I came to believe that, to make a fast change, you must give people what they want and make it clean. Giving people what they don't want and making that cleaner is not enough. Many people will just ignore it. You can't force people to like something they don't want. People need to have what they are accustomed to having. Science and technology need to provide it in a clean way. Go with the flow. That was my thinking.

In 2011, we started a company called Pono, to rescue the art of recorded music by bringing a quality listening alternative to the marketplace. I had a Pono sound system installed in Eldora with a sub-bass woofer in the trunk, new speakers and amplifiers through-out, and a demo development version of Pono. The idea was to take the car to places where my artist friends were playing their music and expose them to the Pono sound by taking them for little rides in the Caddy and giving them demonstrations.

The 1978 Cadillac Eldorado Biarritz became the Pono messen-ger. Sitting on those plush leather seats, listening to great music and full high-resolution twenty-first-century digital sound was a won-derful experience. I began to listen to all of my new records in El-dora before I signed off on them for release.

But every time I started the engine I realized the car smelled of carbon dioxide, and every time I smelled it I wanted to change it. There was something incongruous about a pure sound coming from a smelly and destructive, obsolete car. When I showed the system to Jac Holzman, a world-renowned audiophile and record company pioneer, he commented first about the pollution of the car and sec-ond about the greatness of the sound. "Neil, this car reeks of pollu-tion. I hope it sounds better than it smells."

Eldora continued her service, as the Pono Caddy, polluting music lovers' environments while spreading the word about highest-resolution music. Ultimately, Eldora's days were numbered. The massive V8 was running on just six cylinders and needed to be re-built by Bruce Ferrario at Four Star Automotive, putting Eldora out of commission for a long time. With her special history with Amber and Pono, Eldora occupied a unique place in my heart. I couldn't let it go. I had to fix it and bring it back. I had an itch to take out the original engine and replace it with something I could run biofuel in. I could not enable Eldora to continue as another destructive gasoline-guzzler. There were already too many of them on the roads, and the automobile companies were making more of them every day, presenting them with increasingly desperate and outrageous marketing schemes.

I approached Bruce Ferrario about the idea of rebuilding Eldora's engine into a flex-fuel engine. A California law prohibited the conversion of Eldora because it was not permitted to change the car's emissions. This certain California law prohibited changing the engine in models built after 1976–'77 to protect the environment. Here before me was a case where a law stopped the process of making Eldora a cleaner car by running ethanol as opposed to fossil fuel. That same law also prohibited changing the engine to diesel and running biodiesel. A 1978 Cadillac had to stay the same and burn gasoline. Changing it was illegal. The law was seeking to preserve the emissions control system included in the original car, yet it should not have applied to a cleaner-running replacement engine.

I had purchased another 1978 Cadillac from Texas through eBay that was identical—well, almost identical. The white was not as warm. The interior was nearly the same but did not have John McKeig's special touches. I still liked Eldora because of my history with Amber and the car. I wondered if I should put the engine from the Texas car in Eldora. That engine was running on all cylinders and would be a little cleaner. The cost of doing that was almost the same as the cost of changing to an even cleaner, yet illegal, biofuel engine. I was stymied. How could I make Eldora cleaner?

I am still working on this. I may have to take Eldora out of state to do the work and bring it back into California after. That seems wasteful and possibly illegal. I am looking into it, and in the meantime not using Eldora for long trips. I am restricting her use to Pono demos, transporting her in the mobile garage that is part of my road gym. After years of service, Eldora sits alone in a garage on the ranch, waiting for her next assignment, hoping for another ride to the theater with Amber or a night out on the town with music. Such is the lot for cars. They serve and then they are left behind. But some rise above and live, again and again.

2004 Ford Excursion "Ray White"

ur family had a beautiful home in Hawaii on a point with a tremendous surf break. Manta rays were plentiful in these waters. One day Pegi and I were swimming across the bay, north of our point, and on the return swim we took the outside, meaning we were as far out into the water as we usually went, crossing the bay to the point where our home was located. It was a fair swim and the water was about forty feet deep. Sea life was plentiful in those waters. We could see fish far below us. It was as if we were flying as we looked down on them through our snorkel masks.

Those fish making their way along the sandy bottom were probably no more than two feet long. Looking ahead as I usually did, I saw four huge forms approaching us. I took Pegi's hand in mine and brought her in close to me, and then she saw them, too. She was squeezing my hand tight and I put my arm around her, continuing forward by gently kicking and using my other hand to stabilize. The forms approached. The biggest one was about twelve feet across, and we were on a direct course toward them.

These were manta rays, moving toward us like giant slow-motion bats; the biggest things we had ever seen in the water with us, bigger by far than the dolphins we had first swum with a few years before. The rays continued toward us. I remembered that they were very mellow, like sea cows, and probably were just going about their own business, feeding on the small life in the water. They were getting blurry in our masks as the small creatures they fed on made the water around us look like jelly. At the very last moment, the giant creatures parted ways and went over and under us, gently flying by.

The manta ray is Pegi's *aumakua*. *Aumakua* is a Hawaiian word describing a spirit guardian from the animal world, a bridge between humans and spirits. Sharks and other life of the sea and land can also be *aumakua*. Larry Johnson's was a whale, so every year when the whales showed up at our home on the Big Island, we were reminded of Larry and were both happy and sad. The whales show up less regularly now, perhaps disturbed from their age-old pattern by changes in the earth's climate, just as the jet stream has been disturbed by warming ocean water temperatures, resulting in erratic and extreme weather patterns. The disturbance is caused by global warming, which is caused by humans creating more CO_2 than the planet can consume with plant life. The CO_2 rises in the atmosphere and creates a layer around the earth, keeping heat in.

Living on an island, the damage from fossil fuels and the massive CO_2 emissions seemed even more obvious to us. We felt bad that our island's power was coming from fossil fuels that crossed the ocean in polluting, diesel-powered tanker ships and we were doing what we could, using biodiesel renewable fuel from Maui with up to a ninety percent reduction in CO_2 emissions, and hoping to be a small part of turning the tide toward preserving the earth's balance for our grandchildren and their children after them.

When we purchased a brand-new diesel-powered, white 2004 Ford Excursion to carry big groups of people to events and enjoy one another's company, we named it Ray White in a not so subtle reference to Pegi's *aumakua*. Diesel is much better for mileage than gasoline. Even regular petro diesel reduces emissions because of the better mileage it gets compared to gasoline. When we use biodiesel, Ray White, our biggest vehicle, puts out less CO_2 than any of our others.

Ray is now in his tenth year of service to our family and is showing no signs of weakness with his big diesel motor, powered by plants through indirect solar energy.

When we lived at the ranch, which was a much larger percentage of the time than in Hawaii, I wanted to have a clean-running vehicle and was beginning to wonder what part I could play in raising awareness of the attributes of alternative fuels. Celebrity has to have some value, and using it to raise awareness is a good thing. That is when I discovered the Hummer H1. At first, the Hummer became known because of roadside bombings in the Iraq War. We saw them on TV nightly, some jury-rigged with armor by soldiers for their own protection. Those were the H1's. They were so huge that they took up the width of a whole lane. Then the H1's started showing up on the streets of America, painted in bright colors and driven by a variety of folks for various reasons, which could be the subject of another book on human behavior, which I would be starring in.

The Hummer was attacked by environmentalists as the epitome of wastefulness. No cars or trucks have created the negative reaction that the Hummer did. The thought of soccer moms picking up their kids at school in these huge behemoths really turned off a lot of folks who saw it as a wasteful, CO_2-spewing symbol of all that was wrong with America. In the USA's still wild west, some Hummer dealerships were even attacked and burned by extremist environmentalists.

To complicate matters more for the environmentalists, the conservation regulations passed by Congress, which were energetically lobbied for by big oil company lobbyists, were written specifically for cars, not SUVs. Hummers were classified as trucks, which put them outside these regulations, even though SUVs were designed and used as family vehicles. When the slightly smaller H2 came along, a lot of soccer moms got those. Next, the H3 appeared, a compact SUV smaller than the previous models. These were designed to sell more because they were smaller, but alas, still classified as trucks and outside the government's fuel conservation regulations. Intensive lobbying of politicians backed by money from oil interests is one of the biggest problems facing America's quest for a cleaner world.

The effect of lobbying on conservation regulations in the SUV example shows us quite clearly that government "by the people and for the people" is practically nonexistent. We have government by the corporation and for the corporation. Corporate money makes American laws. Separation of Corporation and State, a twist on "Separation of Church and State," may be what we need. Until we have that, all laws will be made essentially by corporations and based on corporate strategies and values.

Corporations are not people. They do not have the conscience of a parent guarding a child's safety. Corporations are driven by three-month financial reports, and until corporations lose the power they are wielding, laws will be made primarily with a view toward short-term financial gain. About $3.5 billion in lobbying is spent yearly by about 12,000 lobbyists to influence laws supposedly written in the interests of the people by 435 members of Congress and 100 senators. The majority of money to run the election campaigns of the representatives and senators who write the laws comes directly or indirectly from corporate interests.

All you have to do is step back and take a look at corporate-run government to begin to understand why the media has not presented global warming and its cause to the public as the real story of our times. Because of the corporate-occupied Federal Communications Commission, network television and printed media are now serving the corporations by not exposing the true story of climate change and the future of mankind.

There are some brave representatives and senators who oppose these laws, but so far they seem unable to overcome the forces they are up against. The people themselves will have to drop their complacency and rally behind fundamental change, take their country back, and support brave leaders.

However, this is a book about cars.

2000 Hummer H1

n the fall of 2005, Pegi and I were attending a memorial service at a church near the Bridge School, a school Pegi started with two other folks that's for teaching kids like Ben. She couldn't find a school for Ben in the beginning, so in a move that typifies her resolve, she started one herself, and it is now in its twenty-ninth year. We have been to enough of these services to know that life is precious and fleeting. Courtney Jones, a beautiful little student there, had passed away. Our students are sometimes very delicate and frail. Courtney was very young. It was a sad day.

The school was well represented, and Pegi stayed behind after the service, talking with parents of Courtney's classmates and some Bridge School staff. I had stepped outside to get some air and reflect, and was walking around the neighborhood when I saw an H1 Hummer parked in a driveway about a block from the church. Walking over to it for a closer look, it struck me that because the H1 was diesel powered, it was a perfect candidate for biodiesel.

I had been thinking a lot about the future of fuel in general, and

I realized that a Hummer might be the perfect vehicle for a mission to stimulate awareness of biodiesel. By using the fuel in the traditionally anti-green vehicle, I thought awareness could be raised. After finding a used one at a dealership a few miles away from the ranch, I hinted to Pegi that I would love one of them for Christmas, and lo and behold, that Christmas there was an H1 parked in the barn, painted olive green, the definitive military color.

Jon McKeig had painted it for Pegi. Jon really had a great sense for color and had done a stunning job, applying army stencils to the exterior that read GO EARTH (instead of GO ARMY) and BIODIESEL on the back hatch in big letters. EARTH FRIENDLY and FARM FUEL were stenciled on other areas of the exterior. The H1 ran on renewable fuel, one hundred percent biodiesel made from used vegetable oil for a ninety percent reduction in CO_2 emissions, compared to petro diesel fuel. The giant Hummer had taken on a new mission, protecting the environment by being green in more than just color.

There was no conversion needed; no cost to move to biodiesel. The cost of conversion of a relatively new vehicle is nothing. All of the materials in the new cars are perfectly suitable for biofuel. The Hummer's fuel filters did have to be changed more often because biofuel cleaned out all the sludge from inside the engine from running on dirty fuel for seven years. That was the only cost. Over time, we changed the filters less and less.

I drove my green H1 everywhere, and the reactions I got were pretty radical, first pissing people off because they disliked the Hummer and then making them think when they saw that the vehicle was powered by biodiesel. Larry Johnson would rarely ride in it with me, though. I don't think he liked it. Larry's military roots might have had something to do with that. Maybe he didn't like to see civilians driving them. As he was proud to say, he was an army brat. I thought the Hummer's statement was a good thing, though, and I thoroughly enjoyed its new mission.

In 2006, I was thinking about buying a car I could run on biodiesel. I had seen some very nice new Mercedes-Benz sedans in Europe that were diesel-powered, but I couldn't buy a new one in the USA because there weren't any available here. They were banned. America had banned new diesel cars, missing the point that diesel has higher emissions than gasoline. However, because of the added efficiency of diesel, total emissions are significantly lower per mile, so the American laws just didn't make sense. In Europe, people use it because diesel cars are much more economical to maintain and the fuel is cheaper. Thankfully, by 2013, the US ban on diesel cars was finally lifted and advertisements touted the amazing mileage like it was a new thing.

We stored biodiesel fuel on the ranch in a dedicated tank that was filled regularly by a company from Princeton, California, and I was driving the Hummer a lot and leaving the gasoline cars parked, preferring to not burn gas if I could help it. Even the cost per gallon was less with biodiesel. The ranch trucks were now all running on diesel, again with a ninety percent reduction in CO_2 per gallon.

I had noticed a lot of old Mercedes-Benz diesels on the road, which must have been bought before the US ban, and reasoned that they must be very reliable. I researched the models available and found one I really liked, a little two-door coupe called a 300CD. I got on eBay and found one that looked good, called the owner of the car, talked to him, and flew with Pegi and Carl the Affection Hound to San Diego to pick up our new 300CD.

When we got to San Diego we checked into the hotel and moved our bags into the room, where Carl peed on the drapes immediately; a big stinky pee that Carl was known for, except he usually did not do it inside. As a matter of fact, it was quite unusual that he would pee inside. We gave him a talking-to and he felt pretty bad. He was very sensitive.

In the evening, the seller showed up with the car and told us he had brought it on a flatbed because he didn't have a license and did not have the proper tags and was worried about being pulled over. When we first saw the car, it was parked right in front of the hotel, already running and smoking a bit. I planned on going through this old diesel at the ranch to tune it up. I was excited to get the car and drive north, so I gave the guy a check and he left right away.

When we got up the next morning, ready to start our trip back, I went out to start the car but it ran rough and smoked a lot. I mean it *really smoked a lot*. The windows wouldn't go up or down, either. The air-conditioning was also nonfunctional. For being too trusting, I had gotten screwed on eBay again. The car was no good.

I kept remembering that the guy was sweaty and reminded me of a crackhead. Why had I not tried the car before I paid him? That would have been easy and smart. Pegi named that car "Malaisey." She reminded me that she was a menopausal woman and would not be going anywhere in a car with no working windows or air-conditioning. I rented another car and arranged to have Malaisey transported to the ranch warehouse on a flatbed. Not driving that car before I bought it proves that no matter how old you get, you can still do things that make absolutely no sense.

Our rental car was a really nice, new gasoline-powered Mercedes sedan with every option known to man. Driving it on the way home, we stopped in LA overnight, and I looked on the Internet and found a second diesel Mercedes 300CD coupe in Paso Robles, a town halfway up the state toward the ranch. It was identical to Malaisey except that it actually worked. The next day we drove our gasoline rental car north, from LA to Paso Robles, and bought the 300CD.

The previous owner had been running the 300CD on biodiesel and it ran well. We needed to get rid of the gasoline rental car, so we left it in a Denny's parking lot with the key on the left front tire and called Elliot's office. Two of his staff drove out and retrieved the rental car for us. Away we went farther north, not a worry in the world. Such is the life of a rock and roll star.

PEGI HAD NAMED our new little yellow Mercedes "Miss Daisy Green." We elected to take California Highway 1 along the coast to enjoy the scenery and stop at a bed-and-breakfast we knew in Big Sur for the night. It was going to be great! On the coast, where the road started curving a lot, we headed north along the side of a steep cliff that went straight down to the Pacific Ocean.

1982 Mercedes-Benz 300CD "Miss Daisy Green"

About fifty miles from Big Sur, night fell. We were running low on fuel when we discovered that the dash lights did not work and we needed a flashlight to see the speed, oil pressure, and fuel level. We were a bit nervous because we were in the middle of nowhere and did not know the car very well, including how accurate the fuel gauge was. Onward we traveled to Big Sur, where there were no rooms available.

We continued north to Carmel and a place called Trade Winds Motel, where we stayed overnight. The next morning, running on fumes, we got another tank-full of biodiesel from a biofuel station in Santa Cruz. I remember feeling that we were really in the future. At the time, this was one of the only biofuel stations in California.

In 2006, there were 136.8 million passenger cars on the road, and the great majority of them ran on gasoline, which was priced at about $2.59 per gallon. Biodiesel cost about the same. We traveled from Paso Robles to the ranch, a distance of about 205 miles, getting around 27.2 mpg on biodiesel from recycled vegetable oil, and put only 20.3 pounds of CO_2 into the atmosphere. We would have emitted 200 pounds using gasoline.

1959 Lincoln Continental "Lincvolt"

CHAPTER FORTY

Years passed and the world evolved. I had become hypercon-
scious of the damage fossil fuels had done and continued to
do to planet Earth, our home and the home of our children's children. I was becoming obsessed. Although I had gained knowledge
about biofuels, I knew there was much more to learn. My friends
Willie Nelson, John Mellencamp, and Dave Matthews were all
part of Farm Aid and we all had started running our touring vehicles on it. Domestically produced and renewable, biofuels were a
reasonable, if partial, solution to our dependence on foreign oil. But
they had their own set of problems, too.

An argument that biofuels, such as ethanol, disrupted food supply was gaining momentum, but there was another side to that
story. Sales of corn for food were holding steady and had been for
years, indicating that people were not losing their food supply to
fuel. The corn used for ethanol was not used for human consump-
tion; it was used to feed cows, especially in factory farms, which
are another one of the largest sources of CO_2 greenhouse gases.

Naturally cows are grazing animals, not corn eaters, but polluting, corporate factory beef farmers still complained that ethanol production raised the price of corn. In addition to corporate factory beef farmers, behind every campaign against ethanol, Big Oil was lurking, lobbying, and working the back rooms of Washington.

And there's still another side. Biofuels were relatively new, still in their infancy. What we were using was the first generation. Interestingly, when government started to support biofuels with subsidies, business increased and reached the growth goals that were set. At that point, rather than continuing to support the new industry's growth by mandating a further increase in ethanol content in motor fuel from ten to fifteen percent, the government stopped the subsidies. Folks who had invested in biofuels began feeling the pinch, and business started to decline. During that same time, oil subsidies continued unabated. The strength of corporate lobbying at work in Washington was killing the biofuel industry.

It was in this climate that I suddenly woke up one day and was a dinosaur. Looking at my huge collection of gas-guzzlers, I realized that I was in love with something that needed to be replaced, something that had become obsolete. I had turned to biodiesel but I knew there was a lot more I could do.

I talked to a friend, Dale Djerassi, my intelligent and stimulating neighbor who I have known for a long time. He argued for the viability of electric cars. He made strong points with lots of good reasoning behind them and took me to see Tesla, a new company just getting ready to produce its first electric car. The building and operation they had was impressive. I saw the batteries, motors, and bodies they were using and took a ride in one of the first prototypes with Martin Eberhard, the founder. That car was the Tesla Roadster, not available at the time, an extremely fast car with excellent handling and efficiency. Although it was a bit small for me, I was impressed with the power and the battery configuration Tesla had developed. As a result of that visit, I started thinking that maybe electricity and biofuels could work well together.

In 2007, when I decided to repower the biggest gas-guzzler in my car barn, I thought about which guzzler would be the perfect candidate. At the same time, I searched around on the Internet and found a man who made biodiesel muscle cars. His name was Jonathan Goodwin and he lived in Wichita, Kansas. I called him. We spoke for a while, and he was very enthusiastic. I liked his energy.

I can sometimes become so obsessed with a new idea that I lose perspective and start dreaming really big. Predictably, I was always very enthusiastic. That has been good and bad, and has produced mixed results over my life. I wanted to raise awareness of electric transportation and I was very high on the project, naively thinking we were going to change the world.

We settled on a plan to build a series hybrid, different from a regular hybrid because an electric motor always provided power to the wheels. The internal combustion engine would only generate electricity for long trips. For daily commutes, plugging it in overnight would eliminate the daily need for liquid fuel of any kind.

I talked to my friend Marc Benioff, a successful businessman and philanthropist, about the project. Always full of great ideas, he suggested that I make a movie about the conversion. Larry Johnson, my partner in Shakey Pictures, was ready to make the movie about repowering the American dream as soon as he heard about the idea.

Looking over my collection of old cars, I saw my 1959 Lincoln Continental. It was the most outrageous car of them all and would be perfect. It looked great on film, as I knew from *Greendale*. I reasoned that a big American classic car like that would attract the most attention as an electric car and would provide the most exposure. When it was new it got nine miles per gallon. Nobody thought electric cars could be big. Or old.

Larry and I planned our trip to Wichita and made an appointment to meet with Jonathan Goodwin. Our initial plan was to film the trip to Wichita in the Continental, do the conversion, and drive the car back to California to have Roy Brizio finish it after the repower was done. There was a lot of dreaming going on. By my reasoning, Jonathan was the expert for the electric repowering and Roy was the right man to finish and detail the job. His shop was convenient to me and his level of work was legendary. He was just inexperienced at the electric repowering side of the project. That was my plan, although I had not yet met Jonathan Goodwin and really had not done any research about his experience with electric conversions.

Before we left, there was a family birthday party for Pegi's grandma at her home that our whole family attended. I took the Lincoln down there. I showed my young niece and nephews the Continental and told them it was going to be converted to an electric car. Having never even seen a car like the Lincoln Continental before and thinking about it being electric, they just stood there shaking their heads. At the time, there were no electric cars on the market.

After the party ended, Ben Young, Amber, and Pegi all went back to the ranch in Ben's van. I took the Continental and picked up Larry and the crew, which included Ben Johnson, Larry's son, and Will Mitchell, who followed behind the Continental in a van we rented and filled with cameras, lights, and other equipment.

My old friend Larry and I were very comfortable cruising in the old convertible. It was what we both lived for—making movies, traveling, and having a good time. It was mid-September 2007. We left for Wichita and a future beyond our imagination.

The sun was setting on the second day as we hit the outskirts of Vegas. The neon lights were already on. They are on twenty-four hours a day. The van raced ahead and caught a lot of shots of the old convertible cruising into town. With a chrome license-plate holder that said BEVERLY HILLS MOTORCARS on it and several worn decals on the windshield, we could just *feel* that the car had been there before. None of the old decals said "Las Vegas, Nevada," specifically. In the right front seat, while he was holding his camera and shooting, Larry did his voice-over, kind of a newscaster-interviewer personality, shooting me driving the car with the splashy backgrounds of Vegas floating by behind. We were having a blast even though we were not smoking or drinking. We stayed focused, busy doing what we loved. It took a lot of concentration to drive the old Lincoln in a straight line, as it was a little out of alignment and tended to wander on the road.

As we passed by, Larry commented on the many new buildings and empty lots, as well as a huge dark old hotel that was no doubt about to be blown up and replaced by a new one. The giant building was where Elvis Presley had played his first Vegas shows. Such was the way of progress in Las Vegas. Out with the old and in with the new.

The Continental rumbled along, taking this in, no doubt noting that it was much older than that aging hotel, now slated for demolition. We were beginning to feel that the Continental had a soul, memories of the past and feelings about where we were going and what we were doing. Spending a lot of time with a car can do that. The Continental had a fiery spirit about it, and we could feel it.

Like it was a key to the past, a magic memory potion, older folks just opened up when they saw this car. It drew them like magnets. When we arrived at the Hoover Dam, one person who remembered the Continental when it was brand-new was instantly transported back to the past. He enthusiastically led us to the edge of the parking lot where we had stopped and pointed over the wall to the reservoir's cement bottom, hundreds of feet down.

Speaking with a deep Alabama drawl, he said, "Back then, this all used to be full of water right up to the edge here," pointing just a few feet from where we stood. "Carp were right here swimming around the surface. They used to be visible from right here. We came and looked at 'em every time we passed through."

He paused as if he were looking directly into the past, and we all stood there, staring a long way down, hundreds of feet, at the dry concrete floor. Things were really different now. The old Continental was a little worn-out and aged, but it was still here with us. The water he talked about was *gone*.

There was a little moment of silence, and then we said goodbye, walking back to our cars. After a while, Larry and I started the Continental and left for Kingman, Arizona. Again, we filmed the turning of the key, the accelerator being pressed, and the tailpipe for fumes. A lot of soot was coming out during start-ups, causing a floating black cloud.

Outside of a Napa Auto Parts store in Kingman, Arizona, we watched an oil-tanker train roll by for what seemed like forever, while Will and Ben were replacing a headlamp in the old Lincoln. An employee came out and stood, watching the tanker train with us. "Four or five of those go by every day," he commented.

The train was well over a mile long and every car was the same. Long black oil tanks on wheels rumbled by, *clickety-clack, boom-*

boom, boom-boom. We watched silently. The headlamp was fixed and the Continental breathed a sigh of relief. "That feels good," she said quietly.

We headed for Route 66, my old friend the Mother Road, where America traveled west in the fifties. This was the road I had traveled in the old hearse to California! When we finally got rolling on it, we saw a lot of old gas stations boarded up and surrounded by steel fences. Closed motels, abandoned in the sun, stood with open doors creaking in the breeze. A large Standard Oil Products sign could be seen from about a mile away, the paint peeling from it as it barely stood on two giant steel poles and gave slightly to the wind.

Tumbleweeds rolled by a deserted adobe fuel station and gift shop covered by Indian graffiti. *Navajo* was painted on the adobe wall. Windows on both sides of the old structure were smashed out and gone. I drove the Continental off the road and watched a tumbleweed rolling over the sand behind the station. The desert vista was clearly visible through the broken building. This had been a big fuel stop, really a lot more than just a gas station; this was a travel center with all kinds of articles for the traveler, including a big family restaurant, but it was all gone now except for the ruins.

Back when gas was cheap, people drove all over America, chasing their dreams and taking family vacations in their new cars, stopping for the night with their kids and staying in motels along the way; motels decorated like Indian teepees with swing sets out front and nearby drive-in movies. I thought to myself, one day all of these gas stations will be gone. Things that are taken for granted today can easily be gone tomorrow. Time can do a lot. I wondered what would replace gasoline. We traveled on toward Colorado and then through the Rocky Mountains.

STAYING ON TWO-LANE highways really gave us a trip full of feasts for the eye. Small mountain towns and awesome mountain peaks covered in snow flew by between gas stations and fill-ups. When we finally got through the Rockies, we arrived at a place called Trinidad in a rainstorm and sustained our first mechanical failure: a windshield-wiper arm had dislodged itself from its revolving post and was badly stripped so it could not be reapplied.

Larry's exuberance was unique. I can still remember his voice as he described Black Jack's Steakhouse in Trinidad, a former brothel with bedrooms upstairs. Larry had found it and he was very excited, reading aloud from the menu with great enthusiasm. Checking in, we each had our own rooms named after ladies of the night, and some of them had four-poster beds. My door had LILY written above it. I had a four-poster.

We ate steaks downstairs that night where there was a good salad bar and a real bar.

Upstairs on the floor with all of our rooms, there was a kitchen at the end of the hall where Internet reception was good. Later that night, we were all there with our computers, communicating with home and planning the trip. A lady walked in and asked us how we were doing. One thing led to another. She told us that Trinidad was the sex-change capital of the United States; she was in town for her operation and had originally been a man but was unhappy leading a man's existence.

Larry told her what we were doing with our car, that we were going to electrify the old Continental, changing it from gasoline to electricity using a biofuel generator, noting that she, too, was making a big change, and asked if we could interview her. "Sure. I am an ethanol scientist and I am very interested in what you are doing," she said. It was during the interview that she told us she thought we should ask permission from the car before we made the big change. That made sense to us, although we had never thought of it before.

I HAD BEEN GIVING her dashboard an occasional pat and talking to her for a few hours when I asked her for permission to make a change to her drivetrain. Traveling down a Kansas highway at sunset, the idea came as a bit of a surprise to the old Lincoln. We had begun to think of her as feminine. Larry filmed as I talked to her about what we were planning to do, explaining what a great future it would bring. We got the feeling that she was nonplussed by the idea. Shortly after that, the Continental had electrical problems and we lost all lights except the headlights.

The next day, when we finally arrived in Wichita and met Jonathan Goodwin, nicknamed "Johnny Magic" by his Wichita friends, we found he had a very impressive garage. We were optimistic about getting the car on the road as a series hybrid. Work started immediately, and after a few days Larry and I went back to California with Will and Ben and left the Lincoln in Wichita with Johnny Magic, thinking we would be back soon and everything would be done. Before we left I told the old Continental her new name was going to be Lincvolt. We figured the repowering of the Continental would take a few months.

Johnny Magic had a way with metal
Had a way with machines
One day in a garage long ago
He met destiny

In the form of a heavy metal Continental
She was born to run on the Proud Highway.

—"Johnny Magic"

It was a big dream. In the end, nothing for the repower was ever completed in Wichita, but there was a lot of experimenting. Delay upon delay piled up. The months dragged by. The years dragged by. We kept filming and trying to complete the transition, but nothing seemed to work. We made mistake upon miscalculation, attempting to build a clean, efficient drive system to power a big car. Two and a half years into the project, after trying many different ideas, ranging from water-gas power to vaporized fuel systems and giving them all a good shot, trying in vain to get high mileage, all we had was proof that an onboard generator could recharge the batteries while we were driving down the road. A proof of concept. Lincvolt was still just an idea, not a working car.

We left Jonathan Goodwin's garage in Wichita and moved the project back to Brizio's in California in early 2010. During this time, I had toured the world playing concerts and completed three records, traveling back to Wichita with Larry and our crew in between.

With gasoline priced at $2.35 per gallon, vacillating wildly from year to year on its overall steady climb, I had recorded a song called "Fuel Line," featuring the choruses "Fill 'er up" and "Keep fillin' that fuel line." I was writing and performing a lot of songs about Lincvolt and the subject of electric powered cars. *Fork in the Road*, the album we made, was released in 2009. A lot of people were pissed that I made an album about that subject and I got bad reviews, but it was what was on my mind and I can be obsessive. Being obsessive is not such a bad thing for creativity.

TIME CONTINUED to pass for the project, mostly in trying to find the right generator system for a heavy car, and by 2010, with work going on at Brizio's installing a turbine generator, I found myself in Hawaii with Pegi, getting some rest. I flew back to California for a short trip to be with my friend Conan O'Brien on his final *Tonight Show*. Upon my arrival in Los Angeles, I learned Larry Johnson had passed away from a heart attack. My lifelong friend was gone without warning. It was shattering news.

I kept thinking about Larry, processing the fact that he was gone. I saw him in the hallway of my hotel, heard his voice in the lobby. Pegi took it particularly hard. It took Pegi and me several months to recover and get back on our feet. Larry was very close to both of us in different ways. Ben Johnson, Larry's son, took over finishing the Lincvolt picture with me and we kept on rolling. That's what Larry would have wanted, so that's what we did.

> *You're in heaven with nothing to do*
> *The ultimate vacation with no back pain*
> *And all we do is work work work.*
> *You're on vacation*
> *We're workin'*
> *You're in heaven*
> *I'm workin'.*
>
> —"YOU NEVER CALL"

A while later, one night on the ranch, it was a full moon. Billowing clouds were rolling by and we had a good fire going in the junkyard. Ben Johnson and I were shooting a scene. Some Canada geese flew over, honking in the sky, as I was talking about Larry's long history with the Lincvolt project with Dave Toms, an old Canadian friend of mine. Nearby, junkyard cars sat listening in the moonlight.

I noticed the 1951 jeep pickup right where I had left it years before. The jeep pickup's paint had worn over time to show the original construction-orange color in more places, giving it a rich patina. Weeds grew up all around it. The light from the fire played on the windshield. The jeep was talking to me. It was saying it missed Larry.

One time on the road, Ben Johnson and I sat in Lincvolt's front seat and talked frankly about how to treat Larry's passing in the movie we were making. It couldn't have been easy for Ben, yet he just kept looking and trying to figure out the best way for us to go forward. He had the same quality as his father, had the same focus, patience, and energy, and was born to do his own life's work and, like Larry, he would do it in his own way.

Again I hit the road on tour, doing a solo show across Canada. In summer of 2010, I was on the Trans-Canada Highway. While I was somewhere between Cypress River and Winnipeg, Manitoba, on that old road, a sweeping steel guitar came down from the clouds. I got the word from Pegi that my old friend Ben Keith had died on the ranch. It was the end of an era for me and my music.

I was devastated by the loss of Ben, known as "Long Grain" to his friends. I played "Old Man" solo that night on the same guitar I had used on the original recording in Nashville the night I met Ben. I looked over to my right to where he always sat with his steel, still hearing his sweeping tones in my heart.

With Long Grain gone, and his steel guitar silenced, it is hard for me to do all those songs we did together and not hear that steel echoing in my soul. Now I do them only as solo performances. I don't want to hear anyone else attempting to play Ben's parts on those songs with me.

LINCVOLT, now more than three years into the project, was equipped with a Capstone turbine at Brizio Street Rods. She was sounding like a quiet jet. However, as unique and cool as she was with her futuristic Batmobile-like sound, we could not yet go on a sustained journey, one of our primary goals. We had a maximum range of just over a hundred miles before we ran out of electric power and had to stop and regenerate. The system did not have enough power to regenerate more than what we were using when the car traveled at highway speeds. Everything we tried had taken a lot of time, and we still seemed to be aimlessly drifting, our lack of experience catching up with us.

After climate change brought us Hurricane Katrina and the BP oil disaster, we were on a Gulf Coast benefit tour, playing concerts with super-low ticket prices, traveling along the Gulf of Mexico and working with Tyson Foods, gathering food that folks brought to the shows, and donating it to food banks to bring some help to the devastated area. The gulf had lost both its fishing income because of the oil in the water and the tourist trade because of the tar on the beaches.

After the Gulf Coast tour, still filming Lincvolt, and carrying her in one of her tour semitrailers that doubled as a gym and garage, we headed north toward Milwaukee and Farm Aid, and then on to Michigan. We hit Detroit as the country continued reeling from the economic downturn that began in 2008.

In Detroit, my friend Bob Krepsky, official historian at Ford

Motor Company, introduced us to Bill Ford, and we were invited to tour the old Wixom plant, where our Continental was built back in 1959. There we were introduced to the man who had headed up all Lincoln builds at the factory for years, Gary Cooper, and he showed us the facility. Mr. Cooper rode shotgun with us as we eased Lincvolt through the giant multi-acre plant to roll along the Lincoln assembly line one last time. It was an emotionally intense visit.

The giant Wixom Assembly Plant, where our Lincvolt Continental began her life of service, was being demolished around us. We moved slowly along the floor in the Continental. As we edged through the sparks that cascaded down on the cement floor from the metal torches of the demolitionists working above, giant pieces of steel fell from the ceiling, clattering loudly throughout the massive building. The welders did their work. Outside, Ben Johnson captured a shot of flocks of blackbirds circling over the plant. The sun was setting. It was a solemn day in Motor City. Times had changed.

The "mound" was historic. It was used to proudly display the latest models coming out of the Wixom Assembly Plant and was located out at the far edge of the plant's expansive parking lot. One of Lincvolt's sisters definitely had had her big moment on the mound, as did many other seminal cars of the fifties and sixties. Mr. Cooper made sure the old spotlights were turned on as Lincvolt climbed to the top of the mound. We were exposed to passing freeway motorists, and cars were honking their horns in salute, witnessing the beautiful old Lincoln Continental resting in the bright spotlights below a windblown American flag. Everyone knew the plant was closing. This was a moment of pure emotion and sense of history. Larry Johnson would have loved to have captured it. His son, Ben, shot it.

It was 2010. In the elections, the politics of change were being tested. Many politicians were denying the scientific fact that global warming was a man-made problem. Some even maintained that it wasn't happening at all, and they were gaining power in Washington, ignoring science and practicing their politics of denial. They ridiculed President Obama repeatedly for even trying to address the issue. That CO_2 was threatening the climate's stability was dismissed as a myth.

When Lincvolt appeared at a trade show that year in Las Vegas called SEMA (Specialty Equipment Market Association), I spoke about the future of electric cars with batteries charged by clean, domestic biofuel. We had to transport the car there by truck because it could not handle the distance to make the trip. We had been working for three years to make an example of a successful electric biofueled car. I knew we could get there if we just kept at it, but costs were mounting and time was passing.

The car was beautiful and it was electric. People were intrigued by it but its generator still ran on gasoline. We were still trying. It had proved to be endlessly fascinating, rewarding, and challenging, but we were definitely not there yet.

Needing a rest, a few weeks later, Pegi and I were together at a retreat in the desert, a place Larry had shown us, where he had often visited for relaxation and rejuvenation. Very early on the second day of our vacation, the phone rang in our room. It was an anxious call from Ben Johnson, telling me that a fire had destroyed the car. The sound of his voice told the whole story. Sitting in bed, I Googled the news and watched TV coverage of Lincvolt burning on my laptop.

The announcer did not know that Lincvolt had caught fire because it was left charging with an untested system. He was talking about me being a rock star and this being my warehouse, a much more interesting story, but I could clearly recognize the chrome and taillights of Lincvolt. Flames danced on the chrome as the plastic taillight lenses melted.

I couldn't believe what had happened, but I had seen it with my own eyes. I was in shock. Pegi and I left the retreat and headed home immediately to see the damage firsthand. A terrible fire had ravaged the warehouse. For a while I was hard on myself. I had really let the car down. Now Lincvolt had the stigma of being an electric car that had burned, but the fire was not the fault of electric cars. It was our own fault for not being careful and following safe procedures. No one was there to monitor Lincvolt in case a problem developed, and she was left charging with an untested system. It was our fault, not the car's. It could have easily been averted.

There was still a lot left in the warehouse that survived or only suffered a few paint ripples from the extreme heat, including Taylor Phelps's 1948 Buick Roadmaster hearse. That was November of 2010. It was a devastating loss and we were reeling from it. It was then that I realized the fire might have been a blessing in disguise. I learned that the insurance money was almost enough to rebuild the Continental completely, and with all of the new information we had gathered over the past three years and the people we had met, we could finally do it right.

MY SOUL MATE PEGI bought me a parts car, a 1958 Continental convertible with identical matching metal, as a birthday present to replace the melted and deformed parts of the original car's body. After that, Roy Brizio named the car "Miss Pegi," and we had a custom chrome plate engraved with MISS PEGI to replace the old Continental emblem that had melted into the original dashboard in the fire. Roy's suggestion to name the car Miss Pegi was a very thoughtful and sensitive idea. He understood the connection between a guy's car and his wife or girlfriend. Roy had probably learned that from many years of experience working with fanatical hot rod guys and people like myself.

Starting over, I called Bruce Falls at AVL. Bruce was a professional when it came to building series hybrids, a person I knew and respected. Bruce, too, saw that the future of transportation was electric. He had seen it long before we did and had made it his life's work. When we talked, Bruce explained to me that none of the generator systems we had tried over the years were anywhere near big enough to maintain the giant Continental's energy needs, so the car's range would always have been extremely limited. He suggested a Ford Atkinson four-cylinder engine as a generator, the same flex-fuel engine used in the Ford Escape Hybrid. I was excited. Now we were finally going to be able to build the real thing.

WHEN WE ADDED the next-generation biofuel to our new generator system, we finally succeeded in creating the system we had been searching for. I had done a lot of research and found cellulosic ethanol, a fuel of the future being made at a pilot plant in Scotland, South Dakota, by POET. This second-generation biofuel, made domestically, provided a very large reduction in CO_2 emissions compared with gasoline. It did not have a negative effect on the world food supply. The biomass used for this fuel was corn stover, the waste of food crops, nonfood crops, and other waste. It was a sensible solution. Our world has an abundance of waste.

I kept reading, probing, and learning about biomass. Interestingly, speaking for the USA at a world conference on biofuels in 2005, Thomas Dorr, the undersecretary of the US Department of Agriculture for the Bush administration, had said: "In fact, not too many years down the road, once we get cellulosic ethanol up to speed, just about everything on a farm except the machinery, the buildings, and the proverbial squeal of the pig will be a potential energy source. From the sunlight glinting on the fields to the wind rippling through the trees, to the corn stover that today mostly rots in the field; tomorrow it will be powering our vehicles."

Paul Wolfowitz, former leader of the World Bank Group and an early Bush administration proponent of the war on Iraq, added: "In the long term, the manufacture of ethanol from cellulose offers one of the greatest hopes. This technology, which is so far only developed on a pilot scale, uses new catalysts and enzymes to speed up natural processes. The advantage is that it does not rely on valuable crops. It can use waste products such as straw corn stalks or agriculture debris."

The discovery that people connected to the Bush administration had been advocating cellulosic ethanol seven years before I knew it existed was a real eye-opener for me. I was surprised. It goes to show that the world is not black and white. The farther you look, the more you see.

With the help of Ford Motors, we had the motor specially set up in Detroit to run on one hundred percent cellulosic ethanol for our generator. Setting the engine to run on this specific fuel got a lot more energy out of it than the compromised E85 vehicles. They sacrificed energy to be able to also run on gasoline and E85. Both fuels suffered from this idea. Our generator did not. This biogenerator, coupled with a larger fuel tank, gave Lincvolt a range of well over four hundred miles. Because it was maximized for second-generation biofuel, the motor would barely run on normal gasoline at all. It didn't want to anymore. Neither did I.

Although I had no interest in using gasoline myself, I did see the immediate need for a carburetion system that could recognize the type of fuel and adjust automatically, allowing several different fuels, including gasoline, to be used freely. I saw that as a key piece in the mass transition to renewable fuels, allowing people the freedom of choice they deserved.

Brizio Street Rods brought it all together. Roy Brizio organized the rebuild. We used my birthday gift from Pegi and repaired the fire damage to Lincvolt's body at Camilleri's Auto Works in Sacramento. Shavers Auto Interiors created a masterpiece. When the car went back to AVL for a last tune-up and calibration of the new electric drivetrain, Miss Pegi was born.

It was the end of 2012. During the run-up to the 2012 presidential election, President Obama's support of electric vehicles became a political issue for his adversaries, who got most of their funding from the oil company lobbyists. They said uninformed and negative things about electric cars in general. They painted the president's conviction as folly, a waste of time, something America was not ready for. Obama cars.

After Hurricane Sandy hit the East Coast that year, the realization of global warming's effects and the fears of more storms started to take hold. People in New England states actually started cutting down the beautiful, big trees around their houses in fear of the *next* superstorm, prompting a front-page news story in the *New York Times*.

Climate chaos continued to produce unprecedented tornadoes in Oklahoma, historic flooding in Europe, the US, and Canada, and record-breaking heat waves around the world. The predictions made by scientists of the world and Al Gore's 2006 documentary film, *An Inconvenient Truth*, were resonating.

Weather forecasters on television discussed the extreme conditions as proof that the worst winter on record was right now, but they stopped short of mentioning climate change and drawing a connection—the connection science had verified—and were followed by a commercial that was for a gas-burning, CO_2-spewing car. It wasn't until 2014 that I saw a major television network fully acknowledge climate change and its impact. It was ABC.

On our journey across America we visited Utah, and in Canyonlands National Park we met inspiring and dedicated activist Daryl Hannah, who traveled with us on part of our journey. Daryl had been studying biofuels and carbon abuse for longer than I had, and had taken a similar path, with some of her own cars running alternatives to fossil fuels, to make an example of what could be done with the kinds of cars America loves; a Trans Am and an El Camino. She was interested in Canyonlands because oil companies were looking at that national treasure as an oil sands opportunity. After a few days of meeting people and learning about the history of the oil companies in the area, we traveled on, discussing the challenges and wondering about the solutions. It was a once-in-a-lifetime experience, all of us together, enjoying the beauty of Canyonlands, and continuing our dedication to preserving and protecting Mother Earth.

WHEN WE RETURNED to California, during post-trip maintenance by Bruce Ferrario at Four Star Automotive, something very weird happened. Bruce finished his work and washed her for the drive back to Brizio's, but Miss Pegi would not start. Turning her key would result in a normal start but then her power would go dead. *Click, click. CLICK.* The first two clicks meant she was on. The third click meant she had turned herself off. It was like she changed her mind. When he finally got her going for the short trip back to Brizio's, Miss Pegi stalled right on the road halfway there. This was highly unusual and totally unexplained. The next day, when we came into Brizio's shop to see how she was, everything was fine. She was running perfectly.

After we drove to Southern California, Bruce Falls looked for the problem, but there was nothing obvious. He would have to see the car while it was exhibiting the problem, to locate and diagnose it. It was an unsolved mystery.

At that time, we changed fuels to straight cellulosic ethanol, rather than the E85 blend, and completed testing Miss Pegi on one hundred percent cellulosic ethanol, finding even more CO_2 emissions reductions compared to gasoline, and we had improved again. Miss Pegi had gotten even cleaner!

As a reborn E-Lincoln she was very fast and sure, handling the tight curves and mountain roads near the ranch incredibly well. She was as ready as we could make her for the fossil fuel–free journey to Washington and the final filming of segments of our movie. We were all in high spirits, anticipating a great finish, although that unsolved mystery was still there.

The first day of our gasoline-free trip across America to Washington got off to a late start and was uneventful. After staying overnight in Sacramento, about ninety miles from the ranch, we started up the long grade over the Sierras. I noticed that the battery-power level was falling as we climbed the Donner Pass into Truckee. Checking the generator, I saw that it was running, but when I looked to see how much power it was making, I saw zero. Miss Pegi was slowly running out of her precious reserve power.

I decided to conserve energy and travel slower on the shoulder until we reached the next exit. Less speed equals less energy used over the same distance. At that point, the California Highway Patrol began to assist, traveling behind us with their blinkers on. A few miles later at the next exit, we pulled off and stopped. Someone recognized me. A small crowd gathered and soon cameras were out and everyone was taking pictures of Miss Pegi, the highway patrolman, and the rocker.

I called Bruce Falls and told him what had happened with the generator. He said we should reboot the car by turning it off and on and then try again. We did. The generator came on and started charging, but as soon as I started to drive, Miss Pegi's batteries started to lose charge. The highway patrol escorted us to headquarters to park the car in a secure place and regroup. No one wanted to leave Miss Pegi by the side of the road.

I noticed that the generator would charge the batteries as long as the car was not moving. I ran Miss Pegi's generator in the highway patrol lot for a few minutes and we recharged the batteries while she rested, making enough power to easily reach the summit and then glide down to Reno, easily recharging the batteries with regenerative braking on the long decline.

The highway patrol had been very helpful. There were many more cameras. As I stood in the lot, a couple of patrolmen and -women approached and we took a few more pictures, one with a little guitar that I signed before we headed out for Nevada. As we left, Miss Pegi seemed to be enjoying all the attention.

We arrived in Reno and checked in at a big casino hotel. Slot machines rang out as stale air settled on the giant gaming-hall floor. Folks shuffled in and out, working people getting a break and enjoying their time off. We had parked outside across the street at an electric car–charging station provided by the hotel. From my room on the fifth floor I could see Miss Pegi parked in the lot beside a new Tesla Model S sedan. Times were changing.

I had arranged for Bruce Falls to ship us a data recorder. A data recorder connects to the car's computer and records everything the car does. The next morning we would connect the data recorder, capture the generator event as it happened, and email the data back to Bruce at AVL for analysis. Miss Pegi Continental was really becoming a twenty-first-century car!

In the morning, we met four ladies from Petaluma who were traveling in the Tesla. We took a few pictures with them and interviewed them for the film. They were characters, traveling in their electric car to go gambling in Tahoe. Miss Pegi enjoyed showing up the Tesla, while the Tesla pretended not to notice. We laughed a lot about that.

When we connected the data recorder and took off to the interstate, climbing back toward Truckee, the generator malfunctioned right away, running but not charging the batteries. This time we captured the data and sent it back to Bruce, who analyzed it and discovered that the fuel pump was not working correctly and that the motor was starving for fuel.

It was all making sense.

Miss Pegi was once again the center of attention.

Roy Brizio had found Jerry Price for us. Jerry verified that the fuel pump in Miss Pegi was completely trashed, crammed with debris and broken beyond repair. It turned out that my vintage pumps at Feelgood's had delivered contaminated fuel, the cause of Miss Pegi's original wound. My pumps were installed incorrectly.

It was Sunday, and when the service department at Jones West Ford, Reno's biggest Ford dealer, couldn't locate the part, they gave us a used Ford Escape Hybrid to remove the fuel pump from in order to replace our broken one. The good folks at that Ford dealership had been extremely helpful and generous.

After the repair was done at Jerry's, we went to Jones West Ford and had pictures taken with the courteous staff. Miss Pegi enjoyed her photo shoot there immensely with the staff all taking pictures around her striking beauty, her chrome shining in the morning sun.

Then we were back on the road and all was well again, although we had lost a few days. Soon we were out of Nevada and well into Idaho, but we were not yet out of the woods. According to Bruce Falls, we may have done more unseen damage. He was still worried that running Miss Pegi while she was starved for fuel had overheated and possibly damaged her. That stuck in the back of my mind.

AMID ALL THE NUMBERS and emissions calculations there was something new that I found hard to explain. I was starting to have a relationship with Miss Pegi. Every morning I would polish and clean her beautiful metal and chrome lines, caressing her classic American Metal Dream shapes with soft cloths. She was truly one of a kind, beautiful in form and function, performing flawlessly in her completely new way, a truly magnificent machine. And she was definitely feminine. She loved attention and would do things to get it. Having a lot of guys standing around trying to figure out why she would not do something seemed like it was fun for her. She was unpredictable and predictable at the same time. If you did not do the right thing, she would always let you know.

It felt so good to be on the road again with Miss Pegi in her element, the open highway, cruising along in the quiet natural splendor. The countryside was beautiful, especially Montana's majestic mountain ranges, and we continued onward to the great prairies, crossing rivers, passing peaceful serene lakes and green-carpet meadows. Turning north toward Alberta, we crossed the international border the next day. The enchanting scenery and vastness of North America was a feast for our eyes. We savored and captured some awesome traveling shots as the miles rolled by.

Every morning I would get up to clean and polish her beautiful rims, accenting her graceful metal lines, making sure Miss Pegi was ready for the road again and looking good. Those were my peaceful times, meditative morning beginnings that I really enjoyed as I rubbed off the insects and grime that we had accumulated over the miles.

Grating on my mind was the CO_2 of all of the cars and trucks we saw every single day. I knew it was a vast amount, and I knew trying to change that would not be easy. Not easy for anyone. We had a habit. I thought about it long and hard. Miss Pegi had a convincing message. She proved you didn't need to use fossil fuel to move from place to place. Nothing spoke like the presence of the car. She existed.

LOOMING ON THE HORIZON· was an unknown. We had heard about it: the Highway of Death. That was the name the locals had given to Highway 63, which ran north from Edmonton to Fort McMurray, the nearest Alberta town to some of the dirtiest oil on planet Earth. Oil from there polluted so badly that it made Alberta equal to the country of Switzerland in CO_2 emissions.

Alberta was naturally beautiful, a Canadian jewel, but when we rode on the Highway of Death we found that it had earned its name by being an extremely dangerous two-lane road often occupied by giant double-wide loads that traveled in both directions while busily supplying the oil industry. When these trucks met on the road it was unbelievable that they almost always missed one another.

Along with the giant double-wides, hundreds of fast-moving, newly purchased pickup trucks owned by the oil workers flew by, passing whenever they could. Their drivers had toiled long hours for wages to take or send money back home to their families, alongside temporary foreign workers who stayed in camps of dwellings made out of storage containers. They were the hard workers.

For me, it was an unsettling journey. The fight against CO_2 abuse was turning personal. In my heart I knew that CO_2 emissions must be scaled back, way back, and social awareness of this danger to the earth was a key to reversing the trend of abuse. I also knew that many hardworking people depended on this dirty, oil-harvesting activity as their source of livelihood. If I fought back on CO_2 and oil companies, I was directly hurting these working people. That bothered me. I struggled to find a balance with it.

I respected them but was compelled to go against those hard workers because they were digging us into a hole that future generations would have tremendous trouble climbing out of. I am talking about my own grandchildren.

CO_2 EMISSIONS are disproportionately large in tar sands extractions, the most inefficient and wasteful way to harvest fossil fuel on the planet. It is this oil that will flow through the Keystone XL pipeline if it is approved by President Obama. A new study in the USA concluded that the pipeline would not add to the CO_2 emissions meaningfully, reducing pressure on the president to make a decision that might be unpopular with oil interests. Anyone with reasoning power could see that this study was not valid. Why would the oil companies build anything that was not going to increase the flow of oil? I can't ignore the fact that it was being built to carry the dirtiest oil on the planet—oil with three times the carbon emissions of conventional oil—to the world market through a tax-free zone in Texas, virtually ensuring none of the wealth from it went to America except for the few temporary jobs to build it. Such misleading information is common in a corporate government overrun with oil lobbies. And then there's climate change to consider. This was an opportunity for the leader of the free world to stand and deliver. It was a real world-history moment.

Once we safely arrived in Fort McMurray, we could smell petroleum in the air and taste it in our throats. It was in our eyes and in our nostrils even though we were still some twenty-five miles away from the nearest tar sands site, which happened to be the only site open to the public. All of the other ones in the area were verboten. Those roads just disappeared into Alberta's pristine boreal forests on their way to what could only be described as a series of ugly scars on the history of Canada, a lasting testimony to what men blinded by quick money will do.

Fort McMurray had boomtown features: exceptionally high-priced food, bars and prostitutes, money and drugs. The most recent years had seen huge growth, which caused traffic jams for miles. Odd for a rural town. I wondered how the original residents felt. Mixed feelings, I imagined.

We had hired a helicopter to film Miss Pegi from the sky as she traveled around the only tar sands development operation that we could get access to. The pilots were very nice folks who did a wonderful job for us. They usually worked for the oil companies, and went back to doing that as soon as we left.

As Miss Pegi approached the oil sands operations site on the perimeter road, we passed the many poisonous tailings ponds (some as large as lakes) that surround each development area. Those ponds were where the oil companies stored the poisonous water left over from the process of extracting oil from the sands. The water was originally from the river but now it was poison. The flawed idea was that the poison in the tailings ponds would be absorbed into the land and somehow go away. Air cannons were firing constantly to stop wildlife from entering the poisonous water and killing themselves. When I noticed metal scarecrows installed in the toxic lakes to further discourage the wildlife from entering, I was reminded of a story a First Nations woman had told me the previous day about a family of bears that tried to swim across a tailings pond, only to die a few hundred feet from shore.

There were 182 square kilometers of toxic and deadly tailings ponds already in Alberta. I had learned that many of the tailings ponds from the other operations sites were located close to the Athabasca River and were silently leaching into its freshwater. The danger of one of these tailings ponds breeching and filling into the river was unspeakable. Everyone knew it could happen. Two months after my visit, the first one did.

Ancient Canadian treaties, now broken, gave the local First Nations peoples the right to hunt and fish in these lands to sustain their life. Native descendants were now dying of cancer. The great Athabasca River was polluted, enough to make the fish the First Nations people used to eat deformed and inedible, and the water they once drank undrinkable. According to the First Nations peoples, animals that used to be their food were now all too sick to eat.

The oil companies had fought long and hard to avoid the blame for this injustice, but science and discovery had proven their guilt. The giant oil interests continued to fight on with their vast resources, contending that they were not responsible for the devastation they caused. Doctors who identified rare cancers among First Nations peoples living near the area were discredited with false stories that were later debunked. But the damage had been done to the physicians' reputations. Some physicians were hesitant to treat victims of diseases connected to the industry as the oil companies intimidation and fear spread.

First Nations peoples were dying of cancer at elevated rates. The *Edmonton Journal* and CBC reported that many of the physicians' and scientists' stories were true, and quoted notable groups such as Queen's University in Kingston and Environment Canada, who in a joint study looked at core samples from six lakes within ninety kilometers of the oil sands. The authors focused on cancer-causing chemicals that are released when things are burned. They can occur naturally, but burning petroleum leaves a unique fingerprint, so the scientists were able to trace the source: the Alberta tar sands development. The Alberta Cancer Board found elevated rates of rare malignancies 280 kilometers north of Fort McMurray.

Miss Pegi floated silently through it all, shining in the sun, her ultimate power source.

Daryl Hannah joined us again, bringing information about the First Nations peoples and the impact of the tar sands on their community and land. She traveled with us and interviewed some of the First Nations people to help us gain another perspective for the film. It was then that we realized that the best way to slow the reckless oil sands CO_2-intensive development in Alberta was to tell people about the ancient treaties between Canada and the First

Nations. Canadians needed to be aware of the terrible secret that these historic and binding documents, part of Canada's constitution, were being broken by their government.

We met with the local tribes and chiefs and vowed to do a series of concerts across Canada called "Honour the Treaties," to raise awareness and funds for the Athabasca Chipewyan First Nation legal defense as they took on the oil companies and the Canadian government, a government currently led by a science denier and treaty breaker, Prime Minister Stephen Harper.

After a few more days in Alberta, we left the area and journeyed southeast across the border toward Washington, DC. I had an appointment there to speak to the National Farmers Union about biofuels. I knew I would have a lot to say about Fort McMurray oil sands and the coming end of the fossil fuel age, and I thought about it all the way down there.

I was polishing away early one morning in a motel parking lot, making Miss Pegi shine in the sun. A pile of rags was growing on the asphalt. Miss Pegi's chrome was done and the sun was fully up. I could feel the heat. Then I was on her rear fins, working and thinking that, on our present course, by 2050 the world would use seventeen terawatts more energy than it is using now. That's twice as much as today. We would have to look to the sun for energy, master-storing it and converting it to electricity, and using it to power civilization.

As I scrubbed Miss Pegi's windshield clean of bugs and dirt, I remembered an article in the *International Herald Tribune* headlined "Polar Thaw Opens Shortcut for Russian Gas," about one of the first energy projects to take advantage of the thawing in the Arctic. Global warming had melted enough Arctic ice to open up new direct polar routes to ship natural gas from Russia to China to create more CO_2! "If we don't sell them the fuel, someone else will," a Russian Novatek spokesman had said with a shrug, ending the article.

Working on her driver's window, I started making plans. In the film we were making, activists like Daryl would have a chance to speak, and folks who disagreed would have a chance as well, just to keep it real and interesting with opposing points of view represented, kind of like responsible journalism used to be before corporate sponsors chose the news and controlled the topics.

Looking through her passenger window as I cleaned and polished it, I saw Miss Pegi's beautiful dashboard and instrument panel, her repurposed gauges illustrating electric energy levels. I marveled at how much less maintenance electric cars would need with their simple technology and reduced number of parts; no transmissions to adjust, no manual brakes to wear out, less to pay to gasoline stations. That servicing would all disappear with a future of bioelectric transportation.

Polishing the chrome above where her old tailpipe used to be, I could vividly remember the smell and soot that stained the ground whenever I started her up, leaving her very tangible carbon footprint behind. As I polished away, I was getting intense, obsessing on ideas and starting to get into a big loop of repetition, feeling a bit angry about how hard it was for responsible people to change their lives and make their own choices. Why were today's cars not smart enough to run on different fuels like Henry Ford's Model T was? Why couldn't they analyze the fuel that was on board and adjust carburetion for that fuel with twenty-first-century sensors and computers? People need freedom to choose at the pump.

I got a new rag and dipped it in the chrome polish.

I was polishing feverishly, almost removing the chrome as I obsessively tackled it, thinking to myself: If you don't use a fossil fuel in your car or truck today, the warranty will be invalidated. There was one exception; flex-fuel (E85) vehicles, but it was practically impossible to find flex fuel on the freeway system. A Big Oil monopoly existed on the federal interstate system. Where was freedom of choice? Why couldn't I buy an alternative fuel on the interstate? Where was the legislation to make a clean alternative available at all of those service areas along the federal highway system?

I did need to take a break from this thinking.

I was pleading to imaginary car dealers, "Please, someone sell me a great new car."

Suppose I could buy a new car capable of burning different fuels that sent an email to the owner every month to say how it was doing: reporting CO_2 emissions for the month based on the fuel it was using and driver habits and what service it needed. Why not send that email to the carbon tax division of the Energy Department, too? Tax CO_2 emissions. Reward conservation. Charge for abuse. There are easy ways to determine whether the driver is being (a) responsible, (b) very responsible, or (c) abusive. Motivate drivers to use cleaner fuels and save the planet for our grandchildren with capitalism.

I was sure freedom lovers would fight that idea.

Hey! Was I running for office? What was I thinking? *Rub, rub, polish, polish.* That bumper was looking tremendous! There is nothing like polished chrome. A diverse fuel market, carbon taxes, and rewards for responsible driving could maybe pay for infrastructure repairs and rebuild American roads, which would employ hundreds of thousands while helping to save the planet.

It was capitalism! (If I didn't want to make waves, I didn't really have to tell anybody about this. I could just think it to myself, couldn't I? Of course not.) I was talking like a socialist or something. There were many bad words to describe my thinking. I should have just turned myself in.

Folks may think that idea will never work, but it already has been accepted by more than two dozen of the nation's biggest corporations, including the five major oil companies! They are planning their future growth on the expectation that the government will force them to pay a price for carbon pollution. They see it coming. Coca-Cola recently announced that global warming was hurting the company's bottom line because of a lack of water in some countries. Hurting the bottom line? Could carbon abuse be un-American?

I stood up and looked at my work. Miss Pegi was radiating beauty in the morning sunlight, practically blinding me with the brilliance of her chrome and eggshell paint. What a beauty she was, inside and out. I could have this forever. Forever? What did that mean? What would it look like?

So there I was again, thinking about my grandchildren.

I wondered, *Am I worrying too much? Am I too concerned about CO_2 and global warming?* I didn't think so.

TRAVELING ALONG THE HIGHWAY, toward Washington, DC, on a beautiful day with the top down, I decided to try driving faster, maybe cruise at seventy-five miles per hour like many of the other cars. Miss Pegi did not *have* to be slow, although I usually liked to travel about sixty because that uses around half of the fuel of seventy-five miles per hour and produces about half of the CO_2. Tracking these numbers was fun for me, but I needed to be careful not to go too far and bore the hell out of everyone. What a great conversationalist I was turning into.

Miss Pegi rode like a dream. It was like she always wanted to be going that speed. Seventy-five miles per hour! She was built for this. She was clean! I was grooving along, driving on future fuel *and being responsible.* This was cool!

As I traveled, I thought about the things I would say to the National Farmers Union in Washington. As an advocate for renewable fuel, I was scheduled to talk about biofuels and the Renewable Fuel Standard (RFS) in a positive light. The standards were coming up for a vote and oil interests wanted them to go away and for the amount of ethanol used as an octane booster in gasoline to be reduced or eliminated. Big Oil's solution to octane boosting was a cancer-causing chemical that they own themselves. They like that better. They wanted to shut the door on biofuels.

Driving along at seventy-five miles per hour, like there was no tomorrow, I smelled fuel. Looking at the dashboard instruments I saw that the generator had stopped and was automatically trying to restart. I realized Miss Pegi was out of fuel. I slowed her down to save energy and cruised to the next gasoline station on electric power alone. She had no problem reaching it. She still had about forty to forty-five miles' range left. Going fast had quickly charged her generator to the maximum so I had full electric range.

It was a hot afternoon and we had electric power to spare as we silently pulled into the shade next to the only gas station in Reliance, South Dakota, and filled up with some cellulosic ethanol we carried in the chase vehicle. We had started calling it "Freedom Fuel." The owner of the station, a man named Lowell, came over and was watching us. The guys got out their cameras. We started to talk, and told Lowell what we were doing, how clean Freedom Fuel was, and why we were using it instead of gasoline. Lowell said that all the farmers in the area would use Freedom Fuel if they could, but there was no place to get it. We talked about that unavailability for a while, about America's reliance on fossil fuels and no choice available for alternatives at the fuel stations along all the highways. It was a good talk, and we felt that Lowell would be selling and using clean renewable Freedom Fuel if and when he could. We shook hands and drove away, with Lowell standing by his gas station listening to the sound of an electric car quietly pulling away into the future.

Going slower again, about sixty-two, I was watching the fuel gauge like a hawk, but of course it didn't matter. It had never worked right and still wasn't. How had we missed that? I had to calculate miles and speed in my head as we traveled along to come up with an approximate amount of fuel remaining in the tank. When we were going seventy-five miles per hour, twice as much fuel was required compared to sixty miles per hour, and I had miscalculated that badly. Maybe I was having too much fun! I made a note to get that gauge fixed as soon as we got back home to Brizio's.

The next morning I was up polishing Miss Pegi's rims in the sun. Everyone commented on how beautiful they were, simple yet elegant stainless steel with the name LINCVOLT emblazoned on each one. Soon we were on our way again, pulling onto the road, rolling along in a beautiful silence with the wind blowing through our hair and the top down. That day we met a farming family living in Iowa with a cornfield in their backyard and talked to the farmer and his wife for a while about the weather, filming. Suddenly the Lincvolt movie was all about climate change. His wife was looking out on the field behind their home.

"Things have changed so much I don't know why people don't see it," she said, looking off into the distance, kind of talking to herself as well as us. "It has never been like this in all of our years."

Farmers experience the effects of climate change on a daily basis more vividly than anyone else. They are on the front lines. Around the world, disappearing topsoil and unsustainable farming methods create the largest amounts of displaced CO_2 of all the known factors, including transportation. Living soil is the best carbon sink we have, and chemical fertilizers are destroying it. A carbon sink is anything that absorbs more carbon than it releases. It's the balance of nature. Science is sometimes inconvenient.

Later, sitting at a rest area with the generator on, I heard a weird sound under the car. It sounded like something metal was banging around in the exhaust system. I called Roy. The next town we hit, we stopped to get our muffler replaced by a farmer and car guy Roy had contacted. We found his place, got Miss Pegi in his barn, and put her on a lift. When he saw how she was built, with all of the custom work underneath, he called a friend who owned a real muffler shop and made arrangements for us to go there. When we arrived, we found we had to get a new catalytic converter. By running on fumes after I ran out of fuel, we had burned a hole the size of a golf ball in Miss Pegi's catalytic converter. That was hot. A piece of the converter had blown through and was caught in the muffler, rattling around. That's what we had heard in the rest area.

When we called Bruce Falls to report on the converter, he repeated that he was worried there might still be more damage. Things were fine now, though, so we hit the road in the afternoon, Miss Pegi gliding like a dream on a mellow two-lane blacktop through the heartland.

Thinking about what I would say to the National Farmers Union in Washington, as I drove Miss Pegi east, suddenly it dawned on me that I was not Jimmy Stewart. This was not *Mr. Smith Goes to Washington*, and probably no one would listen to me there once I started talking about the climate. I was becoming too used to second-guessing myself.

I sat in a long line of cars outside of the capital. A gentle rain had started to fall and the roadway was shining like a mirror, reflecting the shapes of the thousands of vehicles around me. I pondered how hard it would be to get someone to pay attention to CO_2 or second-generation biomass fuel. I made a promise to myself to speak anyway, so I could sleep at night knowing I had done everything I could. I had used my voice.

Eventually we found ourselves on a road that ran along the Potomac River. There were no buildings, just a line of pavement through an incredibly green wonderland. The rain had stopped and we were almost at our Washington hotel, cruising Miss Pegi through this endless verdant passageway. Everything was green. The after-rain mist was still hanging in the air. Several miles of this euphoric living green fantasy passed before there was a slight turn toward tall buildings. I saw a traffic light ahead.

At this point, I heard *CLICK*, and Miss Pegi's motor lost all its power! The sound stayed about the same, but there was no power to accelerate. I slowly eased Miss Pegi's massive form toward the shoulder, where she stopped in a perfect position just off the road. What could have happened? I remembered the unsolved mystery.

This was disconcerting, to be sure. I turned off the key, waited about a half minute, and then turned it back on, rebooting Miss Pegi like a computer. She liked that. *Click-click*, that familiar sound. Soon we were back on the street heading for the hotel, and I was really wondering what the heck was going on with Miss Pegi. Luckily, Bruce Falls was on his way. He was coming to Washington to help me introduce the concept of a Bio-Electric Transportation Model. We had an appointment with Senator Harry Reid, the

Democratic majority leader, and his staff. It was a valuable opportunity to get some input from them.

That night, outside the hotel, Bruce was working on Miss Pegi right where we had parked. The mystery problem had continued haunting us. It was consistent. Bruce said those relays clicking were protecting us from a threatening condition. He had to learn what that condition was. We had a scent. We were tracking.

Our meeting with Senator Reid and his staff went well. We had a chance to present our concepts and ask questions about barriers to implementation that we might expect. The senator and his staff were very helpful in directing us toward solutions to some of the legislative challenges that were surely before us, roadblocks to change. We had a second staff meeting in the Capitol the next day with our fuel supplier, POET Ethanol, an important potential partner in the Bio-Electric Transportation Model.

The next day our meeting with the National Farmers Union was scheduled, and we had always said that Lincvolt would be there. We were ready with our message. I had written it out:

> *There is no silver bullet to replace fossil fuel. It will take versatile combined systems and it can already happen now. With the Bio-Electric Transportation Model, electricity and biofuels born from the sun can ultimately become the dominant source of transportation energy, replacing fossil fuel. The economics of standardized car batteries being leased by the car manufacturers, then the owners, and then to public utilities after they are too depleted to function in cars, could drastically lower the cost of electric cars and fully extend a car battery's useful life. The leasing model greatly reduces the cost of new electric cars by removing the cost of expensive battery purchase,*

up to $10,000 in cost reduction. Utility Electric power will be generated by many different means in the future, moving toward solar and renewable, and legislation is already in place to mandate battery storage for utility companies to enable renewable energy use. That is the versatility and freedom electricity enables.

For daily transportation, electric power and biofuels working together can make a substantial difference. Dramatically less liquid fuel is used by long-range bioelectric cars compared to standard fossil fuel cars because of the design of a series hybrid. The biogenerator is just there for rare long trips and emergencies outside of the normal daily commute average (thirty-three miles), a range that is completely covered by an overnight charge. That's the model Lincvolt exemplifies.

At the Washington park, located near the Capitol, where I was speaking, the National Farmers Union was interested in seeing Miss Pegi, a bioelectric car that traveled across the country without using any gasoline. It was to be a big moment for Miss Pegi, but she had other ideas. She was demonstrating that unpredictability that we had come to know.

When the time came for me to speak, Miss Pegi was still back at the hotel on the side of the road with Bruce, being uncooperative. She always seemed to miss the last chapter of the plan, her big moment. I had grown to accept her for the way she was.

I spoke to the National Farmers Union about the clear choice between dirty fuel and clean fuel, but not from my notes. I shared my experience visiting Fort McMurray's tar sands projects, referring to them as a wasteland similar to Hiroshima. There happened to be a Canadian minister of the environment in Washington that same day, touting how good the tar sands development was for the future. Our stories clashed and the oil interests began trying to discredit me and bury me any way they could. In Fort McMurray, radio stations banned my music. Conservative oil supporters broke out all of their anger. Although the name Fort McMurray is synonymous with tar sands development in the area, pictures of a beautiful Fort McMurray were shown on TV and in the press, intending to prove that it did not look like Hiroshima or a wasteland, but ultimately only proving that they did not understand a metaphor. A website, neilyounglies.ca, was started.

The desperate moves of the oil interests were counterproductive to their goals. It made folks in Canada aware that there was a real issue with the tar sands and CO_2, and it became a topic of conversation across Canada. That was just what the government and Big Oil didn't want. The more they talked me down for not knowing what I was talking about, the more people read what I said, and it made it clear to a great many that some important facts were on our side.

Right after the National Farmers Union event, Miss Pegi started to run perfectly again. Turning the key now started the car, just as it was supposed to. All good. Again behaving perfectly as she had all across America and up into Canada.

It was foggy and drizzling a few days later when we arrived in New York City to stay at the Carlyle, a great old hotel in Manhattan with a parking garage below it. After a lot of maneuvering in close proximity to other cars, we parked Miss Pegi there, safely out of the rain and wind, ready to go in the morning to shoot her two last big scenes with media celebrities Bill O'Reilly and Stephen Colbert for the Lincvolt movie. We were all very excited about both Colbert and O'Reilly, knowing both of their strong personalities and viewpoints would add a lot to our story.

Sleeping well, we were up with the sun. After a hearty "Larry Johnson breakfast" at our favorite nearby restaurant, it was time to go. The garage was quiet and the attendant was very impressed with Miss Pegi, having watched over her for quite a few hours. When we explained that she was an electric car, he was fascinated and could not wait to see her moving. We planned our routes carefully as we mounted a camera inside on the dashboard for the shoot. We had all the right permits to get to Wall Street.

I got in the driver's seat and turned the key. *Click Click . . . CLICK.* She was doing it again. It was uncanny. She was not co-operating, refusing to stay powered up. I remembered what Bruce, who had already returned to California, told me.

"The car has sensed a condition that could cause problems. It is protecting us."

I tried rebooting. On the fourth try, she stayed on. I was very nervous about going out on the street, not wanting to get in trouble stalling in New York traffic, especially with all the pushback press we were getting about what I had said in Washington.

Exposure had kept growing, and I had requests to do interviews and radio shows, which we turned down, waiting for when I went to Canada with the Honour the Treaties tour. We really didn't want to have video taken of Miss Pegi in trouble in Manhattan appearing in the media at that time. That would have made some of the Big Oil interests very happy and would have been extremely damaging for our message. We didn't want that. There was no choice. We had to cancel our big interviews. It was not a good day for us.

Back in the garage a little later, I tried starting her again, and she was fine. Obviously we had to get Miss Pegi out of New York City somehow. We decided to drive her to New Jersey, load her onto her mobile garage truck, and transport her back to Bruce at AVL for a complete check to solve the issue once and for all. That was a risky thing to do, but she was now acting fine. We decided to go for it, but it turned out that there was something we had missed, a danger we had not considered.

The trip through midtown New York was fine at first with the taxis and traffic all around us. We made our way down the avenues. What a great city. It was my first time with Miss Pegi Continental in New York and it was exhilarating. Once again the center of attention and enjoying it very much, Miss Pegi was in her element, right at home. Traffic gave her a lot of room on the avenues, seeming to appreciate the beautiful old Continental. We turned on a crosstown street, and less than halfway down the block, she clicked off and stalled. I coasted her to the side of the street and luckily we did not hold up traffic. My heart was racing. Turning her key off and waiting a half minute, I tried to reboot the computer again. It worked. She liked it.

We were rolling again and I was a nervous wreck. Miss Pegi stalled two more times in heavy traffic on the way across town. We were on the edge. She seemed to not know whether she had a problem or not. Finally, she settled down and we went a long way with no more incidents. I was just starting to relax when I saw it. Something I had forgotten about completely and now was on my way directly into.

Trapped, we were slowly moving toward the entrance in heavy traffic and we had to go in. There was no way out of the flow. It was a done deal. We had to go in. Miss Pegi was already committed. I thought about all of the things that could have gone wrong to this point and this was the worst thing I could imagine. What if we stalled *in the tunnel*? What could attract more attention than that? I am sure my knuckles were cold white as I held the wheel, and we finally entered, lights shining on the walls as we slowly passed by. With every bump I wondered if she would stop. I was almost praying for a miracle. *Just let Miss Pegi get through this tunnel one time. Please avoid stalling and getting national press. That would be bad for everything we are doing.* The tunnel went on and on. Traffic was slow. How could I have missed seeing this coming? I thought of scenarios to myself: *What if I'm between two buses and I have to stop? That will be pretty safe with one big bus behind us.* As I thought of many other worse scenarios, I looked ahead for a light, a reflection of sunlight on the wall, any sign that the tunnel was ending. By then I was just hanging on, actually praying for a miracle. I saw the light. Miss Pegi finally had made it, emerging out into the bright sunshine.

The Secaucus Holiday Inn, where Miss Pegi's mobile garage truck was parked, was only a couple of miles away. She headed right for it and up the ramp into her safe spot. Secure at last! A one-of-a-kind prototype vehicle of this kind needed a safe home on the road for maintenance and security, and I was never more thankful for Miss Pegi's mobile garage than I was that day.

As I sat there composing myself, gathering my things from the front seat and console, I thought what a great experience the trip had been—all of the people, the problems we overcame, the scenery and beauty of North America—and I felt good. Then I looked at the dashboard one more time. The keys were hanging there in the ignition. The car was like a drug. I wanted more. I wanted to try the key again. I could still drive back to California! What would happen? I turned the key.

Click Click. CLICK. No go. I tried a few more times. Nope. She was not staying on. Each time she just said no. She had given up. We had to find the problem now. It was up to us to figure out what was haunting this car. It was our time to solve this and she was going to go back to the right place: AVL and Bruce Falls, where we could find it once and for all.

After we loaded her into the garage and locked her down with straps, someone showed me a magazine with a picture of a highway patrolman and me. Miss Pegi was behind us on the side of the road, looking good. The story was all about our breakdown back in California. There was no mention of driving across the country free of fossil fuels.

We still had a lot of work left to do to spread the word, what we had accomplished and why.

As for Miss Pegi's mystery, we would find out the answer.

It was water.

There was a small hole where some outside moisture made its way inside the battery pack from the windshield cowling. Just a small opening, but any amount of moisture in her battery compartment would trip her sensors and make her shut down to protect her passengers. The problem had always happened after a rainy trip or a wash. Moisture would slowly make its way through the small opening and into the battery compartment. Water and electricity don't mix.

I think she was grateful. She was a one-of-a-kind prototype doing what she had been designed to do, protecting herself from malfunction and keeping her passengers safe. Miss Pegi was just doing her job. It occurred to me that that was all she had ever done.

After going back to Orange County and getting into the car again, ready for the road, I drove home on Highway 101 through a torrential rainstorm and we had no problems. What a ride! I loved every minute of it; even the part where the windshield wipers stopped working. Miss Pegi was not done with me yet. We continued north with the rain falling intermittently and the wind blowing beads of water off the windshield.

WHEN WE VISITED CANADA AGAIN, supporting First Nations people with the Honour the Treaties tour, raising both legal defense money and awareness, we played a part in bringing light to the situation in Canada. Environmental abuse in the name of commerce had been slipping by Canadians unnoticed under the careful stewardship of the oil companies and the Canadian government.

On the last night of the Honour the Treaties tour, a young man stood protesting against me, holding his NEIL YOUNG LIES sign. Never shy about asking questions, my friend Snowbear walked up to the guy and asked, "What lies?"

"Well, that electric car for one," said the young Canadian. "He never drove across the country in an electric car with no gasoline."

On February 12, just three weeks after the Honour the Treaties tour ended in Calgary, Royal Dutch Shell PLC told regulators it was halting work on its mine in Northern Alberta's oil sands and that it had no idea when it would revive the blueprints. To us this was welcome news, a battle won. First Nations treaties protected the native people, but they also protected the planet. We had maintained that Canada had to honor the treaties and keep her word.

As of this writing, President Obama has not revealed his final judgment on the Keystone XL pipeline, but oil interests are reasonably sure he will back them, and environmentalists are worried. The Keystone XL pipeline approval would enable strong pressure on Canada to break her ancient treaties and proceed with tar sands expansion. The jury is still out for me about what the president's decision will be, but it will be his defining moment, the moment his legacy will be built on.

WHEN I WAS YOUNGER, a boy growing up in Omemee with my family and my dog, the seasons came and went with rhythm, like clockwork. I have seen the changes over the years. Things are not the same now. They are losing the beat. I am doing what I can to hold on to it, preserve it. I didn't know the damage I was doing with my cars, neither did anyone else, but now I do. I had my love relationship with big gas-guzzling cars for a lifetime, yet even I can see the writing on the wall. I am listening to the heart-beat of the earth.

Global warming is a threat like no other, slow-moving and deadly. Miss Pegi needs all the help she can get. This is the beginning of the end for the fossil fuel age. We have a long way to go, but we're going to make it. Henry Ford had wanted to build both electric cars and cars powered by American farmers. That was a dream he started. I am still living that dream, behind the wheel of the unpredictable Miss Pegi, on the Road to Tomorrow.

A few weeks ago, a big rain had just brought welcome relief and green to California's drought-ravaged landscape. I was driving silently through the forest with the top down, listening to some beautiful-sounding classical music. As we broke out of the red-woods and into open farmland, I felt good.

Heading into the sun, I was thankful to be alive and on my way home.

1951 Monarch Sedan "My Dad's Car"

1947 Buick Roadmaster Convertible

ACKNOWLEDGMENTS

JACK HARPER

Jack supplied much of the backup and research for the early days with the Squires in Winnipeg.

PAUL WILLIAMSON

Paul was always there to help with my cars in the beginning, both as a driver/mechanic and as a friend.

JON MCKEIG

Jon's bodywork and detailing on my special cars have made them stand on their own. The unique care he applies to his body, paint, and upholstery work is unmatched.

ROY BRIZIO

Roy's support and friendship at Brizio Street Rods, where much of the fine work on Lincvolt and other cars was accomplished, as well as his understanding of the relationship between owners and their machines, has made him a close friend and key figure in my life as it relates to cars and people.

BRUCE FERRARIO

Bruce's expertise and the perfection, organization, and ongoing support he brings to every project, from Lincvolt to many other cars and trucks I have owned, have made him a valued friend and greatly appreciated mechanic, my "go-to guy" whenever I am in trouble on the road. He is always there to serve and help with the highest professional standards.

BRUCE FALLS

Bruce, the man behind Lincvolt's power train design and a tireless campaigner for system safety, brought the Lincvolt project to a successful and rewarding victory along the road to acceptance of electric transportation. As the designer of Lincvolt's elegant series hybrid system, Bruce Falls and the team at AVL played a pioneering role in electric car history, providing an example that has been followed by the largest carmakers in the world.